Frege on Sense and Reference

D1522584

Gottlob Frege (1848–1925) is considered the father of modern logic and one of the founding figures of analytic philosophy. He was first and foremost a mathematician, but his major works also made important contributions to the philosophy of language.

Frege's writings are difficult and deal with technical, abstract concepts. *The Routledge Philosophy GuideBook to Frege On Sense and Reference* helps the student to get to grips with Frege's thought, and introduces and assesses:

- the background of Frege's philosophical work
- Frege's main papers and arguments, focussing on his distinction between sense and reference
- the continuing importance of Frege's work to philosophy of logic and language.

Ideal for those coming to Frege for the first time, and containing fresh insights for anyone interested in his philosophy, this *GuideBook* is essential reading for all students of philosophy of language, philosophical logic and the history of analytic philosophy.

Mark Textor is a Reader in Philosophy at King's College London, UK. His main interests are in logic and metaphysics, epistemology, philosophy of language and the history of analytic philosophy. He is editor of the *The Austrian Contribution to Analytic Philosophy*, also published by Routledge (2006).

ROUTLEDGE PHILOSOPHY GUIDEBOOKS

Edited by Tim Crane and Jonathan Wolff
University of Cambridge and University College London

Routledge Philosophy GuideBook to

Frege on Sense and Reference

Mark
Textor

Routledge
Taylor & Francis Group

LONDON AND NEW YORK

This edition published 2011
by Routledge
2 Park Square, Milton Park, Abingdon, Oxon OX14 4RN

Simultaneously published in the USA and Canada
by Routledge
270 Madison Ave, New York, NY 10016

Routledge is an imprint of the Taylor & Francis Group, an informa business

© 2011 Mark Textor

Typeset in Sabon and Scala by
Swales & Willis Ltd, Exeter, Devon
Printed and bound in Great Britain by
TJ International Ltd, Padstow, Cornwall

British Library Cataloguing in Publication Data
A catalogue record for this book is available from the British Library

Library of Congress Cataloging in Publication Data
Textor, Markus.
   Routledge philosophy guidebook to Frege on sense and reference /
   by Mark Textor.
   p. cm. — (Routledge philosophy guidebooks)
   Includes bibliographical references (p.) and index.
   1. Frege, Gottlob, 1848–1925. 2. Sense (Philosophy)
   3. Reference (Philosophy) I. Title.
   B3245.F24T48 2010
   193—dc22
   2010007852

ISBN13: 978–0–415–41961–1 (hbk)
ISBN13: 978–0–415–41962–8 (pbk)
ISBN13: 978–0–203–84590–5 (ebk)

Contents

ACKNOWLEDGEMENTS

I have given two seminars and one lecture series on Frege in Bern and Zurich. These seminars were immensely helpful in writing this book. I want to thank the participants for challenging me to explain Frege's ideas, which, in turn, made me understand Frege better (I think). I am grateful to Gabriel Segal and David Papineau, my heads of department during the time I wrote this book, who supported me by granting me leave and to Andreas Graeser and Katia Saporiti for giving me the opportunity to teach in Bern and Zurich. While working on Frege, a number of talks supplied valuable feedback. I want to thank my audiences in Bern, Dublin, Geneva, Hamburg, London, Warwick and Zurich (twice). I have presented material on Frege repeatedly in the King's Philosophy Department Staff Seminar, Oliver Black's discussion group, the Metaphysics discussion group and the Tuesday discussion group. I am grateful to these groups for their critical input. Many people have helped me greatly by reading individual chapters or drafts and giving me detailed feedback. I want to thank Will Bynoe, John Callanan, Chris Cowie, Hanjo Glock, Fabian Gmuendner, Chris Hughes, Brian King, Dominique Kuenzle, Guy Longworth, Fraser MacBride, Christele Machut,

Christian Nimtz, Benjamin Schnieder and Ulrich Stegmann. Many thanks to Alexander Davies, Tim Pritchard and Christoph Pfisterer who have read large parts of the manuscript and whose comments have helped me a lot. Many thanks also to Jessica Leech. She has read the complete first and second draft and helped me again and again to get clear about important points. I have worked with David Galloway in a weekly two-person seminar through most of the manuscript. I am grateful to David for asking me so many hard questions that resulted in changes in the book. I also want to thank Wolfgang Künne. He taught the seminar in which I first learned about Frege's ideas (I hope my grasp of Frege's views has improved over the years). We managed to discuss the first draft in an (almost) six-hour phone call. His comments to the manuscript prevented me from many mistakes. I am grateful to three anonymous referees whose extensive comments led to significant changes. I want to thank Tony Bruce and Katy Hamilton for support and guidance. My final thanks go to Tim Crane and Jonathan Wolff for including the book in their series.

Abbreviations of Frege's works

BL	*Basic Laws of Arithmetic*
BS	*Begriffschrift und andere Aufsätze*
BW	*Gottlob Freges Briefwechsel*
CN	*Conceptual Notation and Related Articles*
CO	'On Concept and Object' (1892), translated in CP
CP	*Collected Papers on Mathematics, Logic and Philosophy*
CSR	'Comments on Sense and Reference'
CT	'Complex Thoughts', translated in CP
FA	*The Foundations of Arithmetic*
FC	'Function and Concept', translated in CP
FLL	*Frege's Lectures on Logic: Carnap's Jena Notes, 1910–1914*
GGA I	*Grundgesetze der Arithmetik*, I
GGA II	*Grundgesetze der Arithmetik*, II
N	'Negation', translated in CP
NS	*Nachgelassene Schriften*
PMC	*Philosophical and Mathematical Correspondence*
PW	*Posthumous Writings*
SR	'On Sense and Reference', translated in CP
T	'Thoughts', translated in CP
VB	*Vorlesungen über Begriffschrift*

INTRODUCTION

The philosopher and mathematician Gottlob Frege (1848–1925) pursued throughout his career a single project. He strove to settle an important question in the philosophy of arithmetic, the science of numbers: what is the source of our knowledge of arithmetic? According to Frege, the truth of arithmetic can be known merely by exercising the faculty of reason:

> In arithmetic we are not concerned with objects which we come to know as something alien from without through the medium of the senses, but with objects given directly to our reason and, as its nearest kin, utterly transparent to it.
>
> (FA: 115)

Frege published four books in his lifetime: *Concept Script, a Formula Language of Pure Thought Modelled upon the Formula Language of Arithmetic (Begriffsschrift, eine der Arithmetischen nachgebildete Formelsprache des reinen Denkens*, 1879), *The Foundations of Arithmetic (Die Grundlagen der Arithmetik*, 1884) and *Basic Laws of Arithmetic I (Grundgesetze der Arithmetik I*, 1893 and *II*, 1903). In the last two books he sets out to prove the truths of arithmetic from the laws of logic on the basis of suitable definitions of concepts such as number. Frege's first book, true to its title, develops a formula language for conducting inferences. Why does Frege first develop such a language? Why is he, in general, concerned with the meaning of language? He himself feels the need to answer this question. In a representative passage he writes: 'Symbols have the same importance for thought that discovering how to use the wind to sail against the wind had for navigation. Thus, let no one despise symbols! A great deal depends on choosing them properly' (CN: 84, 49). When we discovered how to sail against the wind, we discovered how to overcome the limitations imposed by an instrument by using this very same instrument. Language is an indispensable instrument of inferential thinking, but it has its limitations. Yet, we can overcome its limitations if we choose the symbols with which we think properly. Or so Frege argues. He attempts to design a language that expresses thoughts without the intermediary of sound. ('Begriffsschrift' translates as 'concept script' or, better, 'ideography'. Later Frege remarks that 'concept script' is not the best name for his language. Perhaps 'thought script' would have been better.)[1] In addition, the design of the Begriffsschrift answers to further specific demands arising from Frege's scientific project. He aimed to give proofs of the laws of arithmetic in which every step is clearly set out. In the Begriffsschrift everything relevant for inference and nothing else is expressed in signs. The *Begriffsschrift* contains a logic and a theory of judgeable content, that is, a theory of what a statement says or how a judgement represents the world to be. Every Begriffsschrift sentence has as its judgeable content a circumstance, a complex constituted by particulars and properties.

In the 1890s Frege starts to revise this view. He devotes a series the papers 'Function and Concept' (1891), 'On Sense and Reference' (1892) and 'Concept and Object' (1892) to develop the theory of sense and reference that is supposed to supersede the theory of judgeable content. (A further unpublished paper, 'Comments on Sense and Reference' (1892–5) contains helpful elaborations of and additions to his points.) The most important of these papers, 'On Sense and Reference', has become over the last forty years pivotal in philosophical discussions of language and mind. 'No paragraph', says Perry, 'has been more important for the philosophy in language in the twentieth century than the first paragraph of Frege's 1892 essay "Über Sinn und Bedeutung"' (Perry 2001: 141). Why is this?

When thinking about language everyone faces a fundamental and profound question: does the significance of a sentence such as 'Mont Blanc is more than 4,000 metres high' lie in its being correlated with a configuration of objects, a *state of affairs* or *circumstance* that contains Mont Blanc itself, and a property, *being more than 4,000 metres high* or does the significance of the sentence lie in being correlated with or expressing what Frege will call a 'thought', containing among other things a mode of presentation of Mont Blanc? More generally: do our sentences stand directly for circumstances or do they, first and foremost, express presentations that can exist independently of such circumstances?

Early Frege took the first option. He argued that a sentence describes a circumstance and the constituents of the sentence are mere stand-ins for objects. Russell also pursued this option. He writes in a letter to Frege:

> I believe that in spite of all its snowfields Mont Blanc itself is a component part of what is actually asserted in the sentence 'Mont Blanc is more than 4,000 metres high'. We do not assert the thought, for this is a private psychological matter: we assert the object of the thought, and this is, to my mind, a certain complex (an objective proposition, one might say) in which Mont Blanc is itself a component part. If we do not admit this, then we get the conclusion that we know nothing at all about Mont Blanc. This is why for me the *meaning* of a sentence is not the True, but a certain complex which (in the given case) is true.
>
> (PMC: 169; BW: 250–1)

The meaning of 'Mont Blanc is more than 4,000 metres high' is a situation or circumstance. Consequently, the basic task of the theory of meaning is to explain how sentences are linked with situations. A recent example of this strategy is the aptly named *situation semantics*.[2]

Frege's paper 'On Sense and Reference' is of such great importance for the philosophy of language and mind because it takes a stand on this foundational issue. In it, mature Frege argues against his former self and puts the second view of meaning on the map. He also set the agenda for further work. He proposed that every grammatically well-formed expression has a sense (*Sinn*), whose main ingredient he suggestively characterised as a mode of presentation (*Gegebenheitsweise*) of at most one thing. If there is such a thing, it is the reference (*Bedeutung*) of the expression. If one goes the later Frege's way, one needs to know more about sense and reference. Theoretical development of reference and sense has therefore become a fundamental task for the philosophy of language. At the same time, the idea that sentences stand for or describe circumstances has lost nothing of its attraction to philosophers. Even better, some will say, philosophers such as Saul Kripke and John Perry have provided new reasons to endorse a view that favours states of affairs as the meanings of sentences. Friends of Frege have countered with new arguments and the debate is still in full swing. Philosophers agree or disagree with Frege, but they still agree or disagree with *Frege*. His work shapes the philosophical tradition in which we work today and it defines the problems philosophers are currently try to solve. If you do philosophy, you will find it difficult to avoid engaging with Frege's ideas.

Frege's writings are important and philosophically profound, but they don't bestow their content easily on the reader. Especially if one reads on after the first pages of 'On Sense and Reference', his remarks start to sound bizarre: there are two strange objects, the True and the False; every true assertoric sentence names the True, every false assertoric sentence the False. In other papers he assures us that the concept *horse* is not a concept. He himself is well aware of how remarks such as these will strike his readers:

> I have moved further away from conventional views and thereby given mine a paradoxical imprint. If in cursorily browsing one spots here and there an expression that makes one wonder, it will easily seem strange and create an adverse prejudice. I can to some extent estimate the reluctance with which my innovations will be met, since I needed to overcome a similar feeling in myself in order to make them. I have

arrived at them not arbitrarily and out of a craze for novelty, but because the facts themselves forced me to.

(GGA I: x–xi. My translation.)

This book aims to guide the reader through the main ideas of Frege's mature philosophy as he presents them in 'Function and Concept', 'On Sense and Reference' and 'On Concept and Object'. Although the book will touch upon the development of Frege's views by others, the primary aim is to reconstruct and assess the arguments and distinctions presented in these papers. The focus will be on the distinction between sense and reference. I will bring those facts to the fore that forced him to develop his views and give them a paradoxical imprint. My discussion will be driven by the problems with which Frege engages. In working through these problems his distinctive take on them will become clear.

'On Sense and Reference' is for Frege not a philosophical starting, but a mid-career turning point. He argues against parts of his former position, but he will also modify and preserve important parts of it. Hence, a *GuideBook* needs to take into account what he thought before this turning point. I will therefore not start with 'On Sense and Reference', but provide in Chapters 1 to 3 the philosophical background that one needs to understand this paper and its companion pieces. Let me start here by outlining the place of 'On Sense and Reference' in Frege's philosophical development.

As already pointed out, Frege's philosophical theories are to a large extent in the service of his mathematico-philosophical project. Only if one has this project in view can one understand his philosophy. Chapter 1 is therefore devoted to presenting and clarifying the questions he pursues in the philosophy of arithmetic. He attempts to determine whether the truths of arithmetic are analytic or synthetic truths. He argues that every truth of arithmetic can be proved from the laws of logic along with suitable definitions of arithmetical concepts. Before we can discuss Frege's thesis about arithmetic further we need to know what a ground of a truth is and how the laws of logic are distinguished from other laws. Answering these questions will take up large parts of the first chapter. The discussion of the laws of logic will prepare the reconstruction of Frege's theory of the reference of assertoric sentences.

In order to give gapless proofs of the truths of arithmetic Frege designs a new language: the Begriffsschrift. The second chapter is devoted to the Begriffsschrift. It will explain what a Begriffsschrift is and why he designed one.

Chapter 3 introduces the main ideas of the *Begriffsschrift*. Implicit in the design of the Begriffsschrift is an important philosophical point: while pre-Fregean logicians conceived of concepts as building blocks of judgements, and judgements as parts of inferences, Frege turns the order of explanation around: one should start from judgement and inference and finally arrive at concepts. An inference is a judgement made on the basis of other judgements and conceptual content is *what is acknowledged as true in judgement*, it is a *judgeable* content. In this chain of connected logical notions, inference as a variety of judgement is fundamental. A further important part of Frege's re-orientation of logic is his insight that the grammatical decomposition of a sentence into subject and predicate has no logical import. For logical purposes one needs to see sentences as articulated into argument and function-expressions and their contents into arguments and functions (concepts). Chapter 3 reconstructs Frege's arguments for these logical innovations.

In Chapter 4 I will present and assess Frege's argument for splitting up conceptual content into sense and reference. I am sorry for making the reader wait for three chapters. But without knowing what conceptual content is, one will hardly understand why Frege splits it into sense and reference. More importantly he has established many of the central distinctions and theses already before the split. After the split he is busy in re-jigging his theory: does a distinction already made apply in the realm of reference, or in the realm of sense, or in both? I will start my discussion in Chapter 4 by outlining Frege's treatment of statement of sameness of conceptual content in BS and the problems it gives rise to. This will provide the background necessary to understand his argument for splitting up conceptual content into sense and reference. In Chapter 4 I will reconstruct the argument in detail and tease out its consequences.

Frege conceived of the distinction between sense and reference as a major change to the Begriffsschrift. Nearly all philosophers who either accepted or rejected the distinction have taken for granted that it applies to natural language. They take sense and reference to be the basic notions of a semantic theory for English etc. However, there are considerable problems for the application of the distinction to natural language. These problems, I think, fuel anti-Fregean arguments. In Chapter 5 I will go through the main challenges to the Fregean framework when applied to natural languages. One of the main worries is that in natural language the reference of the same expression can shift from one utterance to another. A prominent example is indirect discourse in which, according to Frege, words refer to their normal sense and not to their normal reference. This and other examples of reference shift will be discussed. Chapter 5 is less a guide to Frege's work on the distinction between sense and reference than a guide to responses to his work. The reader should take it as a, I hope, useful extension of the *GuideBook*.

I will discuss in Chapter 6 Frege's theory of sense and reference for assertoric sentences. This is on the one hand fundamental for him, since he recommends a top-down approach to the investigation of sense and reference: one starts with the sense of sentences and moves from there to the sense of sentence parts. On the other hand, he proposes the view that the sense of an assertoric sentence is a mode of presentation of a special object, a truth-value. An assertoric sentence that refers at all refers either to the True or the False. To put it mildly, not many philosophers have adopted this theory. For one thing it is neither clear what truth-values are nor whether there are any. Hence, I will assess Frege's arguments intended to show that there are truth-values and that in uttering a sentence with assertoric force we refer to its truth-value. The core of the chapter is a discussion of his conception of judgement in 'On Sense and Reference'. If we articulate our understanding of what it is to judge, argues Frege, we will recognise that judgement is a relation to an object, the truth of a thought. The objects we discover in this way can serve as the referents of sentences and values of concepts. I will outline and assess the main arguments against his position and find them all wanting. All in all, his prima facie bizarre theory of sense and reference for sentences emerges with considerable credit.

Frege develops and defends in FC and CO the view that concept-words refer to concepts, that is functions from objects into the two truth-values. In Chapter 7 I will compare and contrast his theory of concept-word reference with alternative views. One of his most startling claims is that one cannot refer to concepts using proper names or complete expressions. This leads to the famous 'paradox of the concept *horse*': the expression 'the concept *horse*' does not refer to a concept. In the second half of the chapter I will investigate Frege's reasons to accept that the concept *horse* is not a concept.

A note about translation and quotation. The book is written on the basis of Frege's German texts. I have found it often necessary to re-translate passages from Frege. Re-translations are labelled as such. I will follow the following convention in quoting: first, the abbreviation of the title of the paper containing the passage; second, the page numbers in the original print of the paper. All quotations from FC, SR, CO and the later paper 'Thoughts' (1918), 'Negation' (1919) and 'Complex Thoughts' (1923) are from Frege's *Collected Papers*. Austin's translation of *Die Grundlagen der Arithmetik* has the page numbering as the original. Hence, I will not give the original page numbers in addition.

1

SEARCHING FOR THE FOUNDATIONS OF ARITHMETIC

KANT'S PHILOSOPHY OF ARITHMETIC

In *The Foundations of Arithmetic* and *Basic Laws of Arithmetic* Frege is concerned with arithmetic and its philosophical problems. The titles of these books are programmatic. We know many particular and general arithmetical truths. (Frege called the latter 'laws'.) Frege's project is *not* to find new arithmetical truths. He wants to establish on which *foundations* arithmetic rests by identifying its *basic laws*. Many of his original contributions to philosophy are in the service of this project. Hence we can understand his logical innovations through understanding their role in his project. The nature and point of this project are best appreciated by considering the view Frege opposes: Kant's philosophy of arithmetic.

According to Kant, mathematics is the pure formal science of quantity or magnitude: geometry studies spatial magnitude; arithmetic studies numerical magnitudes. Arithmetic is the science of number, geometry the science of space. Kant argued that the truths of geometry and arithmetic are synthetic a priori. What does that mean?

Kant introduced synthetic/analytic and a priori/a posteriori as properties of judgements, mental acts of accepting a proposition. Take as an example of a proposition the law of identity, that everything is identical with itself. The proposition is neither a judgement nor a sentence. For example, when you and I judge that everything is identical with itself, there are two judgements, but not two laws of identity. The synthetic/analytic distinction concerns how different concepts are related in judgement; the a priori/a posteriori distinction concerns the type of justification one has for the judgement.

Kant defined an analytic *judgement* as one whose subject-concept contains the predicate-concept. (See, for example, Kant 1781/8: B 11/A 7.) How should one spell out this containment-metaphor? Consider the judgement that every bachelor is unmarried. The definition of the concept of a bachelor is: someone x is a bachelor if, and only if, x is an unmarried eligible male person. Hence, the concept of being unmarried is definitionally contained in the concept of a bachelor. Kant also characterised analytic judgements in a second, related, way, as judgements of conceptual explanation (*Erläuterungsurteil*) and synthetic judgements as ampliative judgements (*Erweiterungsurteil*). Analytic judgements merely explain or 'analyse' the subject-concept; synthetic judgements 'amplify' the subject-concept by adding something to it with the predicate-concept. Furthermore, Kant held that analytic judgements can be known through the principle of contradiction. For instance, if one denies that every bachelor is unmarried one arrives at the contradiction that not every unmarried eligible male person is unmarried. In order to be justified in an analytic judgement we only need to exercise our logical (and conceptual) abilities; the exercise of perceptual faculties is not required. Kant's second characterisation of the analytic/synthetic distinction is more fruitful than the first. For, as Frege pointed out, not every judgement has subject-predicate structure (FA: 100). For example, the judgement that everything is identical with itself does not have the right structure, yet it seems analytic. However, one can still say that such a judgement can be justified by exercising one's ability to analyse or define concepts. Moreover, in order to explain what it means that the predicate-concept is contained in the subject-concept we need to invoke the notion of explanation or definition anyway. Frege argues further that Kant's definition is based on a too narrow view of definition: concepts are defined by providing a list of properties something must have to fall under the concept (ibid.). But which exact form the exercise of our ability to define a concept takes is not important. The crucial point is that the judgement can be justified by an exercise of this ability. Hence, one can say that for Kant a judgement is analytic if, and only if, it is justified by an exercise of the ability to define a concept, and synthetic if, and only if, it is not analytic.

Where this analytic/synthetic distinction is concerned with a relation between concepts that bears on the justification of judgements, the a priori/a posteriori distinction is directly concerned with the justification of judgements. Kant characterises an a priori judgement as a judgement that is independent of experience. (Kant 1781/7: A 2) 'Independent' in which sense? It is plausible to hold that most judgements are genetically dependent on experience. I could not even make the judgement that every tree is a tree if I had no experience to acquire the relevant concepts. However, this judgement can still be a priori in that it can be justified independently of particular experiences. An a posteriori judgement is a judgement that is not a priori.

Kant argues that the *sentences* of arithmetic and geometry are synthetic a priori (Kant 1781/8: B 14/A 16). 'Sentence' seems here to mean the proposition expressed by a sentence. However, the concepts of syntheticity and a priority have been explained for judgements and not for propositions. Moreover, the same proposition may be recognised in an a priori and in an a posteriori judgement. For example, I may decide that the door is closed or not closed is true by looking whether it is closed or by applying elementary logic. Is the truth that the door is closed or not closed a priori *and* a posteriori? This problem motivates in part Frege's redefinition of the distinction between a priori/a posteriori and synthetic/analytic, which I will discuss later in this chapter. But let us first press on and assume that the truths of arithmetic and geometry are synthetic a priori in the following sense: a thinker can make judgements that are a priori and synthetic in which he comes to know these truths. A judgement that is synthetic a priori will not be justified by the exercise of an ability to define a concept, but it will be justified independently of experience. Kant's discussion is fuelled by the question what this justification might be. For example, he argued that defining the concepts of 7, 5 and plus doesn't suffice to justify my judgement that 7 + 5 = 12 (Kant 1781/8: B 15–16). How can such a judgement be justified without being based on empirical reasons?

Kant's answer to this question is contained in the following passage:

> Philosophy confines itself to universal concepts, mathematics can achieve nothing by concepts alone but hastens at once to intuition, in which it considers the concept *in concreto*, although still not empirically, but only in an intuition which it presents *a priori*, that is which it has constructed, and in which whatever follows from the universal conditions of the construction must be universally valid of the object of the concept thus construed.
>
> (Kant 1781/7: A 715/B 744)

This quotation contains the main point of disagreement between Kant and Frege. Frege claims, against Kant, that in arithmetic we don't need to have intuitions, representations of particular things in space and time, to justify our judgements. Our ability to define general concepts and to draw inferences is our source of arithmetical knowledge.

Before we can discuss this issue further we need to understand Kant's view better. Kant's own example is helpful. He considers the geometrical judgement that in any triangle the three interior angles are equal to two right angles. This judgement seems to be a priori. However, the geometer 'can analyse and clarify the concept of a straight line or of an angle or of the number three, but he can never arrive at any properties not already contained in these concepts' (Kant 1781/7: A 715/B 744). How can the geometer justify the above judgement *independently of experience*? He

> at once begins by constructing a triangle. Since he knows that the sum of two right angles is exactly equal to the sum of all the adjacent angles which can be constructed from a single point on a straight line, he

prolongs one side of his triangle and obtains two adjacent angles, which together are equal to two right angles. He then divides the external angle by drawing a line parallel to the opposite side of the triangle, and observes that he has thus obtained an external adjacent angle which is equal to an internal angle–and so on. In this fashion, through a chain of inferences guided throughout by intuition, he arrives at a fully evident and universally valid solution of the problem.

(Kant 1781/7: A 716–7/B 744–5)

Kant's geometrical example is, he thinks, representative of the methodology of mathematics. In mathematics we have to construct instances of general concepts (the concept *in concreto*) to extend our knowledge. When perceiving that a constructed instance of a general concept *F* is *G* we can come to know that necessarily every *F* is *G*, *although it is not analytic that every F is G* (being *G* is not contained in the concept of an *F*).

A priori judgements are strictly universal and necessary (Kant 1781/7: B 15). How can 'constructing' and perceiving a *particular* triangle justify holding that *necessarily* for *every* triangle the three interior angles are equal to two right angles? Simply seeing a triangular figure will not give us strictly universal and necessary knowledge about triangles. The idea that the instance of the concept is constructed must explain how we can acquire such knowledge. In constructing a particular geometrical figure I am solely guided by my knowledge of the general concept of the figure. The particular constructed figure is therefore a representative of all instances of the general concept.

Why is construction an a priori method to acquire knowledge? We can construct geometrical figures on the basis of our knowledge of the corresponding concepts independently of our actual perceptions of such figures in the imagination. The justification of our knowledge acquired by perceiving the construction does therefore not depend on how our experiences of actual objects in space have been.[1]

The construction of instances of general concepts is also supposed to explain how *arithmetic* can be synthetic and a priori. To explain Kant's answer in detail would take us too far. But here is the gist of it. He writes in the *Critique of Pure Reason*:

> [S]tarting with the number 7, and for the concept of 5 calling in the aid of the fingers of my hand as intuition, I now add one by one to the number 7 the units which I previously took together to form the number 5, and with the aid of that figure [the hand] see the number 12 come into being. [...] Arithmetical sentences are therefore always synthetic.
>
> (Kant 1781/7: B 15–16)

At bottom, synthetic arithmetical judgements are justified by perceiving properties of constructed sequences that represent numbers ('see the number 12 come into being'). Each constructed sequence consisting of say three strokes is a particular, but it is exemplary of the general type *sequence of three elements*. We have the ability to see the particular sequence as of this type and come to learn about the type by visually attending to the particular sequence.[2] For example, representing the number 3 in stroke notation as '///' can make one aware of the general truth that every number has a successor. One sees that one can keep adding new strokes without limit and thereby generate new magnitudes. We can generate an infinite sequence of strokes that is a model of the infinite sequence of the represented numbers. For Kant, only constructing arithmetical concepts and intuiting the constructions can justify synthetic knowledge of arithmetic.

Of course we can't always construct representative instances by using our fingers or other objects. Fingers are replaced by symbols:

> Once it [mathematics] has adopted a notation for the general concept of magnitudes so far as their different relations are concerned, it exhibits in intuition, in accordance with certain universal rules, all the various operations through which the magnitudes are produced and modified. When, for instance, one magnitude is to be divided by another, their symbols are placed together, in accordance with the sign of division, and similarly in the other process; and thus in algebra by means of a symbolic construction, just as in geometry by means of an ostensive construction (the geometrical construction of the objects themselves) we succeed in arriving at results which discursive knowledge could never have reached by means of mere concepts.
>
> (Kant 1781/7: A 717/B 745)

What is symbolic construction? Kant exegetes are divided about how to answer this question. Does Kant mean that the mathematical symbols are the constructions that enable us to come to know the general truths we are interested in or does he take these symbols only to encode concepts that guide us in making the construction?[3] We need not enter this debate. The important point for our purposes is that arithmetical knowledge is based on constructing instances of concepts.

FREGE'S ARGUMENT FROM SIMILARITY

In FA Frege agrees with Kant on the epistemology of geometry, but not on arithmetic. Yes, says Frege,

> [i]n geometry, [...], it is quite intelligible that general sentences should be derived from intuition; the points or planes or lines which we intuit are not really particular at all, which is what enables them to stand as representatives of the whole of their kind. But with the numbers it is different; each has its own peculiarities.
>
> (FA: 20. I have altered the translation.)

Points, planes and lines are, of course, particulars, but every point (plane, line) shares its intrinsic properties with every other point (plane, line). The particularity of a point consists in its relations to other things. In contrast, numbers are not intrinsic duplicates of each other (FA: 20). For example, 2 is the smallest prime. It does not share all its intrinsic features with 4, which is not prime.

Fair enough. But Frege misses his target. Kant claims that we can come to know general truths of geometry and arithmetic by having intuitions of particular objects we have constructed on the basis of our knowledge of concepts. In the case of arithmetic, the objects will be particular sequences constructed by us in virtue of our knowledge of the number concepts. All sequences that are constructed on the basis of our knowledge of the concept '3' are alike in the properties that we need to instantiate to construct instances of this concept. The fact that there are further intrinsic properties which different numbers can differ in is compatible with Kant's basic thought.

Frege goes on to present in FA a whole battery of prima facie reasons against the view that the power to construct representations of numbers and to intuit them can be the source of our knowledge of particular arithmetical truths. I will not assess these objections here. Instead I will focus on Frege's systematic argument against Kant that has a constructive point: it makes Frege's own view of arithmetic plausible. The building blocks of this argument are contained in his letter to Stumpf from 1882:[4]

> The field of geometry is the field of possible spatial intuition; arithmetic recognises no such limitation. Everything is countable, not just what is juxtaposed in space, not just what is successive in time, not just external phenomena, but also inner mental processes and events and even concepts, which stand neither in temporal nor in spatial but only in logical relations to one another. The only barrier to countability is to be found in the perfection of concepts. Bald people for example cannot be counted as long as the concept of baldness is not defined so precisely that for any individual there can be no doubt whether it falls under it or not. Thus the domain of the countable is as wide as the domain of conceptual thought, and a source of knowledge of more limited scope, for instance, spatial intuition, sense perception would not suffice to guarantee the universal validity of arithmetical sentences. And to enable one to base oneself on intuition it does not help to let non-spatial objects be represented by spatial ones when counting. For the admissibility of such a representation needs to be argued for.
>
> (PMC: 100; BW: 163–4. In part my translation.)

Let us first consider Frege's concluding consideration. If one holds that the truths of arithmetic are synthetic a priori, one may propose that one comes to know them via analogy. One constructs spatial sequences that represent or model numbers. For example, just as there is a series of stroke sequences '/, //, /// …', there is a series of numbers. However, how do we know that the stroke sequences correspond in these respects to the numbers? In order to do so we need to draw on independent knowledge of the numbers.

This is a good objection, but it does not directly apply to Kant. According to him, we gain synthetic a priori knowledge by

(1) constructing instances of a concept (2) seeing that some of the properties of the constructed instances are exemplary of all objects falling under the concept. Hence, the stroke sequence '///' is exemplary of the type of manifold that has three members. Kant may have described how we come to have synthetic a priori knowledge of such types. But now it is unclear whether such types are numbers and, if they are not, in which relation they stand to the numbers. Kant's account seems to be incomplete.

Frege's main point against Kant is that everything that falls under a (non-vague) concept can be counted.[5] Hence, the domain of the countable is the same as the domain of things falling under precise concepts. Countability does a lot of work for Frege here. In its current standard meaning 'countable' applies to sets. A set is countable if, and only if, its members can be put into a one-to-one correspondence with either the set of natural numbers or a subset of this set. If every thinkable is countable, this notion of countability is too narrow. For instance, the points between points A and B on a line are countable, but the set containing these points cannot be put into a one-to-one correspondence with the set of natural numbers. 'Countable object' should therefore be understood as 'object of a kind that is amenable to counting'.

The domain of the countable is wider than the domain of the spatio-temporal; the domain of the objects of which we can have intuitions. If the laws of arithmetic hold for everything that falls under a precise concept, we cannot come to know them by constructing instances of concepts of spatio-temporal objects. In this way we can only come to know general truths that hold of spatio-temporal objects, not general truths that hold of everything whatsoever. We need a further reason that supports the generalisation from the spatio-temporal to the unrestricted case. This further reason must draw on knowledge of arithmetic that is not grounded in spatio-temporal intuition.

Frege concludes that spatial intuition is not the source of arithmetical knowledge. Kant draws the opposite conclusion. He sticks to the view that spatial intuition is the source of arithmetical knowledge and rejects therefore that every thinkable object can be counted:

[W]hen all is said and done, we cannot subject any object other than an object of a possible *sensible* intuition to quantitative, numerical assessment, and it thus remains a principle without exception that mathematics can be applied only to *sensibilia*. The magnitude of God's perfection, of duration, and so on, can only be expressed by means of the *totality* of reality; it could not possibly be represented by means of numbers, even if one wanted to assume a merely intelligible unit as measure.

(Kant 1788: 285)

Kant's restriction on what is countable seems unmotivated and counter-intuitive. In order to count some things I must be able to distinguish and re-identify them. But we can distinguish and re-identify things that are not in space and time in many ways. Take as a paradigm case sets. Set *a* is the same set as set *b* if, and only if, *a* and *b* have the same members. When asked to count sets we don't need to construct sensible representations of them. Sets are countable (in Frege's sense) because one can distinguish and re-identify them via their members. We can develop similar accounts for other non-spatio-temporal objects: thoughts, numbers. However, Frege's own example, concepts, will turn out to be problematic (see Chapter 7).

In FA Frege integrates the assumption that everything is countable into what I will call *the argument from similarity*:

For purposes of conceptual thought we can always assume the contrary of some one or other of the geometrical axioms, without involving ourselves in any self-contradictions when we draw deductive consequences from the assumptions that conflict with intuition. This possibility shows that the axioms of geometry are independent of one another and of the basic laws of logic, and are therefore synthetic. Can the same be said of the fundamental principles of the science of numbers? Does not everything collapse into confusion when we try denying one of them? Would thinking itself still be possible? Does not the ground of arithmetic lie deeper than that of all empirical knowledge, deeper than even that of geometry? The truths of arithmetic govern the domain of the countable. This is the most comprehensive of all; for it is not only what is actual, not only what is intuitable, that belongs to it, but everything thinkable. Should not the laws of number then stand in the most intimate connection with the laws of thought?

(FA: 20–1. My translation.)

Frege points out that the *truths of arithmetic* and the *laws of logic* are strikingly similar in important respects:

1   The laws of logic hold for every object, whether it is intuitable or not. So do the laws of arithmetic.
2   The rejection of the laws of logic will make thinking impossible. So does the rejection of the laws of arithmetic.

Both (1) and (2) are in need of development and defence. I will start by discussing (2) in more detail.

When Frege argues that one can neither deny the laws of logic nor the 'fundamental principles' of arithmetic, we should not understand him as claiming that one cannot make mistakes about these laws. Of course we can make such mistakes. What is then the point that underlies his argument? In order to answer this question we must consider his notion of a law of logic.

Take Frege's standard example for a law of logic:

(L1)

(CN: 137; BS: 26)

(L1) is a general truth, not a norm of judgement: (L1) does not prescribe when to judge something, the law itself does not mention judgement.

But if one wants to judge truly whenever one judges, one had better obey the laws of truth in one's judging. A rule of or prescription for judgement derived from a law of truth is:

One may: If one judges *a*, judge (if *b*, then *a*).

'We must assume that the rules for our thinking and for our holding something to be true are determined by the laws of truth. These are given with those' (PW: 128; NS, 139. My translation). He is too optimistic: the rules for correct judgement cannot be read off directly from the laws of truth. For example, one law of logic says, roughly put, that the truth of *p* and (if *p*, then *q*) guarantees the truth of *q*. But:

One may: acknowledge the truth of *q*, if one acknowledges the truth of (if *p*, then *q*) and *p*,

is not a good rule for judging.[6] If I already have good reasons against the truth of *q*, I should not judge *q*, but re-evaluate my premises. Sometimes one ought to reject the truth of *p* instead of acknowledge the truth of *q*.[7]

The rules for (correct) judgement need to be distinguished from empirical laws of holding true. Such a law might be:

For every thinker *x*, if *x* is capable of inference, *x* will infer *q* from (if *p*, then *q*) and *p*.

When people make inferences, they often do not infer in accordance with the laws of logic. I have made many incorrect inferences in my life, some falsified the law above. But of course none of my faulty inferences will falsify a prescription for correct judgement or the primitive law that grounds it.

Not only laws such as (L1) yield rules for inference and judgement. If I want to do geometry correctly, my geometrical judgements had better respect the laws of geometry. In later work, Frege responds to this objection as follows:

Any law asserting what is, can be conceived as prescribing that one ought to think in conformity with it, and is thus in that sense a law of thought. This holds of the laws of geometry and physics no less than for laws of logic. *The latter have a special title to the name 'laws of thought' only if we mean to assert that they are the most general laws, which*

> *prescribe universally the way in which one ought to think if one is to think at all.*
>
> (GGA I: xv. My translation and emphasis.)

The laws of logic yield norms for correct judgement. Our thinking need not conform to these norms; however, it must be assessable in their light.[8] These norms determine, at least in part, when one has made a mistake in one's truth-directed thinking. If we rejected the laws of logic, we would indirectly also reject the most fundamental and general prescriptions for the assessment of truth-directed thought. But if we reject these prescriptions as standards for assessing our thinking, we will 'reduce our thought to confusion and finally do without all judgement whatsoever' (GGA I: xvii). Episodes of thought that cannot be evaluated in the light of the relevant prescriptions do not qualify as judgements or inferences.

Now contrast the laws of logic with the laws of Euclidean geometry. The latter only yield rules for the assessment of our thought about spatial things. If we reject the corresponding geometrical norms, our thinking can no longer qualify as thinking about spatial objects. However, we will still count as making judgements and inferences. Riemann and other non-Euclideans make rational judgements about ways space can be. They go on to reason about space in a discursive fashion, solve logical puzzles etc.

This brings us to the second similarity between the laws of logic and the truths of arithmetic that Frege points out in FA. If we reject the laws of arithmetic, we indirectly reject norms for thinking about the realm of the countable. But, argues Frege, *the realm of the countable includes everything thinkable*. If the countable includes the thinkable, the laws of arithmetic yield norms that have the same range of application as the laws of logic. Thinking is only truth-directed if it is evaluable with respect to the norms that follow from the laws of arithmetic.[9] Consider an example to see the force of Frege's point. If you endorsed that Hesperus is a planet while simultaneously rejecting that the number of planets is larger than or equal to 1 and you see on reflection no problem with this, it becomes hard to say that you are still judging, endorsing or rejecting something.

Frege proceeds to give an explanation of the similarity between the laws of arithmetic and logic:

The argument from similarity

(P1) The laws of arithmetic govern the domain of everything thinkable and cannot be denied without forsaking the possibility of truth-directed thought.

(P2) The laws of logic govern the domain of everything thinkable and cannot be denied without forsaking the possibility of truth-directed thought.

(P3) The best explanation for this similarity is that the laws of arithmetic stand in the most intimate connection with the laws of logic.

(C)   Therefore: The laws of arithmetic stand in the most intimate connection with the laws of logic.

What could the 'most intimate connection' (*'innigste Verbindung'*) be? The most intimate connection is identity. However, prima facie, the truths of arithmetic cannot be identical with the laws of logic: the former are about numbers, the latter about everything. What is the less 'intimate connection' between these laws? The laws of logic form a finite core from which infinitely many truths of arithmetic are supposed to follow. Hence, the latter are supposed to be theorems of the former. For instance, Frege compares the relation of the laws of logic to those of arithmetic with the relation between the axioms and theorems of geometry (FA: 24). This suggests that arithmetical truths are theorems of the laws of logic. I cannot deny a theorem that I have inferred from a law without thereby denying the law.

Frege's argument from similarity is not deductive, but it makes plausible (1) that the source of our arithmetical knowledge is not symbolic construction of magnitudes and (2) that the source of arithmetical knowledge is the same as the source of our knowledge of logic.

FREGE ON ANALYTICITY AND A PRIORITY

Let us now see how the argument from similarity bears on the question whether the truths of arithmetic are synthetic a priori as Kant assumes, or analytic a priori as Frege wants to argue (see FA: 3). Frege applies analytic/synthetic and a priori/a posteriori directly to *truths*, not to judgements. In order to do this he explains the Kantian terminology in FA in a new way. We need therefore first to get clear about Frege's understanding of a priori/a posteriori and analytic/synthetic before we can return to the question above.

The basis of Frege's new explanation can already be found in the preface of BS:

> In apprehending a scientific truth we pass, as a rule, through several stages of certainty. First guessed, perhaps, from an inadequate number of particular cases the general sentence becomes little by little more firmly established by obtaining, through chains of inference [*Schlussketten*], a connection with other truths – whether conclusions which find confirmation in some other way are derived from it; or, conversely, whether it comes to be recognised as a conclusion of sentences already established. Thus, on the one hand, we can ask by what path a sentence has been gradually established; or, on the other, how it is finally most securely groundable. The first question possibly has to be answered differently for different people; the latter is more definite, and the answer to it is connected with the inner nature of the sentence under consideration.
>
> The firmest method of proof is, obviously, the purely logical one, which, disregarding the particular characteristics of things, is grounded solely on those laws on which all knowledge rests. Accordingly, we divide all truths that require grounding [*Begründung*] into two kinds, those for which the proof can be carried out purely by means of logic and those for which it must be supported by facts of experience. But that a sentence is of the first kind is surely compatible with the fact that it could nevertheless not have come to consciousness in a human mind without activity of the senses. Therefore it is not the psychological mode of origin but the most perfect method of proof [*vollkommenste Art der Beweisführung*] that is the basis of the classification.
>
> (CN: 103; BS: iii)[10]

There is a subtle shift in this passage from a distinction between more and less certain ways of apprehending a truth to a distinction between ways of coming to know a truth that correspond to its nature and those that do not. I take it that this is more a shift in focus than in topic. Frege tries to articulate the idea that for a given truth there is a way of coming to know it that is appropriate to the kind of truth it is. To get a grip on this idea consider the following example. How do I know that $2 + 2 = 4$? I have confirmed that $2 + 2 = 4$ over and over again by counting. My belief that $2 + 2 = 4$ is justified by induction: I have never encountered a counter-example, but only many positive cases. My current epistemic reason (warrant) for believing that $2 + 2 = 4$ is inductive. I take it that most others have the same type of warrant or they are warranted to believe mathematical truths on the basis of the testimony of experts (maths teachers etc.). Is arithmetic therefore an empirical science that discovers and justifies truths by induction? Mill and others have answered 'yes' and concluded that arithmetic is an empirical science.

But this just seems wrong. Even if everyone knew that $2 + 2 = 4$ only by induction, this way of knowing that $2 + 2 = 4$ does not conform to the kind of truth it is. There are other ways of coming to know the same truth, which are, in a way to be made precise, more suited to its nature. In order to make room for the required distinction between ways of coming to know a truth, Frege distinguishes between *epistemic reasons* and *grounds of truth*; in his later work he will speak of *reasons for holding true and reasons for truth*. The distinction can be introduced by means of an example.[11]

After reading the outside thermometer I conclude that it is cold outside. What justifies me in making this judgement, my *epistemic reason*, is another judgement, namely my judgement that the thermometer reads such and such. My epistemic reason will be specified in an answer to the question: what entitles me to judge now that it is warm outside? Something is a *thinker's* epistemic reason for a judgement at *a time* if it entitles *him* to make the judgement that initiates a belief. The same thinker can have different epistemic reasons for the same belief at different times (I may have now better epistemic reasons for a belief than I had previously).

Similarly, different people may have different epistemic reasons for judging the same truth at the same time. Frege identifies epistemic reasons with judgements: making one judgement entitles one to make further judgements.

While the observational judgement that the thermometer reads thus-and-so (together with background knowledge) entitles me to judge now that the weather is warm, there is another relation between these facts that is the other way around: the thermometer reads thus-and-so *because* the weather is warm and not the other way around. Hence, Frege distinguishes between a four-place relation that holds between judgements (beliefs) relative to a time and a thinker that he calls entitlement (*Berechtigung*) or justification (*Rechtfertigung*) and a two-place relation between truths that he calls either simply *dependence* or *grounding*.

The distinction between grounds and epistemic reasons gives us now two options for making distinctions among truths:

1   One can distinguish truths with respect to the epistemic reasons someone has to believe them at some time.
2   One can distinguish truths with respect to their grounds.

Frege opts for (2) and argues that the philosophically interesting classifications of truths concern their grounds. His inspiration is Leibniz:

> [W]e are concerned here not with the way they [the laws of number] are discovered but with the kind of ground on which their proof rests; or in Leibniz's words 'the question here is not one of the history of our discoveries, which is different in different men, but of the connexion and natural order of truths, which is always the same' (*Nouveaux Essais*, IV, §9).
>
> (FA: 23)

Truths are ordered by the ground-relation. Why is this order 'natural'? It is natural because it orders truths according to their nature. The ground-relation holds, if it does, between truths in virtue of their inner nature. Hence, the ground-relation can be used to classify truths indirectly by their inner nature.

The grounds of a truth are discovered in proofs. For some truths there is one *perfect* proof.[12] The perfect proof is, as Frege puts it in BS, connected to the *inner nature of the truth* proved: because a truth has a certain inner nature, that is, I take it, it consists of certain concepts in a certain combination, it can proved in one way and not another. If there is such a connection between the inner nature of a truth and a particular kind of proof, giving such a proof for a truth is an indirect way of establishing something about the truth itself, namely, what kind of truth it is.

For this reason Frege classifies truths by the kind of *proofs* they have. Consider a non-primitive truth *P*, i.e. a truth that is grounded in other truths. Its grounds can be arranged in a sequence starting with *P* and terminating in primitive truths; the grounding-sequence. If *P* has a grounding-sequence that *only* contains laws of logic and truths that can be recognised by defining one or more concepts they contain, I will call it a *truth with purely logical grounds*. If the grounding-sequence of a truth contains at least some truths about particular matters of facts, I will call it a *truth with empirical grounds*. In FA, Frege connects the distinction between *truth with purely logical grounds* and *truth with empirical grounds* with the Kantian distinction between analytic/synthetic, a priori/a posteriori:

> It now depends on finding the proof and following it back to the primitive truths. If on the way only general logical laws and definitions are encountered, then the truth is an analytic one, provided one takes also sentences into account on which, for instance, the admissibility of a definition rests. If it is however not possible to give the proof, without using truths that are not of general logical nature, but instead refer to the domain of a particular science, then the sentence is a synthetic one. For a truth to be a posteriori, it must be impossible for its proof to avoid appeal to facts, that is, to unprovable and non-general truths that contain predications of particular objects. But if, on the contrary, it is possible to give a proof exclusively from general laws, which themselves neither need nor admit of proof, then the truth is a priori.
>
> (FA: 4. My translation.)

A proof is a chain of judgements that, in the ideal case, recaptures the ordering of truths.[13] A synthetic truth is defined as *a truth that*

is impossible to prove from laws of logic and definitions alone.
Why is it impossible to prove a truth in this way? Because the truth
is not grounded only in the laws of logic.

Frege arrives in this way at the following definitions:

> (An) *P* is an analytic truth = df. *P* has purely logical grounds.
> (Syn) *P* is a synthetic truth = df. *P* is not an analytic truth.

As we have seen, the argument from similarity makes it plausible
that the truths of arithmetic are analytic *in this sense*.

The epistemic distinction between a priori and a posteriori is
also explained with respect to provability and, ultimately, types of
grounding-sequences:

> (Ap) *P* is an a priori truth = df. *P*'s grounding-sequence contains only
> laws that are neither in need nor capable of proof.
> (Apo) *P* is an a posteriori truth = df. *P* is not an a priori truth.

The argument from similarity also makes it plausible that the
truths of arithmetic are a priori *in this sense*.

Although Frege defines analyticity and a priority both in terms
of truth-grounds, they don't coincide. For not all primitive laws
are laws of logic (and so not all a priori truths are analytic). The
laws of logic are of unrestricted generality. They hold for everything. The law of identity can serve as an example. Every object is
identical with itself, independently of its particular nature. Now
the truths of geometry can only be proved from primitive laws of
restricted generality. It is a law of restricted generality that every
straight line is the shortest connection between two points. This
law holds for geometrical objects, it does not hold for everything
tout court. A geometrical proposition cannot be proved without
invoking such special laws. Hence, the truths of geometry are *synthetic* a priori, the truths of arithmetic analytic a priori.

(Ap) explains the knowability of a truth independently of
experience in terms of its provability from primitive truths.
Primitive truths have no grounds, therefore they cannot be
proved. However, they also don't need to be proved to be rationally believed (FA: 4). If a truth neither admits of nor needs

proof, how can we be entitled to believe it and come to know it? One cannot prove a primitive truth, but one can make it plausible by supplying epistemic reasons. For example, Frege reports in a letter to Russell that he accepted a primitive logical law because this law alone allowed him to explain how we apprehend the numbers (PMC: 140–1; BW: 223). However, in the ideal case we come to know a primitive truth simply by apprehending it. Everyone who grasps the law of identity that everything is self-identical is entitled to believe that everything is self-identical.

To sum up the discussion so far: one may know a truth, but yet not know it in a way that conforms to its nature. In order to come to know the truth in the right way, one needs to find its grounds. Finding the truth-grounds of already known truths has further advantages:[14]

1   In finding the grounds for a known truth one establishes how the truth can be ideally known. For example, our current reasons for holding true that $2 + 2 = 4$ can be empirical, yet the grounds of this truth are not. Ideally, it can be known a priori (FA: §3).

2   In finding the grounds for a known truth one can come to know it in a more secure way (CN: 103; BS: iii; FA: 1–3). One cannot reject the laws of logic without undermining the ability to make judgements. In this sense believing something on the basis of the laws of logic is more secure than believing it on the basis of other truths that can be doubted and even be rationally rejected.

3   In finding the grounds for known arithmetical truths one will show how these truths can be derived from a small number of axioms. Hence, Frege speaks in BS of finding a core of laws that contain by their power all other truths of arithmetic (CN: §13, 136; BS: §13, 24).

Frege's definitions of analyticity and a priority for truths make substantial assumptions. *First*, we need to understand what it is for one truth to be the ground of another truth to apply the definition. *Second*, there can only be analytic truths if there are *logical* laws. Let us try first to get a better understanding of the grounding-relation.

MORE ON TRUTH-GROUNDS

Frege has the grounding-relation in mind when he says that a proof 'affords us insight into the dependence of truths upon one another' (FA: 2). How can one understand the idea that one truth is the ground of another truth? In the quote from BS he says that the most perfect way to prove a truth is the basis for a classification of truth. This suggests that grounding is an idealised epistemic relation between truths:

> (GE) The truth *P* is a ground of the truth *Q* if, and only if, the most perfect proof of *Q* uses *P* as a premise.

But why does the most perfect proof of Q use P as a premise? A proof does not create a relation between truths; it must capture a relation that already exists.[15] It is possible to prove a truth from other truths because these truths are related in a certain way.

The fact that a truth is the ground of some other truths is not dependent on facts about provability, while facts about provability depend on the obtaining of the grounding-relation. Such an objective understanding meshes with Frege's view that the inner nature of a 'sentence' determines whether and how it is provable. How can one explain this objective notion of grounding further? Unfortunately his writings are not of much help in answering this question. He uses the notion of grounding, but he does not discuss it in detail. I will now try to extract at least the core of his understanding of grounding from his writings.

First, there are basic or primitive truths (*Urwahrheiten*) that have no grounds. Take the law of identity that everything is self-identical. This is a truth, but what could be its ground? One may be tempted to answer that everything is self-identical because the Moon is the Moon, 1 = 1, and so on. These particular truths have in turn no grounds. Hence, there are infinitely many primitive truths. These truths cannot be proved because they have no grounds.

Now Frege takes the assumption of 'infinitely many unprovable truths to be incongruous and paradoxical' because reason demands surveyability of its foundations (FA: 6). But why should a prima facie plausible requirement about known truths hold for the objective grounding-relation?

A more convincing reason to hold that general truths can be primitive is that some general truths have no particular true instances. It is, for example, a general truth that every truly good deed is morally right, even if there are no truly good deeds. If the truth of a general proposition does not depend on its having true instances, why should the truth of a general primitive proposition depend on its having true instances?

Frege assumes that some laws of logic are primitive. But he also provides arguments for the truth of what he calls 'basic laws' that draw on truths about the meaning of words used to express the laws. For example, in BS he writes about the law (L1):

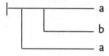

that it says:

> 'The case in which *a* is denied, *b* is affirmed, and *a* is affirmed is excluded'. This is evident, since *a* cannot be denied and affirmed at the same time. We can also express the judgement in words this way. 'If a proposition *a* holds, then it also holds in case an arbitrary proposition *b* holds'.
>
> (CN: 137; BS: 26)

If this is a justification of a law of logic that draws on more basic truths, Frege's practice would contradict his claim that the laws of logic are primitive. However, the law holds independently of the meaning of the sign. Hence, although the argument cannot prove the law from the grounds for its truth, it can help one to come to know the law by furthering understanding of the concepts involved. When the argument has helped one to understand the law one has thereby come to know it.[16]

Second, a truth *P* can only be the ground of a truth *Q* if *P* is more general than Q. This is indirectly made plausible by the previous point. For instance, it is not the case that everything is self-identical in virtue of the fact that every number is self-identical. Numbers are self-identical because everything is self-identical. There is therefore an asymmetry between laws of restricted generality, the arithmetical laws concern all *numbers*, and laws of unrestricted generality, the laws of logic concern *everything*. It is possible that the latter are the grounds of the former, but not the other way around.

Third, Frege remarks that it is natural to deduce more complex from less complex truths in order to establish the relation among truths (CN: 136; BS: 25). When is the truth Q more complex than the truth P? Although Frege does not explicitly state it, it is plausible to assume that he works with the following idea: if the concepts that are contained in Q can be defined in terms of the concepts contained in P, but not the other way around, Q is more complex than P. The laws of logic are the grounds of the truth of arithmetic, in part, because arithmetical concepts such as *number* can be defined in terms of logical concepts (but not the other way around).

If we take these points together, we arrive at least at a necessary condition for the obtaining of the grounding-relation between two truths:

> The truth P is a ground of the truth Q only if P is less complex and more general than Q.

In order to arrive at a full understanding of the grounding-relation one needs to add to this necessary condition the further condition that Q *depends* on P. In his later work 'On the Foundations of Geometry II' Frege will explain what dependence means as applied to truths (true thoughts):

> Let Ω be a group of true thoughts. Let a thought G follow from one or several of the thoughts of this group by means of a logical inference such that apart from the laws of logic, no proposition not belonging to Ω is used. Call what we have just performed a logical step. Now if through a sequence of such steps, where every step takes the result of

the preceding as one of its basis, we can reach a group of thoughts that
contains the thought A, then we call A dependent upon group Ω. If this
is not possible, then we call A independent of Ω. The latter will occur
when A is false.

(CP: 334, 423–4)

It is not far fetched to assume that Frege has this notion of dependence already in mind in his early work. We will look closer at the
notion of a logical inference in Chapter 3. All we need to know for
our purposes here is that a logical inference is a judgement mediated by other judgements (PW: 3; NS: 3). There is a tension
between Frege's view that there is a mind-independent ordering of
truths into grounds and grounded truths and the explanation of
this ordering via the notion of judgement. If the ordering of truth
is objective, it should not be explained by appealing to inferences.
According to him, a truth A is dependent on other truths Ω if one
can reach A in a series of logical steps from Ω. One will immediately ask whether there are intrinsic properties of A and Ω which
are responsible for this possibility. If so, then these properties
should figure in an explanation of dependence. So far, he has told
us how we discover that one truth is the ground of another, not
what it is for a truth to be a ground of another one.

In 'On the Foundations of Geometry II' Frege goes on to sketch
the outlines of what he calls a *new science*. This new science puts
forth laws, which connect logical inference, truth and other properties. The science investigates, among other things, how one can
prove that a truth is independent from another truth. He answers
this question by giving a new characterisation of the notion of
(in)dependence, which is close to the one proposed by Bolzano
before him:[17] The thought t is dependent on the thought t^* if, provided the thought t (t^*) is expressed by the sentence s (s^*) of a logically perfect language, every variation of the non-logical words in
s^* that creates a true variant of s^*, also creates a true s variant. To
illustrate this with an example, consider the thought expressed by
'Venus = Venus' and the thought expressed by 'Everything is
identical with itself'. Every replacement of the non-logical word
'Venus' with a referring singular term will generate a true variant
of our first sentence and vacuously a true variation of the second.

Hence, all variations of non-logical words with referential expressions that make the first thought true also make the second thought true and vice versa. Consequently, the first thought depends on the second and the second depends on the first.

This example can also be used to show why grounding is not exhausted by dependence between truths. One wants to say that Venus is identical with Venus because everything is self-identical, but not the other way around. However, the truth that Venus is identical with Venus and that everything is self-identical are mutually dependent. Hence, Frege needs to add further consideration about complexity and generality to bring out that the truth that everything is self-identical is the ground of the truth that Venus is identical with Venus and not the other way around. But even if we have done so, we cannot be satisfied. For Frege's characterisation of dependence requires that the thoughts under investigation are expressed in a special vocabulary. But to be so expressible is not an intrinsic property of thoughts. Frege himself takes therefore the second characterisation only to approximate the matter (CP: 337, 426).

As far as I know Frege does not give a satisfactory characterisation of the grounding-relation. But he outlines ways to track which truth is the ground of which other truth. That will suffice for our purposes.

WHAT IS LOGIC?

Frege's definition of analyticity by means of the notion of a basic logical law makes it important to get clear wherein the logical nature of such a law consists. Here is why. Kant took Aristotle's syllogistic to exhaust logic: 'It is remarkable also that to the present day this logic has not been able to advance a single step, and is thus to all appearances a closed and completed body of doctrine' (Kant 1781/7: B viii).

Now Frege simplified the language in which Aristotelian syllogistic logic was expressed and added new laws to it. Consider the logical law:

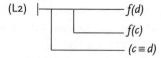

(L2) ⌐ ——— $f(d)$
       ——— $f(c)$
       ——— $(c \equiv d)$

Frege glosses this law as '[t]he case in which the content of c is identical with the content of d and in which $f(c)$ is affirmed and $f(d)$ denied does not occur' (CN: 162; BS: 50). (L2) cannot even be formulated in the language of Aristotelian logic.

The extension of Aristotelian logic makes Frege vulnerable to an objection levelled against Russell by Poincaré:

> We see how much richer the new logic is than the classical logic; the symbols are multiplied and allow of varied combinations which are no longer limited in number. Has one the right to give this extension to the meaning of the word *logic*? It would be useless to examine this question and to seek with Russell a mere quarrel about words. Grant him what he demands, but be not astonished if certain verities declared irreducible to logic in the old sense of the word find themselves now reducible to logic in the new sense – something very different.
>
> (Poincaré 1908: 461)

Assume for the sake of argument that Frege had managed to prove the laws of arithmetic on the basis of the laws of logic and definitions. For him this shows that arithmetic consists of analytic truths known a priori. Frege's modus ponendo ponens is the Kantian's modus tollendo tollens: arithmetic is synthetic, therefore the laws used to prove the truths of arithmetic are not analytic or, more broadly, of logical nature.

Frege's definition of analyticity does not say anything about the status of the laws of logic.[18] It would, however, be surprising if he supposed that the basic laws of logic were synthetic. A conservative modification of Frege's view would be to say that a truth is analytic if, and only if, it is provable from the logical laws and definitions, or it is itself a logical law. But this modification simply stipulates that the logical laws have a special status, while dialectically an explanation and justification of this status is needed. For example, Heck says:[19]

[N]o derivation of the basic laws of arithmetic will decide the epistemological status of arithmetic on its own. It will simply leave us with the epistemological status of the axioms and rules used in the derivation. It thus must be at least an intelligible question whether the axioms and rules of the Begriffsschrift are logical in character. What other question could remain?

(Heck 2007: 31)

The upshot of this is that Frege needs to provide a principle-based answer to the question wherein the logical character of the foundational laws consists that does not beg the question against Kant.

In which sense are then laws such as (L1) and (L2) laws of *logic*? Previously we saw that Frege answered this question as follows: the laws of logic are those primitive laws of unrestricted generality that yield prescriptions for the assessment of truth-directed thinking, independently of its particular subject-matter.

How does this conception of a logical law help Frege to show that the Kantian is wrong? In trying to prove the laws of arithmetic from the laws of logic, he will try to prove the basic laws of arithmetic from the laws to which every thinker who aims to judge correctly is committed. According to Frege, the laws of logic are the primitive and unrestricted laws that everyone who strives for the truth must implicitly acknowledge. He gives a good description of this project in BS when he says about the proofs in BS that they are examples of how

pure thought (regardless of any content given through the senses or even given *a priori* through an intuition) is able, all by itself, to produce from the content *which arises from its own nature* judgements which at first glance seem to be possible only on the grounds of some intuition.

(CN: 167; BS: 54. My emphasis.)

Imagine a rational thinker who lacks all perceptual abilities as well as the ability for perceptual imagination. The thinker can nonetheless strive for truth and make the prescription of judgement intelligible to himself. He can thereby come to know the laws of logic and infer the laws of arithmetic from these laws. Ideally, a judging subject who (1) can articulate the prescriptions for judgement and the laws that these prescriptions presuppose and (2) can infer and define is in a position to come to know the truths of arithmetic.

In FA Frege illustrates his view with a suggestive picture:

> In arithmetic we are not concerned with objects which we come to know as something alien from without through the medium of the senses, but with objects given directly to our reason and, as its nearest kin, utterly transparent to it.
>
> (FA: 115)

A thinker who can make judgements can find out the principles to which this activity commits him. If Frege is right, these principles are based on the laws of logic, which, in turn, are the grounds of the truths of arithmetic. If a thinker can work his way from the pre-scriptions or commendations for judgement to the laws of truth underwriting them, he has the basis to prove the laws of arithmetic.

Let us summarise the discussion so far: what makes a primitive law of unrestricted generality a law of logic? We have seen that Frege applies a test for logicality in the argument from similarity: a law that grounds norms with respect to which an episode of thinking must be assessable to be a judgement or inference, is a logical law. The laws of arithmetic are such laws, but they are not primitive logical laws. They themselves are grounded in the basic laws of logic.

If Frege can prove the truths of arithmetic from the basic laws of logic together with suitable definitions, he has won the day, even if Kant and his followers would disagree with Frege's con-ception of logic. We can therefore set up the dialectic between Frege and Kant without assuming a shared notion of logic by ask-ing: are the grounds of arithmetical truths solely laws of truth that neither admit of nor need proof to which every rational thinker who pursues the truth is rationally committed? Frege says 'yes', Kant says 'no'. According to Kant, arithmetical truths can only be known by constructing and intuiting arithmetical concepts. This way of putting the problem yields a sharp contrast between Frege and Kant *independently of their disagreement over what logic is and which laws it comprises.*

What matters for the further discussion is how Frege understands the generality of the laws of logic and which commitments this understanding brings with it. Hence, I will turn now to the question: what is a *law* of logic?

WHAT IS A *LAW* OF LOGIC?

Laws of logic are *laws* and laws are *general*. What does the generality of a law of logic consist in? In order to see the bite of the question compare it with a law of physics. Such a law holds for *every* particle. For which things does a law of logic hold?

Let us start by looking at Frege's thought about generality. Generality and its expression is the starting point of the *Begriffsschrift*. Section 1 of the *Begriffsschrift* reads as follows:

> The signs customarily used in the general theory of magnitudes are divided into two kinds. The first includes the letters, each of which represents either a number left undetermined or a function left undetermined. This indeterminacy makes it possible to use letters to express the general validity of sentences like
>
> $(a + b)c = ac + bc.$
>
> The other kind includes signs like $+$, $-$, $\sqrt{}$, 0, 1, 2, of which each has its particular meaning.
>
> *I adopt this fundamental thought of a distinction between two kinds of signs that has not been carried out in the theory of magnitudes in order to use it for the more inclusive domain of pure thought.* I divide therefore all signs which I will apply *into those under which one may think different things* and *those that have a particular sense*. The first are the *letters,* and these are to serve mainly the expression of generality. In spite of all indeterminateness one has to require that a letter once it has been given a meaning retains it in the same connection.
>
> (CN: 111; BS: 1. In part my translation.)

Arithmetic textbooks formulate the laws of arithmetic by using letters. Take Frege's example:

The distributive law of multiplication: $(a + b)c = ac + bc.$

The distributive law is what expressed by the statement above by means of letters such as 'a', 'b' etc. The letters do not name particular numbers. Numerals such as '1' do. If we only used numerals we could not formulate the laws of arithmetic. We could say '$(1 + 2) \times 3 = 1 \times 3 + 2 \times 3$ and so on'. But the 'and so on' is too unspecific to make clear which law is under consideration. The expressions of arithmetical laws contain letters, the expressions of particular arithmetical facts don't. How do letters manage to express generality?

The adverb 'indeterminately' provides the clue. Take 'a' to indeterminately indicate numbers. The meaning of 'a' does not therefore pick out one of them as the referent of the term: each number is as good a candidate as any for being the referent of 'a'. Therefore, no number is determinately referred to by 'a' etc. For example, someone who understands the law cannot sensibly ask: 'which of all numbers is a?'

Is 'indeterminate indication' a form of ambiguity?[20] Sometimes it seems so. A letter can indeterminately indicate many things if either its sense is unspecific or it has many senses. In both cases there are many candidates for being its referent. As in other cases of indeterminacy, we are free to make the indeterminate meaning determinate by replacing it with determinate meanings. The only restriction is that every meaning we give to 'a' will be a meaning that makes the letter stand determinately for one number. If we give 'a' the meaning of a numeral, we bring it about that it stands determinately for a number. Let us call a stipulation that endows 'a' with such a meaning 'a sharpening'. If every sharpening of the meaning of the letters contained in a sentence s generates a true sentence about numbers, s is a general truth about numbers (a law in Frege's sense). The sentence '$(a + b)c = ac + bc$' is a law since all 'sharpenings' that make each letter determinately stand for a number yield true sentences about particular numbers. Hence, '$(a + b)c = ac + bc$' is a law of number.

One sharpens the meaning of a letter that indeterminately indicates numbers if one gives it the sense of a particular numeral. If there is for every number a designator, the generality of '$(a + b)c = ac + bc$' implies that one can replace the letters with designators of numbers, and as long as one replaces the same letter with the same designator, the replacement 'generates' a particular arithmetical truth. Hence, the following inference is valid:

$(a + b)c = ac + bc$
Therefore: $(1 + 2) \times 3 = 1 \times 3 + 2 \times 3$

If we want to organise our arithmetical knowledge in such a way that finite minds can grasp it, we need to find the laws of arithmetic from which all particular arithmetical truths can be inferred in this way. The laws cannot be expressed without using letters or signs that have the same function. No wonder that Frege has put letters and generality at the beginning of his work.

He then went on to generalise the use of letters to express the laws of logic. We have already seen how he expressed the generality of the laws of logic by means of letters. Consider again (L1) and (L2):[21]

(L1)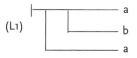

(CN: 137; BS: 26)

(L2)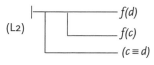

(CN: 161; BS: 50)

As one can infer from the laws of arithmetic particular arithmetic truths, one can infer from the laws of logic particular logical truths. For example,

Therefore:

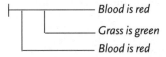

But if letters, in general, indeterminately indicate things, they must also do so in laws of logic. So which things does 'a' indeterminately indicate in the formulation of Frege's first logical law? To see the problem consider a strengthened version of the second law:

$$f(a) = f(b)$$
$$a = b$$

(see PMC: 152–3; BW: 235)

The letters 'a' and 'b' indeterminately indicate objects. So one must replace 'a' and 'b' with the names of objects, for instance, 'the evening star' and 'the morning star'. If we do this, we get 'If the morning star is the same thing as the evening star, the morning star is a planet is the same thing as the evening star is a planet.' The consequent, and therefore this conditional itself, is not a sentence of English. But take: 'If the morning star is the same thing as the evening star, the morning star's being a planet is the same thing as the evening star's being a planet.' This is a bit awkward, but correct English. (Consider: 'Usain's being quick is much talked about'.) Or consider the alternative phrasing: 'If the morning star is the same thing as the evening star, the circumstance that the morning star is a planet is the same thing as the circumstance that the evening star is a planet.' Those working in the field of linguistics talk about an operation that takes a sentence ('John is quick') and yields a noun phrase ('John's being quick'). The result of the operation is often called 'sentence-nominalisation'. A sentence-nominalisation is not the name of a sentence, but a noun phrase that is derived from a sentence.[22] Most sentence-nominalisations retain features of the sentence they are derived from, such as the argument structure of the verb. When Frege talks about sentences flanking the identity-sign, we must understand him as saying that sentence-nominalisations such as 'the evening star's being a planet' flank the identity-sign.[23]

I will devote the next two chapters to Frege's *Begriffsschrift*. But I will anticipate some points here in order to make Frege's view of logical laws intelligible. In BS Frege says:

> We can imagine a language in which the sentence 'Archimedes perished at the conquest of Syracuse' would be expressed in the following way 'The violent death of Archimedes at the conquest of Syracuse is a fact'. Even here, if one wishes, he can distinguish subject and predicate; but the subject contains the whole content, and the predicate serves only to represent this as a judgement. *Such a language would have only a single predicate for all judgements*; namely, 'is a fact' ... *Our Begriffsschrift is such a language, and the symbol* $\vdash$ *is its common predicate for all judgements.*
>
> (CN: 113; BS: 3–4. In part my translation.)

If we translate an assertoric sentence into Begriffsschrift, we must split it up into a sentence-nominalisation and the predicate 'is a fact':

> 'Archimedes perished at the conquest of Syracuse' has the same content as '(The violent death of Archimedes at the conquest of Syracuse) is a fact'.
> 'Sea-water is salty' has the same content as '(The saltiness of sea-water) is a fact'.

What is the point of the replacement of an assertoric sentence with two expressions? Natural language assertoric sentences run *expressing a thought* and *asserting* together. Assertoric force is in natural language carried by the indicative (PW: 198; NS: 214; CP: 247, 377). *If there is no factor that cancels the assertoric force*, to utter 'Sea-water is salty' is to assert that sea-water is salty (FC: 149, 22 fn). But as the antecedent or consequent of a conditional ('If sea-water is salty, it is unhealthy to drink it') or as a disjunct of disjunction ('Either sea-water is salty or sea-water is full of minerals'), an assertoric sentence does not assert anything. Frege aims therefore to find a way to express the content of an assertoric sentence in unasserted form. In a language that can express the contents of assertoric sentences without *eo ipso* asserting them, these contents will be expressed completely by sentence-nominal-isations. He tries to make us see that it would be logically advantageous to have such a language and how we can arrive at it. I will come back to this point in Chapter 6.

Frege's Begriffsschrift is intended to be a language in which one can express a judgeable content without asserting it. It has a special sign to nominalise sentences:

> *The horizontal stroke*, which is part of the symbol ⊢, *ties the symbols which follow it into a whole; and the assertion, which is expressed by means of the vertical stroke at the left end of the horizontal one, relates to this whole.* Let us call the horizontal stroke the *content stroke*, the vertical one the *judgement stroke*. The content stroke serves also to relate any sign to the whole formed by the symbols that follow the stroke. *Whatever follows the content stroke must always have an assertible content.*
>
> (CN: 112; BS: 2)

The content-stroke can be paraphrased as 'the circumstance that'. He offers as alternative 'the sentence that'. If a sign follows the content-stroke that does not express the complete content of a judgement, the resulting complex sign is ill-formed. For example, '—Frege' is ill-formed; '—Frege is a philosopher' is well-formed and can be read 'The circumstance that Frege is a philosopher'. It is obvious that '—Frege is a philosopher' does not carry assertoric force.

In Begriffschrift assertoric force is carried only by the judgement-stroke '|'. It is fused with the content-stroke to the complex sign '⊢' that is used to make assertions. Frege takes '⊢' to be the common predicate of all judgements. It can be paraphrased as 'is a fact' and has the role assertoric form has in natural language: it presents the content, as Frege misleadingly puts it, 'as a judgement' (CN: 113; BS: 3–4). If we combine '|' and, for instance, '—Frege is a philosopher' to make '⊢Frege is a philosopher' we predicate *being a fact* of the circumstance that Frege is a philosopher. This is asserting that Frege is a philosopher.

In his *Basic Laws*, after the introduction of the sense/reference distinction, content-stroke and judgement-stroke will be explained differently. Frege assumes that an assertoric sentence refers either to the True or the False, if it refers at all. (More about this in Chapter 6.) He explains in section 5 of BL that '—ξ' refers to the True, if what replaces 'ξ' refers to the True, and refers to the False otherwise. According to this explanation, '—Frege' is no longer ill-formed; it is a (well-formed) complex name of the False. The sign '⊢—' is now a *sui generis* sign that, prefixed to a sentence, asserts what the sentence says (see FC: 149, 22).

With this in mind we can shed light on the generality of the logical laws. In (L1) the variables indicate indeterminately the referents of sentence-nominalisations. Frege calls them 'circumstances'. He uses a great variety of non-equivalent explanations when he tries to convey how one should understand the laws of logic and their instances. Here is the explanation that is in line with what we have said so far: An *instance* of a law of logic such as (L1) should be understood as follows:

> It is a fact that the circumstance that 2 is less than 3 is a sufficient condition for the circumstance that if 1 = 1, 2 is less than 3 (see CN: 144; BS: 33).

The letters in the formulation of the law (L1) are here replaced by nominalised sentences that stand for circumstances.

The law (L1) itself is about every object; the laws of physics or geometry are about objects of particular kinds ('All *right angles* are equal to each other'). The law (L1) itself is *not* a law of circumstances and the letters in the law statement range over everything. This comes out more clearly in Frege's later explanation of the content-stroke. Because the law is formulated using the content-stroke, every replacement of the letters with something results in truth. For example, if we replace '*a*' with 'Frege' in (L1) '—Frege' will refer to the False and the instance of the law is true.

As the above instance of (L1) shows, such instances don't ascribe the property of *being a fact* or *being true* to an object. This becomes even clearer in Frege's later work where ⊢— is no longer to be read as 'is a fact' but is a *sui generis* sign whose utterance asserts something (FC: 149, 22 fn). Why is this important?

Assume, contrary to what Frege says, that the laws of logic are laws that concern the conditions under which propositions have the property of being true (false) and which are expressed with a truth-predicate ('is true'). Let us use sentence-nominalisations such as 'the circumstance that $2 + 2 = 4$' to refer to the proposition that $2 + 2 = 4$. Can one express (L1) by saying '$(\forall x) (\forall y) (\forall p) (\forall q)$ (x = that p & y = that $q \rightarrow$ [that p is true $\rightarrow$ (that q is true $\rightarrow$ that p is true)]'? No, this is a law of restricted generality; it concerns every proposition. In contrast, Frege's laws of logic are of unrestricted generality. If the laws of logic were expressed with a truth-predicate, they would be laws of a special science: the laws of those objects that are true. This special science cannot be the universal science of logic. For this special science presupposes logic. In any investigation one will make inferences, therefore the scientists of thoughts will also make inferences. Even the basic laws of the new science incorporate the notion of inference. For example, Frege writes in 'Foundations of Geometry II': 'If such and such is the case, then the thought G does not follow by *logical inference* from the thoughts A, B, C'(CP: 336, 426. My emphasis). The laws of logic are more fundamental than the laws of the special science of thoughts. These laws must be formulated without the truth-predicate. Logic does not require a truth-property. However, one may assume the existence of such a property for other reasons.

According to Frege's mature view, the sentence-nominalisations formed by combining the content-stroke with a sentence and the sentences from which the nominalisations are derived refer to something. For he holds in BL that '—ξ' is a functional expression that maps the referents of expressions replacing 'ξ' to the True or the False. Hence, his way of formulating the laws of logic commits us to the thesis that sentences refer.[24]

In Frege's BS an instance of a law of logic that one would now render as "$(\forall p) (\forall q) (p \,\&\, q) \rightarrow p)$" is 'Cassius' being lean and being hungry' is sufficient for 'Cassius' being lean'.[25] The instance of the law demands that the sentence-nominalisations 'Cassius' being lean' and 'Cassius' being hungry' refer to things that are among the things over which the variables 'p' and 'q' range. In BS

Frege has not yet clearly committed himself to the view that the nominalised sentences themselves refer. However, one might wonder how 'the circumstance that Cassius is lean' can refer to something if the unnominalised sentence did not already refer to it.

The question whether sentences refer and to what they refer is directly connected to Frege's view that logic is a science that aims to find laws, general truths. If this question has to be answered negatively, this view will be undermined. But why should one believe that there are laws of logic in the first place? Most contemporary logicians use schemata where Frege used laws of logic. Dummett even says: 'Logic can begin only when the idea is introduced of a schematic representation of a form of argument' (Dummett 1991b: 23).

What is a schema? Take (Sch) 'If P, then (if Q, then P)'. The letters 'P' and 'Q' in (Sch) are neither variables that range over something nor are they terms that name something or sentences that express something. For these reasons a schema is not a sentence, it is neither true nor false. Together with a method of substituting expressions of the right sort and assigning objects to them, a schema is a template to generate interpretations. In the basic case, an interpretation replaces schematic predicate letters with predicates and assigns an extension to them, it replaces placeholders for singular terms with singular terms and assigns objects to them, and it replaces schematic sentence letters with sentences and assigns truth-values to them. The interpretation of (Sch) 'If it rains, then if it snows, then it rains' says something and is true. Current logicians now go on and generalise over interpretations of schemata:

> A schema s is universally valid if, and only if, all interpretations of s are true.
> A schema s_1 implies a schema s_2 if, and only if, every interpretation that makes s_1 true, also makes s_2 true.

Laws of logic are replaced by universally valid schemata, in which all non-logical words are replaced by schematic letters. This of course raises the question: 'What is a logical word?'

Given Frege's project it is not open to him to use schemata. Frege wants to ground the truths of arithmetic on the primitive laws of logic. If this is to be possible, the primitive laws of logic must be *truths*. A schema is neither true nor false. Hence, it cannot be the ground for another truth.

It is a truth that all interpretations of a valid schema are true, but one cannot infer from this truth about a schema the truths Frege is interested in. Moreover, the basic laws of logic are supposed to neither need nor admit of proof. But the fact that a schema is true under all interpretations is not primitive. It is true because of certain semantic truths, for example, that 'is red' applies to x if, and only if, x is red. Such semantic truths cannot serve as the basis of arithmetical truths. The semantic truth just mentioned is contingent and language-relative. It cannot be the ground for the truths of arithmetic that are supposed to be necessary and absolute.[26] Frege's foundational project makes it impossible for him to understand the unrestricted generality of the laws of logic as the universal validity of schemata.

An alternative to the schematic conception of logic is to interpret the quantifiers in the laws of logic substitutionally. According to the substitutional interpretation, '$(\forall p)\ (\forall q)\ (p\ \&\ q) \to p$)' expresses a truth if, and only if, all replacements of the letters 'p' and 'q' with sentences of the language used yield true sentences.

If we read the quantifiers substitutionally, there is a reason in virtue of which a law of logic is true. The law is true because all correct substitutions are true sentences. Hence, the law is not a primitive truth. This consequence is in conflict with Frege's view that the laws of logic are primitive truths that are neither in need nor capable of proof. For this reason he cannot accept the substitutional account as explaining the generality of the laws of logic.[27]

To summarise: for Frege the laws of logic are general truths, their instances are truths in which circumstances are referred to. These circumstances are referred to by Begriffsschrift sentences. He developed a special script to express such circumstances and prove the truths of arithmetic. The next two chapters will be devoted to the Begriffsschrift. Frege's conception of logic requires that unasserted sentences refer to something. So far he has only assumed this, in his later work he tries to provide reasons for the assumption made. These reasons will be assessed in Chapter 6.

2

THE BEGRIFFSSCHRIFT AND ITS PHILOSOPHICAL BACKGROUND

[T]he aim of this ideography was not to provide a means of dealing systematically and rapidly with complicated logical questions, but to enable one to settle the question as to the empirical or merely logical basis of a branch of knowledge – in this case, arithmetic.

(Jourdain 1912: 178)

When listing the results of his work Frege starts with the following comment: 'Nearly everything is connected to the Begriffsschrift' (PW: 184; NS: 200). Indeed. The *Begriffsschrift* introduces a family of ideas, which Frege then goes on to modify in 'Function and Concept', 'On Sense and Reference' and 'Concept and Object'. The aim of this chapter is to explain what a Begriffschrift is supposed to be and what its philosophical import is. I will start by contrasting Frege's Begriffsschrift with a natural language such as English.

WHAT IS A BEGRIFFSSCHRIFT GOOD FOR?

Chapter 1 introduced Frege's mathematico-philosophical project. He has a good reason to suppose that the truth-grounds of the arithmetical laws are *exhausted* by the laws of logic and definitional truths. Arithmetic truths are therefore supposed to be analytic (see Chapter 1, pp. 23ff.). In order to confirm his hypothesis Frege needs to infer the laws of arithmetic from the laws of logic and definitional truths and *nothing else*. An inference is the mental act of acknowledging a truth for a reason or reasons; the reasons are other already acknowledged truths. In the opening of BS Frege describes what he had to do to before he could make the required inferences and ensure that no assumptions beyond the laws of logic and definitional truth were made:

> Now, while considering the question to which of these two kinds [of truths] do judgements of arithmetic belong, I had first to test how far one could get in arithmetic by means of logical deductions alone, supported only by the laws of thought, which transcend all [particularity]. The procedure in this effort was this: I sought first to reduce the concept of ordering-in-a-sequence to the notion of *logical* ordering, in order to advance from there to the concept of number. *So that something intuitive could not squeeze in unnoticed here, it was important to keep the chain of reasoning free of gaps. As I endeavoured to fulfil this requirement most rigorously, I found an obstacle in the inadequacy of the language; despite all the unwieldiness of the expressions, the more complex the relations became, the less precision – which my purpose required – could be obtained. From this need arose the idea of the concept script presented here.* Thus, its chief purpose should be to test in the most reliable manner the validity of a chain of reasoning and expose each presupposition which tends to creep in unnoticed, so that its source can be investigated. For this reason I have omitted everything which is without importance for *the chain of inference*. In section 3, I have designated by conceptual content that which is of sole importance for me. Hence, this explanation must always be kept in mind if one wishes to grasp correctly the nature of my formula language.
>
> (CN: 104; BS: iv. My emphasis. I have changed the translation.)

An inference can only establish that the truth inferred is analytic (synthetic) if every step in the inference is identified. For one needs to check that *nothing but* the laws of logic and definitional truths are used. The chain of reasoning must, as Frege say, be free of gaps. This is no trivial requirement. Many inferences are enthymematic. They leave out assumptions or principles of inferences because these are taken to be uncontroversial or too obvious to be explicitly included. Frege aims to eliminate such reliance on hidden assumptions in inferences.

We can conduct inferences in natural language, that is, we can make deductive inferences from what we say to be so with natural language sentence. Sometimes an inference is represented as a step from one sequence of signs to another (CP: 318, 387). We conduct inferences on paper etc. Thinkers like us can't do otherwise; we make most inferences by manipulating symbols. The question of interest for Frege is therefore whether we can, in general, make *gapless* inferences by manipulating natural language sentences.

Frege's answer is that we can't; natural language has features that make it unsuited for conducting *gapless* inferences (of course we can reason in natural language, but we will assume many things in our reasoning that are not explicitly symbolised). Natural language is a *multi-purpose* instrument: You can write poetry, romance someone, tell the truth, a joke or make a symbolic inference. And, *among many other things*, natural language expressions have logical properties: sentences are true (as uttered in a context), they have a certain form, contain predicates etc. How could we make inferences in natural language if it had no logical properties? From a logical point of view, natural language is inadequate, not because it has no logical features, but because it has many other features as well (see PW: 266; NS: 285).

One of the main purposes of natural language is communication, the transmission of thoughts.[1] A language that primarily answers to the demands of communication needs to satisfy other conditions than a language that is primarily a vehicle of inferential thought, especially if this language shall make gapless inference possible. If I want to communicate with you, I can leave something to guesswork. Consider the following example. The question 'Will Gerrard be able to play in the semi-final?' leaves open which semi-final, for how long (a few minutes, the whole game), in which position etc. Gerrard is supposed to play. We answer such questions all the time with ease. How do I come to know what you ask me? I can only come to know what you asked by making various 'educated' guesses. Frege himself points out that such guesses are in general easily made.[2] We are sufficiently alike to reliably jump within a margin of error to similar enough conclusions to understand each other. Now making guesses is good enough for communication, but not for conducting gapless inferences: '[A] language that is intended for scientific employment must not leave anything to guesswork' (PW: 213; NS: 230).[3]

Deficiency 1: Natural language sentences are incomplete in that their meaning does not *by itself* determine a content that is either true or false. Speakers need to rely on their ability to make additional guesses to come to know which content is expressed.

Why is it unattractive to rely on guesswork? If the language we used in our inferences were to leave something to guesswork, the conclusions of our proofs would depend on the premises *and the right guesses*. The inference might still establish that a proposition is true, but its premises would not exhaust the propositions on which the truth of the conclusion depended. Hence, inferring a truth *P* from the laws of logic and definitional truths would not establish that *P* is analytic. We must make guesses and with our guesses 'something intuitive can squeeze in'. This has to be avoided if we aim for *gapless* inference. On the first page of *The Basic Laws of Arithmetic* Frege describes Begriffsschrift formulas therefore as complete in a strict sense:[4]

> Each of these formulas is a *complete* [sentence] including all of the conditions necessary to its validity. This completeness, not [tolerating] [tacit] attachment of presuppositions in thought [*stillschweigend hinzuzudenkende Voraussetzungen*], seems to me to indispensable for the rigor of the conduct of proof.
>
> (GGA I: vi. Partly my translation and emphasis.)

I will come back to the *completeness requirement* in my discussion of context-dependent sentences in Chapter 6.

Frege lists as a special form of this deficiency that natural language arguments often leave open the logical law that licenses the inference. He says in 'Peano's Begriffsschrift and my own',

> [i]n order to test whether a list of axioms is complete, we have to try and derive from them all the proofs of the branch of learning to which they relate. And in doing this it is imperative that we draw conclusions only in accordance with purely logical laws, for otherwise something may intrude unobserved which should have been laid down as an axiom. The reason why verbal languages are ill suited to this purpose lies not just in the occasional ambiguity of expressions, but above all in the absence of fixed forms for inferring.
>
> (CP: 235, 362)

Fair enough, natural language does not make the logical laws they rely on explicit. However, this is no 'design fault'. We could be more explicit and say not just 'P; If P, Q. Therefore Q', but 'P; If P, Q. Therefore, according to modus ponendo ponens Q'. To lay the blame for the 'absence of fixed forms of inferring' at the door of natural language seems to be unfair. For example, the same criticism can be made with respect to the language of arithmetic (GGA I: 1).

Deficiency 2: Natural language sentences are structurally and lexically ambiguous.

An ambiguous sentence has more than one content. Under 'content' we can understand for the purposes of this chapter what is put forth in an assertoric utterance as true. One form of ambiguity is structural. For example, in 'Flying planes can be dangerous' the phrase 'Flying planes' can refer to planes in flight or the activity of flying planes. Another form of ambiguity is due to the fact that a word can have more than one meaning ('Meet me at the bank'). Now assume that you make an inference from an ambiguous sentence. Which content was your premise, which content your conclusion?

> If sentences having the same wording differ, they can only do so in their thought-content. Just how could there be a single proof of different

thoughts? This looks as though what is proved is the wording alone, without the thought-content, and as though afterwards different thoughts were supposed to be correlated with the wording in different disciplines. Rubbish! A mere wording without a thought-content can never be proved.

(CP: 316, 385 fn)

An inference cannot be expressed in ambiguous words. For which inference is expressed? There are two or more 'conclusions' of the inference. Which one has been proved? The answer seems to be neither. Has the *sentence* that follows 'Therefore' been proved? No, a sentence is not a truth; a sentence of English can express a truth. What we prove is the truth the English sentence expresses, it is not even clear what it means to say that one proves a sentence of English: '"[T]he most important rule that logic must impose on written and spoken language" is therefore the rule of non-ambiguity: *no sign has more than one content*' (CP: 316, 385 fn. See also CN: 86, 52).

Deficiency 3: Natural language sentences suggest contents that are not asserted.

Consider for illustration Frege's example from SR: 'Napoleon, who recognised the danger to his right flank, himself led his guards against the enemy position' (SR: 172, 45). This sentence is composed of two sentences 'Napoleon recognised the danger to his right flank' and 'Napoleon himself led his guards against the enemy position' and it literally expresses the conjunctive thought that

1   Napoleon recognised the danger to his right flank and
2   Napoleon himself led his guards against the enemy position.

But an utterance of the sentence strongly suggests, in addition to (1) and (2),

3   Napoleon's reason for leading his guards against the enemy position was that he recognised the danger to his right flank.

Now imagine that you are interested in assessing which inferences one can make from the judgement voiced by asserting that Napoleon, who recognised the danger to his right flank, himself led his guards against the enemy position. Do we need to take (3) in addition to (1) and (2) into account or not? Without an answer to this question, we cannot determine what we can infer from the content of the sentence.

When we assess an inference represented as a sequence of natural language sentences we need to employ subtle tests and linguistic intuitions to distinguish between *what has been asserted* or acknowledged as true and *what has been suggested* without being asserted. A Begriffsschrift is, in part, designed to simplify matters. It only expresses the content and does not suggest anything above it: 'Everything necessary for correct inference is fully expressed; but what is not necessary is usually not indicated, *nothing is left to guessing*' (CN: 113; BS: 3). For example, Begriffsschrift sentences have no grammatical subject and predicate because the subject position suggests the additional content that the referent of the subject term has special importance.

So what is a *Begriffsschrift* good for? While (most) natural languages are *multi-purpose* sound languages, a Begriffsschrift is a script designed for the *single purpose* of expressing everything necessary for correct inference and nothing else. Since the Begriffsschrift is a single-purpose script, it brings out those logical features that are also present in natural language, but are often hidden by those features of natural language that are in the service of further purposes. For this reason Frege's Begriffsschrift differs in interesting ways from a natural language like English.

First, Frege's Begriffsschrift is *grammatically poorer than natural languages*. Distinctions that can be expressed in natural language cannot be expressed in a Begriffsschrift. As we will see in the next chapter, Frege replaces in his Begriffsschrift the distinction between grammatical subject and predicate with the distinction between argument and function. Every Begriffsschrift sentence consists of the same predicate, 'is a fact', and a sentence-nominalisation (see Chapter 1, p. 42; CN: 113; BS: 4).

Second, Frege's Begriffsschrift *contains signs not contained in natural language*. Take the most striking and theoretically important example: the assertion sign. Natural language sentences are pragmatically ambiguous. The sentence 'Snow is white' can be uttered to make an assertion, but also to make other speech acts. In science, argues Frege, we need to flag those sentences, which express contents whose truth we acknowledge (judge). In the Begriffsschrift the inscription of a sign that expresses a conceptual content is either an assertion or not. If I write '⊢—Frege is a philosopher' I have made an assertion; if I leave the judgement-stroke out and write '—Frege is a philosopher', I have merely put forth a content. In the second case, says Frege, the writer merely evokes the idea of the circumstance of 'John's loving Mary' in his audience (CN: 112; BS: 2). The judgement-stroke is relevant for inference because, argues Frege, one can only draw inferences from contents that one acknowledges as true. (More about this later in Chapter 3, p. 79f.) To see Frege's point consider introducing the logical law of modus ponens via an instance: 'Blood is red, and if blood is red, snow is white. Therefore, snow is white.' In order to grasp the law on the basis of the instance one must be able to distinguish between what is asserted and what not. For example, 'snow is white' is not asserted; what is asserted, among other things, is 'If Blood is red, snow is white.' If one follows Frege's maxim that everything that is essential for inference shall be embodied in a sign, one will need a sign that shows that a content is acknowledged as true. Hence, he criticises Peano's Begriffsschrift for missing such an assertion sign.[5]

THE BEGRIFFSSCHRIFT AS A 'LINGUA CHARACTERI[STI]CA'[6]

Is a Begriffsschrift nothing more that an artificial language designed to conduct gapless proofs? If a Begriffsschrift were *only* a language designed to express what is relevant for inference *and nothing else*, it would be sufficient to strip natural language sentences from every construction that does not bear on the inferential properties of sentences. For example, active/passive transformations could be pruned. Take as an example the language of first-order predicate logic. It is a product of such a 'delete everything unnecessary for inference' process. The language of first-order logic has no plurals, no inflections, no tenses. But other than the language of first-order logic the Begriffsschrift is not only a pruned and disambiguated natural language. It is a two-dimensional script that uses diagrammatic elements: lines and connections between them etc. What motivates those features that set the Begriffsschrift apart from other formal languages?

In order to answer this question we must locate Frege's Begriffsschrift in its tradition. Frege neither invents the term 'Begriffsschrift' nor the idea of the script denoted by it.[7] He mentions Trendelenburg's essay on Leibniz's *characterica universalis* in the *Begriffsschrift* and he seems to have taken the term 'Begriffsschrift' from it. In this essay Trendelenburg discusses Leibniz's notion of a *lingua characterica*.

What is a *lingua characterica*? In his *New Essays*, Leibniz lets Theophile say:

> [W]e could introduce a Universal Symbolism, a very popular one and better than the Chinese one, if in place of words we used *little figures that represented visible things by means of their traits and invisible ones by means of the visible things that accompany them*, also bringing in certain additional marks suitable for conveying inflections and particles. This would at once enable us to communicate easily with remote peoples; but if we adopt it among ourselves (though without abandoning ordinary writing), the use of this way of writing would be of great service in enriching our imaginations and giving us thoughts that were less blind and less word-dependent than our present ones are.
>
> (Leibniz 1764: IV, vi. My italicised correction.)

A *characteristica universalis* is a pictorial language whose signs represent visible and invisible things by sharing features. Among the invisible things, thoughts are especially important. Frege quotes Leibniz as saying that a *lingua characterica* 'peindre non pas les paroles, mais les pensées [does not depict spoken words, but thoughts]' (PW: 13; NS: 14).

Trendelenburg uses 'Begriffsschrift' for a language whose words are pictures that represent concepts:

> The human mind, which owes so much to signs, has here recognised
> the possibility of elaborating signs still further inasmuch as, instead of
> the words already present in the language, *it brings sign and thing, the*
> *form of the sign and the content of the concept, into direct contact*, and
> devises signs which represent as separated and conjoined the charac-
> teristics which are separated or conjoined in the concepts. Science has,
> in certain areas and for its own reasons, already produced the first
> beginnings of such a Begriffsschrift.
>
> (Trendelenburg 1856: 3–4. My translation and emphasis.)

Trendelenburg is not the first to use 'Begriffsschrift'. Wilhelm von
Humboldt explains 'Begriffschrift' in an illuminating way:[8] 'The
script either represents concepts or tones, it is an idea script or a
phonetic script' (Humboldt 1824: 40–2). Humboldt calls a script
that represents ideas 'Begriffsschrift'. The scripts we use, say written English, are phonetic scripts; their written words are phono-
grams. The inscription of the English sentence 'Mind the Gap!' is
a sign of a sign because it represents and is a template for the pro-
duction of an utterance.[9]

To summarise: a script is a Begriffsschrift if it satisfies one or
more of the following three conditions:[10]

1   Its signs are signs of concepts (not of signs).
2   A combination of signs to a complex sign mirrors the combi-
    nation of concepts the complex sign designates.
3   It is universal, understandable by everyone.

Points 1 to 3 are logically independent. There may, for example,
be a script that satisfies 2 and 3, but not 1. Points 1 to 3 are not
necessary and sufficient conditions for being a Begriffsschrift,
rather they go together when pre-Fregean authors shape the idea
of a Begriffsschrift.

Point 3 is of no interest to Frege. But 1 and 2 are. First to point
1. He says later in 'Thoughts': 'What is it that we call a sentence?
– A sequence of sounds, but only if it has a sense (this is not meant
to convey that any series of sounds that has a sense is a sentence)'
(T: 353, 60). If a natural language sentence is a sequence of
sounds that expresses a sense, a *written* sentence is a recipe for the

recreation of such a sequence of sounds. The represented sequence of sounds in turn expresses a thought.[11] Begriffsschrift sentences express content *without the mediation of sounds*:

> Logical correctness should never be sacrificed to brevity of expression. It is therefore highly important to devise a mathematical language that combines the most rigorous accuracy with the greatest possible brevity. *A Begriffsschrift, a totality of rules, which enables one to express thoughts directly in written or printed symbols without the intervention of sounds would be most appropriate to this end.*
>
> (CP: 292, 666. My translation and emphasis.)

Now to point 2. Frege illustrates point 2 in the following quotation:

> [T]he content is to be rendered [in a Begriffsschrift] more exactly than is done by verbal language. For that leaves a great deal to guesswork, even if only of the most elementary kind. There is only an imperfect correspondence between the way words are concatenated and the structure of the concepts. The words 'lifeboat' and 'deathbed' are similarly constructed though the logical relations of the constituents are different. So the latter isn't expressed at all, but is left to guesswork.
>
> (PW: 12–12; NS: 13)

The way a sentence is composed out of parts shall mirror in a Begriffsschrift the way its content is composed out of concepts. This maxim for the design of a Begriffsschrift can only be imposed if Begriffsschrift sentences express contents that have constituents. Frege held such a view of content when writing the BS and FA (see Chapter 3, p. 81f.) After introducing the sense/reference distinction, the maxim can only apply to the thoughts expressed by a sentence. More about this later.

According to Frege, satisfying point 1 helps to satisfy point 2:

> As the name [concept script] indicates, its primitive constituents are neither sounds nor syllables, but written symbols; it is, to use a Leibnizian expression, a *lingua characterica*. This difference from spoken language is not without its consequences, and manifests itself in

two main ways: written signs endure while sounds perish; written signs appear on a two-dimensional surface while sounds occur in unidimensional time. *Because of their persistence written signs are more like concepts, and thus better adapted to logical use than sounds.*

(CP: 236, 364–5. My emphasis.)

Frege's general message is that the properties of inscriptions resemble more properties of their designata than properties of sound sequences. A written word persists independently of our activities. Unlike the spoken word it endures after we have stopped speaking. Why does its persistence make a written sign more like a concept? A concept is something which we encounter and which we can, so to speak, revisit. Something similar goes for written words. We can encounter and revisit them. In revisiting them we may discover new truths about them etc. One point of using a script, instead of a sound-language is that the written signs have similarities to their designata. In contrast, without a special method of recording, spoken words are to ephemeral to have the properties of interest for Frege. Spoken words are similar to ideas that he frequently describes as mental processes or events (PW: 144; NS: 156). The spoken word is itself an event and it excites ideas.

The similarity between inscription and its referent (and later sense) is of crucial importance for Frege. In Leibniz's ideography some ideograms were supposed to stand for invisible things. Frege will often use language as a bridge between the visible (words) and the invisible. Here is a striking passage from 'On the Scientific Justification of a Conceptual Notation':

Without signs we would scarcely rise to conceptual thinking. Thus, in giving different, but similar things the same sign, we no longer designate *[bezeichnen]* the individual thing, but rather what the individual things have in common: the concept. *And we attain the concept only by designating it, for since it is imperceptible [unanschaulich] it requires a perceptible representative [anschaulicher Vertreter] in order to appear to us [uns erscheinen zu können]. (In this way the sensuous opens up to us [erschliesst uns] the world of the non-sensuous.)*

(CN: 84, 50. My translation and emphasis. The English translation omits the sentence in parentheses.)

First, a remark about the translation of the key term *anschaulicher Vertreter*. *Vertreter* can mean, among other things, proxy and substitute. That the concept word is a proxy fits the general point Frege makes in the quote. The adjective *anschaulich* has also different layers of meaning. An '*anschauliches* X' is an X that is or can be perceived; it means literally something that can be looked at. But German also has the idiomatic expression *etwas anschaulich machen*, that is, to explain an abstract state of affairs by means of examples or models. Both meanings are in play here and when Frege says that the task of Boole's logic and his *Begriffsschrift* is 'to depict (*anschaulich darstellen*), by means of a script, logical relations'.[12]

Second, what do the perceptible or sensible representatives do? They make the invisible *appear to us*. This sounds paradoxical. How can a non-sensible abstract object such as a concept appear to us? The perceptible signs represent the concepts they stand for indirectly to the senses by being perceptible models of them. This idea will get clearer when we look at an instructive example for Begriffschrift symbols that Trendelenburg gives:

> Our numerals, which express, following the tenfold law, the progressive formation of numbers are an excellent example showing, as in algebra and higher mathematics, that with *adequate signs* [*zutreffende Zeichen*] man's mastery, insight and art grew in unforeseeable ways.
>
> (Trendelenburg 1856: 3–4. My translation and emphasis.)

We already know the idea of symbolic construction of a concept from the discussion of Kant's philosophy of arithmetic in Chapter 1 (pp. 14–15). The series of the numerals I, II, III, IV, V, … shares properties with the series of the numbers, that is, the things designated. There is a first numeral, and every numeral has a successor, which is determined by a law, and so on. The same goes for numbers. Therefore the series of numerals stands for the series of numbers and is a visual model of the number series, the first series represents the second to the senses.[13] The sensuous signs make features of the designated abstract objects available to the senses because if the signs are produced and arranged according to the law that governs their composition there is a one-to-one

correspondence between the numerals so arranged and the designated numbers.[14]

In his late paper 'Logical Generality' Frege argues that logical
generality is a primitive notion. How can one then come to know
what generality is? The answer is that the sentences expressing
generality make it 'appear' to us:

> If a thought cannot be perceived by the senses, it is not expected that its
> generality can be. I am not in a position to produce a thought in the way
> a mineralogist presents a sample of a mineral so as to draw attention to
> its characteristic lustre. It may be impossible to use a definition to fix
> what is meant by generality.
>
> Language may appear to offer a way out, for, on the one hand, its sen-
> tences can be perceived by the senses, and, on the other, they express
> thoughts. *As a vehicle for the expression of thoughts, language must model
> itself upon what happens at the level of thoughts. So we may hope that we
> can use it as a bridge from the perceptible to the imperceptible.* Once we
> have come to an understanding about what happens at the linguistic
> level, we may find it easier to go on and apply what we have understood
> to what holds at the level of thought:– to what is mirrored in language.
>
> (PW: 259; NS: 279. My emphasis.)

After warning his readers that there are, of course, limits to this
mutual correspondence, he presses on to introduce his readers to
generality by considering law statements.

Frege argued against Kant that we cannot come to know the
properties of the numbers by seeing the series of their visible representative, the numerals. How can then visible signs make the
invisible concepts appear to us?

THE BEGRIFFSCHRIFT AS A PICTURE-LANGUAGE OF THOUGHT

Frege argues in the quote above that sentences of a language L can
only be a vehicle for the expression of thoughts or, more generally,
contents, if they are structurally like the contents they express.
Since thoughts have not been introduced yet, read for 'thought' in
what follows simply 'content' or 'meaning'. In 'Compound

Thoughts' he presented a fuller version of the argument he relies on in 'Logical Generality':

> It is astonishing what language can do. With a few syllables it can express an incalculable number of thoughts, so that even if a thought has been grasped by an inhabitant of the Earth for the first time, a form of words can be found in which it will be understood by someone else to whom the thought is entirely new. *This would not be possible, if we could not distinguish parts in the thought corresponding to the parts of a sentence, so that the structure of the sentence can serve as a picture of the structure of the thought.*
>
> (CT: 390, 36. My emphasis. See also PMC: 79; BW: 127)

Sentences are *pictures* of thoughts in the broad sense of being perceptible representatives. Frege argues that it is only possible to grasp a thought by understanding a sentence S which has not been expressed before only if (1) S can be decomposed into a finite number of simple parts e_1 to e_n, (2) e_1 to e_n express senses, and the thought expressed by S contains the senses of e_1 to e_n arranged in a way that corresponds to the arrangement of e_1 to e_n in S. Since we can express new thoughts, we should accept that the composition of a thought is a picture of the composition of a sentence.

Now prima facie a sign can express independently of its form a content. Why should, for example, a proper name not have the sense of a predicate? Consider the following example. Let the atomic and gap-free sign 'R' express the sense of 'x is between y and z'; let 'London' stand for London, 'Southampton' for Southampton, and 'Bristol' for Bristol. Does 'R London Southampton Bristol' say that London is between Southampton and Bristol or that Southampton is between London and Bristol or ...? Does 'London R Southampton Bristol' say what 'R London Southampton Bristol' says? What is said is indeterminate because the signs don't mirror the things they stand for. Speakers may come to an agreement about the significance of the order of the signs in 'R London Southampton Bristol' when they confront them and the words understood as agreed will express one thought. However, speakers of English can come to grasp new thoughts *without making such agreements*. Hence, our mini-language fails a minimal requirement for the expression of contents (thoughts):

> A propositional question contains a demand that we should either acknowledge the truth of a thought, or reject it as false. In order to meet this demand correctly, two things are requisite: first, *the wording of the question must enable us to recognise without any doubt the thought under discussion [...]*.
>
> (N: 373, 143. My emphasis.)

In view of the context-dependence of most sentences, Frege's 'without any doubt' is too strong. However, that a sentence pictures the thought expressed is at least a necessary condition for us to be able to grasp a determinate thought on the basis of a sentential utterance. If, for example, a relation is not signified by a sign that has in an analogous sense argument-places that can be filled in an order, knowledge of context and language would not enable us to express something determinately and put us in a position to grasp it.

Frege seems to be right: only if content and vehicle are structurally similar can one express the other. We (that is, beings with our cognitive faculties) can grasp thoughts only if we 'put them into words'. However, the signs that enable us to grasp thoughts also have sensible properties that distort them. This is, as he says, 'the greatest difficulty of philosophy' (CT: 45, 400). He brings it out in a late manuscript about logico-mathematical investigations:

> These investigations are especially difficult because in the very act of conducting them we are easily misled by language: by language which is, after all, an indispensable tool for carrying them out. Indeed one would think that language would first have to be freed from all logical imperfections before it was employed in such investigations. *Fortunately our logical dispositions have supplied us with a yardstick by which we are apprised of these defects [the logical imperfections of language]. Such a yardstick is at work even in language, obstructed though it may be by many illogical features that are also at work in language.*
>
> (PW: 266; NS: 285. My emphasis and translation.)[15]

Frege 'designs' a Begriffsschrift in order to express content with signs that have only logical features. As he points out, a script is better for this purpose than a reformed natural language.

Let us take stock before moving further. In Frege's Begriffsschrift signs are inscriptions supposed to do three things at once:

(BS1) They stand directly for conceptual contents.
(BS2) They mirror the structure of the conceptual content they stand for.
(BS3) Some are perceptible representatives (*anschauliche Vertreter*) of their contents.

The signs of natural language often do not satisfy (BS1) and (BS3). But why should they? According to Frege, they are designed to encode sound sequences and these in turn give rise to thoughts and ideas.

We have now an idea why Frege needs a Begriffsschrift. A Begriffsschrift is, as he repeatedly stresses, a language, whose sentences have a content, represent something. In the next section I will discuss the theory of content that underlies the *Begriffsschrift* and contrast it with alternatives.

HOW THE BEGRIFFSSCHRIFT BRINGS JUDGEMENT TO THE FORE

Let us start by putting the organisation of a pre-Fregean logic book and Frege's *Begriffsschrift* side by side. Kant's '*Jäsche Logik*' (Jäsche, 1800) can serve as a representative example (another example I will frequently use is Boole's *An Investigation of the Laws of Thought* (1854)):

Jaesche Logik (Elementarlehre)	*Begriffsschrift*
1 Of Concepts	The Judgement
2 Of Judgements	The Conditional
3 Of Inferences	The Negation
	The Content-Identity
	The Function
	The Generality

Kant works his way from the simple to the complex; Frege from the complex to the simple. Kant starts with concepts and works his way to inference via judgement; Frege starts with judgement, goes on to discuss different kinds of judgements, and only when discussing functions and generality concepts (under a different name) will enter Frege's picture of logic. The order of explanation in the *Begriffsschrift* embodies an important and fundamental change in logic. Frege will retrospectively say:

> What is distinctive of my conception of logic is in the first instance marked out by my bringing the content of the word 'true' to the fore, and secondly by my letting the thought immediately follow as that for which the question of truth can arise at all. I do not begin with concepts and put them together to a thought or a judgement; I come by the parts of a thought by decomposing the thought. This distinguishes my Begriffsschrift from the similar inventions of Leibniz and his successors, despite what the name suggests; perhaps it was not a happy choice on my part.
>
> (PW: 253; NS: 273. My translation.)

The *Begriffsschrift* should better have been called either *Urteilsschrift* (judgement-script) or *Gedankenschrift* (thought-script). For these titles would reflect Frege's view that judgements and their contents are prior in the order of explanation to abstraction and concepts.

Frege's idea to prioritise judgement and judgemental content in logical theorising is revolutionary. Surprisingly, the idea that sparks the revolution can already be found in Kant.[16] When reading Kant the following sentences will have struck Frege:[17]

> We can reduce ['*zurückführen*'] all actions of the understanding ['*Verstand*'] to judgements, so that in general the understanding can be seen as the capacity for judging. [...] Thinking is recognising by means of concepts. Concepts as predicates of possible judgements refer to ideas of a yet undetermined object. For instance, the concept of body refers to something, say, a metal, which can be recognised by means of this concept. [...] It is therefore a concept of a potential judgement, for example, that metal is a body. Hence, the function of the understanding

can all be found if one can represent the functions of the unity in judgement in total.

(Kant 1781/7: A 69. My translation.)

While the detail of this passage is hardly clear, its general thrust
is difficult to miss: concepts are to be understood as predicates
of possible judgements, not: judgements are to be understood as
actual combinations of concepts. Judgement comes therefore in
the order of explanation before concept. For Kant, this is a
particular application of the general principle that all mental acts
are contributions to judgements and must be understood therefore by taking judgement as primitive. Frege argues in
Begriffsschrift that Kant's classification of judgements in terms of
quality, quantity, relation and modality is too baroque. But he
follows Kant's 'judgement-first' principle in *logic*: all *logical*
activity can be explained by taking judgement to be logically
primitive.

Frege frequently distinguishes his own approach to logic from
the Aristotelian one. He characterises it one year after the publication of *Begriffsschrift* in the following way:

> So it transpires that even when we restrict ourselves to pure logic my
> concept script commands a somewhat wider domain than Boole's for-
> mula-language. This is a result of having departed further from
> Aristotelian logic. For in Aristotle, as in Boole, the logically primitive
> activity is the formation of concepts by abstraction, and judgement and
> inference enter in through an immediate or indirect comparison of con-
> cepts with respect to their extensions.
>
> (PW: 14–15, NS: 16. In part my translation.)

Let us expand on this and bring out how Aristotelians start with
concepts and aim to arrive at inference. When Frege criticises the
Aristotelian tradition in logic, he takes Boole's *An Investigation
of the Laws of Thought* to be a representative example of this tradition. Let us therefore have a look at Boole's views.

Boole states his aim in Proposition I of his book: 'To deduce
the laws of the symbols of Logic from a consideration of those
operations of the mind which are implied in the strict use of

language as an instrument of reasoning' (Boole 1854: 30). The operation implied in symbolic reasoning is the definite act of conception (Boole 1854: 31). Frege has this act in mind when he speaks of abstraction. The Aristotelian holds:

A1 The basic logical act is the forming of concepts and extensions.

In conception, we form general conceptions and subsume individuals under them. The objects answering to a conception form a class (extension). The limiting case is a name of an individual where the class is a singleton. The logical operations and symbolism is derivative from the mental operation of conception (Boole 1854: 32). For example, 'A + B' refers to the operation of adding the class of As to the class of Bs.

A1 structures the Aristotelian approach to logic. Concepts have extensions and are related to each other via their extensions. For example, the extension of one concept may be the same as that of another or include the extension of another. In the Aristotelian picture, as developed by Boole, judgeable contents are built up by a limited number of logical operations from concepts.[18] Primary propositions are those propositions that state relations between the extensions of concepts. For example, the proposition that every human is mortal registers that the extension of (human) is contained in the extension of (mortal) etc. Secondary propositions state relations between primary propositions (see Boole 1854: 38). When I say 'If Socrates is a man, Socrates is mortal' I state a relation between the primary propositions that Socrates is a man and that Socrates is mortal. An inference from some statements to another is valid in virtue of relations between the extensions of the concepts involved and the objects denoted. For instance, consider the inference: 'Every man is mortal. Socrates is a man. Therefore: Socrates is mortal.' The fact that Socrates is in the extension of *man*, and that the extension of *mortal* includes the extension of *man* guarantees that the conclusion is true if the premises are.

In his criticism of Boole, Frege argues that the Aristotelians take the wrong mental operation to be logically primitive. In logic one must start from the activity of judging:

F1 The basic logical activity is judging. Judging is taking a judge-able content to be true (CN: 111; BS: 2) or to be a fact (CN: 113; BS: 4).[19]

The *Begriffsschrift* builds on (F1). Here is a preview of Frege's further steps in the *Begriffsschrift*:

F2 Some judgements are justified by other judgements: inferring is judging in the consciousness of acknowledged truths as justifying reasons. If a judgement is justified on the basis of another judgement it is an inference (PW: 3; NS: 3).

F3 The fact that judgements can have the same conclusions with respect to further judgements as premises allows one to introduce the notion of a judgemental or conceptual content:

> Judgement j has the same conceptual content as judgement j* if, and only if, given the judgements j_1 to j_n as premises, the same judgements can be inferred from j and j* together with j_1 to j_n (see CN: 112; BS: 2–3).

F4 The notion of a conceptual content is used to say what a Begriffsschrift sentence represents or stands for. A Begriffschrift sentence usually stands for the conceptual contents of the judgement it can express *and nothing else*:[20] '[S]ymbols are usually only representatives [*Stellvertreter*] of their content – so that each combinations [of symbols] expresses only a relation between their contents [...] (CN: 124; BS: 13).

F5 A Begriffsschrift sentence can be decomposed in different ways into a variable or argument-part and a constant or function part (BS: §9).

F6 *Under certain conditions* not only the Begriffsschrift sentence, but also its content is decomposed into a variable and a constant part. The constant part of a conceptual content is a *concept*.

In the next chapter we will see that Frege moves in the *Begriffsschrift* from judgements to judgeable contents and from judgeable contents to concepts. Concepts are constituents of judgeable contents. For example, the judgeable contents *that Socrates is a man* and *that Aristotle is a man* both contain the same concept.

F6 introduces concepts (under another name). Frege reverses the Aristotelian order of explanation in logic: concepts come after judgements in the order of explanation. Why should one prioritise judging and judgeable content in the order of explanation and individuation over abstraction and concepts?

CONCEPT-FORMATION AND THE CONTEXT-PRINCIPLE

In the Boolean picture, one forms concepts by abstracting them from similar individuals and combining the so abstracted concepts to complex concepts and, finally, judgeable contents. Take the concept *bachelor*. It conjoins the concepts *man* and *unmarried*, the latter concept conjoins the concepts of *negation* and *married*. If we conjoin two concepts, the extension of the new concept is the class of objects that fall under both of the conjoined concepts. Other operations on concepts are disjoining etc. One can use Venn diagrams to picture the relations between the extensions of the defined concepts and their conceptual building blocks:

> If we look at what we have in the diagrams, we notice that in both cases the boundary of the concept whether it is one formed by logical multiplication or addition is made up of parts of the boundaries of the concepts already given. This holds for any concept formation that can be represented in the Boolean notation. This feature of the diagrams is naturally an expression of something inherent in the situation itself, but which is hard to express without recourse to imagery. In this sort of concept formation one must then assume as given a system of concepts, or speaking metaphorically, a network of lines. These already contain the new concepts: all one has to do is to use the lines that are already there to demarcate complete surface areas in a new way.
>
> (PW: 33–4; NS: 37–8)

In 'Boole's Logical Calculus and the Concept script' Frege provides examples of mathematical concepts which are not combinations of already given conceptual building blocks (see PW: 32–3; NS: 36–70). Here is a simpler example that can serve to make his point.[21] Assume that you have the concept *killing*. You can entertain the content that John kills Peter, that Peter kills John, that John kills John and that Peter kills Peter. If you realise a similarity between the last two contents, you can discern in them the concept of a self-killing, although you did not need to possess it before to grasp these contents. You acquire a new concept by decomposing a judgeable content, not by combining already given concepts:

> [W]e see that there's no question there of using the boundary lines of concepts we already have to form the boundaries of the new ones. Rather, totally new boundary lines are drawn by such definitions – and these are scientifically fruitful ones.
>
> (PW: 34; NS: 39)

Frege's line of reasoning goes as follows: there are concepts that are not combinations of basic concepts. These concepts can only be formed by, roughly speaking, taking certain judgeable contents as one's starting points and form new concepts by finding common constituents in these contents.

The observation that some concepts can be (and likely only be) formed by decomposing judgeable contents does not rule out that these judgeable contents contain and combine previously given concepts. For Frege continues: 'Here too, *we use old concepts to construct new ones*, but in so doing we combine the old ones together in a variety of ways by means of the signs of generality, negation and the conditional' (ibid.). On the basis of judgeable contents that combine 'old' concepts with the concepts of generality, negation and conditionality one can form additional concepts that are not mere *combinations* of the old concepts.

So far Frege has discovered a new third way of concept-formation. Some concepts are formed by conception or abstraction, other concepts are formed by combining these concepts, and, finally, some concepts are formed by decomposing conceptual contents expressed by means of the signs of generality, negation and conditionality. Frege criticised Boole for making it impossible to see that there is this third way of concept-formation that is especially important for mathematical concept-formation.

However, Frege advocated in 'Boole's Logical Calculus and the Concept script' also a stronger view. He holds that *all* concepts arise from the decomposition of judgeable contents: 'I allow the formation of concepts to arise *only* from judgements' (PW: 16; NS, 17. My translation and emphasis). In the next chapter I will illustrate how Frege follows this maxim in the *Begriffsschrift*. But so far we have no reason to rule out concept-formation by combining 'old' concepts. Some concepts are formed by decomposing a conceptual content, but not all.

In a letter to Stumpf, written in 1882 shortly after the publication of the *Begriffsschrift*, Frege argues on the basis of assumptions about concepts that one not only can, but *must* start from judgements and their contents:

> A concept is unsaturated in that it requires something to fall under it; hence it cannot exist on its own. That an individual falls under it is a judgeable content, and here the concept appears as a predicate and is always predicative. In this case, where the subject is an individual, the relation of subject to predicate is not a third thing added to the two, but it belongs to the content of the predicate, which is what makes the predicate [unsaturated]. Now I do not believe that concept formation can precede judgement because this would presuppose the independent existence of concepts, but I think of a concept as having arisen by decomposition from a judgeable content.
>
> (PMC: 101; BW: 164)

Traditional logicians say that a concept is something under which other things fall. Frege tries to argue on the basis of this characterisation of concepts that one has to start with judgement in logic because concepts have no independent existence. He renders the traditional characterisation as 'a concept demands that something falls under it'. But it is obvious that nothing can fall under the concept of *being different from itself*. How can an obviously empty concept demand that something falls under it?

In *The Foundations of Arithmetic* he makes a point about

concepts that is free from the problems raised in the letter quoted above:

> [If from the circumstance that the Earth has more mass than the Moon we subtract the Earth and the Moon], the remainder is relation-concept, which has on its own no sense any more than a simple concept: *it always demands completion to a judgeable content.*
>
> (FA: 82. My translation and emphasis.)[22]

Although the concept *being different from itself* does not demand that anything falls under it, it demands to be completed into a judgeable content. To anticipate: some conceptual contents are facts, others are not. No judgeable content into which the concept of *being different from itself* can be completed is a fact. However, the concept still demands completion to a conceptual content, either a fact or a mere circumstance.

If we take the last point into account Frege's argument for putting judgement and judgeable content first can be rendered in the following way:

> A concept always demands completion to a judgeable content by an object.
>> Therefore: a concept cannot exist on its own.
>> Therefore: logic cannot start with concepts.

He describes the feature that a concept demands completion by saying that it is *unsaturated* or *incomplete*. Why should one think that concepts *demand* completion into judgeable contents? It is plausible to hold that there are things that cannot exist 'on their own'. For instance, the axis of the Earth depends for its existence of the Earth. But our understanding of what a concept is does not it make it plausible that a concept cannot exist without a conceptual content of which it is part. It does not commit us to a view on this matter.

Even if concepts, in general, are formed from conceptual contents, concepts can be ontologically independent from judgeable contents. If we talk of 'forming' a concept by decomposing a conceptual content, we describe how we come to discern a concept into a conceptual content. We need a reason to move from 'concepts are discerned in judgeable contents' to 'concepts cannot exist without combining with objects to judgeable contents'. Frege, as far as I can see, has not provided such a reason.

The view that concepts can only be formed by decomposition of judgeable contents raises several difficult questions. If one can split up a judgeable content into parts at all, the judgeable content must already be articulated.[23] There are correct and incorrect decompositions of a content. Which decompositions are correct depends on the nature of the judgeable content: how it is composed out of other contents. A circle threatens: judgeable contents are decomposable because they combine concepts in a particular way; concepts are only formable because they can be distinguished in conceptual contents. Frege acknowledges this problem:

> [I]nstead of putting a judgement together out of an individual as subject and an already previously formed concept as predicate, we do the opposite and arrive at a concept by splitting up the content of a possible judgement. Of course, if the expression of the content of a possible judgement is to be analysable in this way, it must already be itself articulated. We may infer from this that at least the properties and relations which are not further analysable must have their own simple designations. But it doesn't follow from this that the ideas of these properties and relations are formed apart from objects: on the contrary they arise simultaneously with the first judgement in which they are ascribed to things.
>
> (PW: 17; NS: 18–19)

Frege's solution is that neither judgements and judgeable contents are prior to concepts nor are concepts prior to judgements and judgeable contents; they come together. But why should one hold that in judging one decomposes a judgeable content? Which principles guide such decompositions? I will return to these questions in the next chapter (p. 97).

In its strong version, Frege's 'judgement-first' view is controversial. Nonetheless it is important methodological advice to aim to understand concepts, if possible, by considering judgeable contents in which they occur. In FA Frege lists as one of three fundamental maxims that guide his inquiry the following one: 'Never to ask for the meaning of a word in isolation, but only in the context of a sentence' (FA: xxii). This maxim is known as 'the context-principle'. Although the context-principle is not justified by Frege's arguments, it is sound methodological advice. If assertoric sentences express judgeable-contents and some concepts are formed by decomposing conceptual contents and not by combining primitive concepts, one should explore whether one can arrive at a concept by decomposing conceptual contents in which it occurs if one cannot define it otherwise. Frege goes this way in FA:

> How, then, are numbers given to us, if we cannot have any ideas of intuitions of them? *Since it is only in the context of a proposition that words have any meaning,* our problem becomes this: to define the sense of a proposition in which a number word occurs.
>
> (FA: 73. My emphasis.)

If Frege is right in saying that we don't have Kantian intuitions of numbers; we need a new way to say how we apprehend numbers. Now we utter assertoric sentences to express judgements and to make assertions. Frege's 'judgement-first' view recommends therefore that we investigate the role of number-designators in sentences. But there are many sentences in which they occur. Should all sentences with number-designators be investigated? No, only those in which number-designators appear as names of objects: identity-statements such as: 'The number of knives on the table is the same as the number of forks on the table.' If we can give an account of the conceptual content of these statements and an account of how the number-designators contribute to this conceptual content, we have a new answer to the question how numbers are given to us. Numbers are given to us as those objects number-designators contribute to the conceptual content of a particular kind of identity statement.

We know now what Frege's Begriffschrift is supposed to do and how it is organised in a novel 'top-down' fashion. The next chapter will fill out the plan of the Begriffschrift further and start Frege's discussion of judgement, inference and judgeable content.

3

FROM SUBJECT AND PREDICATE
TO ARGUMENT AND FUNCTION

> In particular, I believe that the replacement of the concepts of *subject* and *predicate* by *argument* and *function* will prove itself in the long run. It is easy to see how apprehending a content as function of an argument leads to the formation of concepts.
>
> (CN: 107; BS: vii)

INTRODUCTION

In the tradition of Aristotle, logicians before Frege distinguished in every assertoric sentence three constituents. Boole's logic is a representative example of this view:

> A primary proposition, in the most general sense, consists of two terms, between which a relation is asserted to exist. These terms are not necessarily single-worded names, but may represent any collection of objects [...]. In the proposition, 'All fixed stars are suns,' the term 'all fixed stars' would be called the *subject*, and 'suns' the *predicate*.
>
> (Boole 1854: 42)

Boole holds that every primary affirmative proposition – a proposition that is not about propositions – has a unique tripartite analysis into subject, copula and predicate. Such a proposition states a relation between the extensions (Boole calls them 'collections') of the subject and predicate. The copula is a sign of affirmation and carries assertoric force. It turns a collection of concepts into a proposition that represents things as being a certain way.

Frege disagrees with the core assumptions of the tripartite analysis. There is no plausible distinction between affirmative and negative propositions; the copula is not a sign of affirmation carrying assertoric force; an assertoric sentence has no unique analysis into subject and predicate. The following inference illustrates the last point:[1]

(1) All dogs bite themselves sometimes.
Therefore: (2) Fido bites Fido sometimes.
Therefore: (3) Some dog bites Fido sometimes.

According to the tripartite analysis (2) has a unique predicate. What is it? If we take the predicate to be 'bites Fido sometimes' we can understand how one can infer (3) from (2). It is a case of inferring that *there is an F* from *Fa*. But if 'bites Fido sometimes' is the predicate in (2) we cannot understand how (2) can be inferred from (1). In order to understand this inference we need to take the predicate in (2) to be 'bites itself sometimes'. But if we do so, we have lost the explanation of how one can infer (3) from (2). In view of such problems Frege gives up the assumption that there is a *unique* analysis of an assertoric sentences into subject, predicate and copula. The topic of multiple analyses of a sentence into constituents will concern us throughout the chapter.

Frege argues that one must distinguish parts in a Begriffsschrift sentence, but that these parts are of a different kind than Aristotelians supposed. He calls these sentence parts *variable part* or *argument* and *invariable* part or *function*. In order to prevent a mix-up with established terminology, I will use 'function-expression' and 'argument-expression' instead of Frege's 'argument' and 'function'. He goes on to argue that argues that the division of a Begriffsschrift sentence into argument- and function-expressions corresponds to a division in the conceptual content of these sentences. As a Begriffsschrift sentence is composed of argument- and function-expressions, its conceptual content is composed of arguments and functions. He will call these functions 'concepts'. The assumption that sentences and their contents have an argument/function structure is now conceived as one of his major contributions to logic. In this chapter I will reconstruct and assess his reasons for this assumption. I will start by introducing the philosophical building blocks of the *Begriffsschrift*: judgement, inference and conceptual content.

WHAT COMES FIRST: JUDGEMENT, INFERENCE AND CONCEPTUAL CONTENT

Frege's Begriffsschrift can fruitfully be contrasted with Boole's calculus. Boole aimed to 'deduce the laws of the symbols of Logic from a consideration of those operations of the mind which are implied in the strict use of language as an instrument of reasoning' (Boole 1854: 30). Frege's aim is similar, but he takes judging, not conceiving or abstracting, to be the primitive logical operation.

We have seen in Chapter 1 (p. 41) that all Begriffsschrift sentences have the same predicate, 'is a fact', and that their contents are completely contained in their subject terms. For example, the sentence-nominalisation 'The violent death of Archimedes at the conquest of Syracuse' contains the *whole content* of 'Archimedes perished at the conquest of Syracuse', that is, the sentence and the nominal phrase have the same content. The idea that a sentence and a sentence-nominalisation can have the same content is surprising, but important for many of Frege's purposes. I will come back to it in Chapter 6. Implicit in the idea of a one-predicate language is a view of judgement and assertion. One asserts that John loves Mary by applying 'is a fact' to the singular term 'John's loving Mary'; the latter denotes a judgeable content. Frege takes these contents to be circumstances (*Umstände*). Judging is subsuming judgeable contents under the concept *is a fact*.

Frege's *Begriffsschrift* view of judgement can be motivated by looking at a problem of the traditional view that judging is subsuming things under concepts. Take the judgement expressed by an assertoric utterance of 'John loves Mary'. If judging is subsuming something under a concept, which thing is subsumed under which concept in this judgement? Is John subsumed under the concept of *someone loves Mary*? Why should one not say that Mary is subsumed under the concept *John loves someone* and so forth? There seems no independent reason to single out one of these subsumptions as *the* judgement that John loves Mary.

Frege wants a conception of judgement that brings out that all these property ascriptions are correctly detectable in the judgement that John loves Mary. The problem becomes more acute when we consider judgements of multiple generality, which play an important role in number theory. Mathematicians judge truly that for every number there is one number that is its successor and another number that is its predecessor. Which things are subsumed under which concepts?

Frege starts with judgement and therefore avoids these questions. If judging that John loves Mary is subsuming the judgeable content that John loves Mary under the concept *is a fact*, the judgement is correct if, and only if, John has the property of loving Mary if, and only if, Mary is being loved by John, and so on. Hence, in subsuming the judgeable content that John loves Mary under the concept *is a fact* one makes all the above subsumptions 'in one go'.[2] As we have already seen in Chapter 1 (p. 43), Frege will later abandon the idea that the predicate 'is a fact' carries assertoric force.

Although Frege starts in BS with judgement, his discussion of judgement mainly prepares the way for the theory of inference. In the background of BS is a view that he outlined in his early manuscript '17 Key-sentences in Logic'. It contains seventeen programmatic theses, the thirteenth to the fifteenth of which are:

13. One justifies a judgement either by going back to already acknowledged truths or without using other judgements. Only the first case, inferring, is the subject of logic.
14. The doctrines of concept and judgement serve only to prepare the doctrine of inference.

15. The task of logic is to advance the laws, which govern the justification of one judgement by another, independently of whether they
are true.

(PW: 175; NS: 190. In part my translation.)

When I reason 'Peter is a bachelor. *Therefore*, Peter is unmarried'
I acknowledge one truth because I acknowledge another truth.
The 'therefore' is a stylistic variant of 'For this *reason*'. In §6 of BS
Frege discusses the forms of inference (*Schlussarten*) and how to
write them down on paper (see CN: 118f.; BS: 8f.). One form is:

$$\begin{array}{l} \vdash A \\ \vdash A \to B \\ \hline \vdash B \end{array}$$

Frege uses here a new primitive sign without explanation, namely
the line under the premise judgements.[3] The line corresponds to
the 'Therefore' of natural language. With the judgement-stroke
alone he would not be able to distinguish a mere sequence of
judgements from an inference. An inference is a judgement that is
made in the light of previous judgements and not simply a judgement that terminates a sequence of judgements.

An inference is a judgement made because one is conscious of
grounds for the inferred truth. The grounds are truths, one's consciousness of these truths is one's acknowledging them as true.
The 'because' does not imply a temporal order. My Cartesian
inference 'I think, therefore I am' only goes through if premise and
conclusion judgement are simultaneous.

Two points about inference are important for our further discussion: First, what does it mean to 'make a judgement because
we are conscious of other truths as justifying reasons'? Inference
is a form of judgement, but not one that can be decomposed into
the conceptual building block *judgement* plus X. For example,
making the inference '$\vdash A$, therefore: $\vdash B$' is not judging that if A
is true, then B is true and consequently judging that B is true. For
I can make the inference without judging or even entertaining the
thought that if A is true, then B is true. As Lewis Carrol has
shown, one may assent to the conditional 'If A is true, then B is

true' and 'A' and yet not infer B from A. Similarly, inferring a truth from another is not recognising that one truth stands in the relation of logical consequence (or a broader notion of derivability) to another. I can recognise that B is a logical consequence of A and still not infer B from A. Inference can also not be fully understood in causal terms. I may come to accept A as the result of a causal process that starts with my acknowledgement of the truth of B, yet this process does not qualify as an inference. My acknowledgement of the truth of B may be overheard by someone who then goes on to hypnotise me to acknowledge the truth of A. Even if B must be true if A is true, and I am caused to acknowledge the truth of B because I have acknowledged the truth of A, I haven't made an inference in this case. More refined causal analyses are available, but they will fall prey, I think, to more refined counter-examples.

Inference is therefore a mental act, a *sui generis* form of judgement. This is ideal for Frege's purposes. He starts with two primitives: judgement and inference. These primitives are good primitives. For the practice of judging and inferring are practices we cannot do without and everyone knows what judgement and inference is from his own case. Moreover, inference is the basic practice of mathematics.[4]

Although there seems to be no satisfactory reductive definition of inference, one can characterise it further. If one knows P and infers Q from P, one comes to know Q. One can infer Q from P if one's knowledge of P together with knowledge of the laws of logic suffices to come to know Q. This does not mean that the laws of logic serve as premises of the inference; one does not infer Q from P and the laws of logic. An inference is accordance with the laws of logic if it conforms to prescriptions that are grounded in these laws.[5]

According to Frege's view, an inference is a judgement that results in a distinctive way from other judgements. In BS he allowed that one can infer something from judgeable contents that are merely assumed or entertained:

'[— Opposite magnetic poles attract each other' does not express a thought] but should simply evoke in the reader the idea of the reciprocal attraction of opposite magnetic poles, perhaps, say in order to derive some conclusions from it and with these test the correctness of the thought.

(CN: 112; BS: 2)

For example, if I can infer from a content that is not acknowledged as true, a content that I know to be false, I have found out that the former content is false. We will see in due course that this 'relaxed' view of inference is of great importance to the theory of judgeable content in the *Begriffsschrift*.

Frege holds later that one can only make inferences from (1) acknowledged (2) truths.[6] Here is a representative example of his later endorsement of (1): 'A mere thought, that has not been acknowledged as true, cannot be a premise. ... Mere hypotheses cannot be premises' (PMC: 182; BW: 118. My translation). Prima facie, (1) is counter-intuitive.[7] Don't we often infer something from mere hypotheses?

No, when you *infer* Q from P, you can detach the conclusion Q from the premise P. After you have inferred it, you have come to know Q on the basis of your prior knowledge of P. You have moved from the premise to the conclusion; detached the conclusion for the premises. Frege expresses this, somewhat misleadingly, by saying that the premises 'disappear': 'And this entire or partial disappearance of the premises is what is characteristic of proper inference' (PMC: 23; BW: 37).

In contrast, if you merely assume P, and 'reason' to Q, you cannot detach Q from the assumption. Your reasoning entitles you only to acknowledge that Q is the case, if P is. You are not entitled to acknowledge the truth of Q. The premise has not disappeared, but reappears in the conclusion (ibid.). Frege reserves the title 'inference' for reasoning that entitles us to detach the conclusion and reconstructs 'inferences from hypotheses' as involving asserted conditionals with these hypotheses as antecedents.

Now to (2). You might have committed yourself to the truth of P and reasoned from P to Q. However, later you find out that P is, in fact, false. According to Frege, you have made no inference. One cannot infer anything from a falsehood. This goes against our common practice of inferring. Frege is best understood, I think, as proposing a reform of this practice. His aim is to discover truths. Inferences that *only* comply with the laws of logic don't guarantee that one judges truly. Only if one's starting points are already true judgements one is guaranteed to arrive at truths. One cannot infer anything from a false premise because inferring can only serve as a method that guarantees one to judge truly if one starts with true premises (PW: 175; NS: 190; PMC: 16–17; BW: 30).

We have now an initial grip on judgement and inference and can build on it to understand *judgeable content*. When we consider judgements there are various equivalence relations between them. For instance, the two judgements may have the same emotional effects etc. But Frege is only interested in inferential equivalence:

> Let me observe that there are two ways in which the contents of two judgements can differ: it may, or it may not, be the case that all inferences that can be drawn from the first judgement when combined with certain other ones can always be drawn from the second when combined with the same judgements. The two sentences 'The Greeks defeated the Persians at Plataea' and 'The Persians were defeated by the Greeks at Plataea' differ in the former way, even if a slight difference in sense is discernible, the agreement in sense is preponderant. Now I call the part of the content that is the same in both the conceptual content.
>
> (CN: 112; BS: 2–3. In part my translation.)

In this passage Frege speaks about drawing inferences ('*Folgerungen ziehen*') and judgements that follow from premises ('*Urteile folgen aus*'). Inference is the crucial notion in the theory of conceptual content. On the basis of this notion and our ability to assess claims such as '*P*. For this reason it is the case that *q*', Frege will introduce the notion of same conceptual content:

> If one can infer from the judgement *j* together with further judgements j_1 to j_n the same judgements that one can infer from the judgement $\mathfrak{f}$ together with the judgements judgements j_1 to j_n, then the judgements j and $\mathfrak{f}$ have the same conceptual content.

The following example illustrates the point of Frege's criterion. If you are a rational thinker who follows the laws of logic, you cannot infer from your judgement that Hesperus is Hesperus together with, say, the judgement that Phosphorus is a planet, a conclusion that is not already inferable from each premise alone. However, you can infer from the judgement that Hesperus is Phosphorus together with the judgement that Phosphorus is a planet the conclusion that Hesperus is a planet. This conclusion cannot be inferred from one of the premises alone. Hence, the conceptual content that Hesperus is Hesperus is different from the conceptual content that Hesperus is Phosphorus. This is an important result that will lead Frege to split up conceptual content into sense and reference. I will come back to this in Chapter 4.

The beginning of §8 of BS suggests that a *sentence* whose assertion is the manifestation of the judgement that *p* has the same conceptual content as the judgement. Sentence constituents have contents and a sentence represents relations between the contents of the sentence constituents. Frege goes on to identify the conceptual content of a Begriffsschrift sentence with a circumstance ('*Umstand*'): a structured entity that contains particulars and properties in an order.

So far, so plausible. But a closer look shows that there are severe problems. First, as we have seen Frege will later argue that one can only infer something from acknowledged *truths*. Since, one cannot infer anything from a false judgement, all false judgements have the same conceptual content. This is highly counter-intuitive. The conceptual content that the Moon is bigger than the Earth is clearly distinct from the conceptual content that $1 = 2$. Frege's criterion is therefore based on a view of inference that he will soon reject.

Second, not every conceptual content can be the content of a judgement. For example, some sentences have conceptual contents that cannot be judged. One cannot judge that $1 = 2$. Such *obvious* falsehoods are rejected as soon as they are apprehended. But if one can neither judge that $1 = 2$ nor that $2 = 3$, one cannot distinguish these conceptual contents in terms of the inferences that one can draw from them.

In the literature, Frege's criterion of content-identity has been criticised for different reasons. Here is a representative example:

> [Frege suggests] a criterion of the following form: φ and ψ have the same conceptual content iff [if and only if] (Γ, φ entails ℵ if, and only if, Γ, ψ entails ℵ). But while something of that form must be accepted as a truth about the identity of contents there seems to be no way of converting it into a workable criterion of individuation. If 'entails' were understood in a broadly truth-theoretic fashion, the result would be that all judgements necessarily alike in truth-value, and so for instance all true arithmetical judgements, would have the same content – something Frege plainly did not intend. On the other hand, to understand 'entails' in the proof-theoretic way necessarily implicates the language in which the judgements are expressed and proofs conducted.
>
> (Sullivan 2004: 696)

From Frege's remarks about inference it should be clear that his notion of inference can neither be understood as the truth-theoretic notion of logical consequence nor as the proof-theoretic notion of derivability. Sullivan's remarks give us further reason to disentangle inference, logical consequence and derivability:[8]

1 Inference: the acknowledgement of the truth of a content justified by another acknowledgement of the truth of a content in accordance with the laws of logic.
2 Logical consequence: a semantic relation between sentences (Tarski) or propositions (Bolzano). The sentence s_2 is a logical consequence of the sentence s_1 if, and only if, every assignment of objects (individuals and sets) to the non-logical words that makes s_1 true, makes s_2 true also.
3 Logical derivability: a syntactic relation between formulas in a logical calculus. The formula s_2 is logically derivable from a formula s_1 if, and only if, the rules of the calculus allow one to transform s_1 into s_2.

We cannot take inference to be logical consequence. The proposition Q can be a logical consequence of the proposition P independently whether P is acknowledged as true. But inference is the acknowledgement of one *truth* justified by the acknowledgment of another *truth*. Consider in addition the following 'inference':

Hesperus is Hesperus. Therefore, Hesperus is Phosphorus.

Given that Hesperus is the same planet as Phosphorus, every replacement of the non-logical words 'Hesperus' and 'Phosphorus' that makes 'Hesperus is Hesperus' true will also make 'Hesperus is Phosphorus' is true. Hence, 'Hesperus is Phosphorus' is a logical consequence of 'Hesperus is Hesperus'. But one cannot come to know that Hesperus is Phosphorus on the basis of one's knowledge that Hesperus is Hesperus by applying the laws of logic.

Adding that the speaker must know that P and Q stand in the relation of logical consequence will not help. For then we have added a new premise to the argument and the question arises how we can infer that Hesperus shines from the new premises. A regress threatens if, in general, we need to know whether our new premises and the conclusion stand in the relation of logical consequence. Moreover, we often make inferences without knowing and even entertaining propositions about logical consequence.[9]

An explanation of inference via derivability is precluded by the fact that a thinker can infer Q from P without considering how his or her judgement may be couched in a formal language. Inference is a mental act that is not constrained by the syntactic rules of a language or calculus, whereas derivability is.

If we take these points together, we must conclude that Frege does not provide us with a sufficiently general criterion of content-identity in BS. He might have come to the same conclusion, for he will not use the criterion in later work (see Chapter 4, pp. 140ff.). Our partial understanding of content-identity will, however, be sufficient to follow his further discussion.

VARIABLE AND CONSTANT PARTS OF BEGRIFFSSCHRIFT SENTENCES

Let us start with the assumption about the division of a sentence into parts that Frege wants to replace. Take a simple example

'Socrates is wise'. We are taught that in this sentence 'Socrates' is in subject position and 'wise' in predicate position. The sentence is, so we say, about Socrates and ascribes *being wise* to him. What is the grammatical subject of a sentence? It is an expression that occupies a particular position in the sentence: 'In language the subject place in the word-order has the role of a *special* place [*ausgezeichnete Stelle*], in which one puts what one wishes the hearer to focus his attention on. *(See also §9)*' (CN: 113; BS: 3. In part my translation and emphasis).

School grammars explain what a grammatical subject is by appealing to a particular kind of question. The grammatical subject of a sentence s is identified when we answer the question 'Who or what does something (is thus-and-so)?' with respect to s. For example, with respect to the sentence 'John and Mary went to the cinema' we can ask 'Who or what went to the cinema?' Answer: 'John and Mary'. These words make up the grammatical subject; they are in subject position in the sentence under consideration. The link between position in a sentence and questions will be important throughout this chapter. For example, the phenomenon of questions/answer congruence can be used to shed further light on the grammatical notion of subject position. In uttering a sentence I can make a certain part of it prominent, for example, I can stress it. I will follow linguists who say that the relevant sentence part is then 'in focus' and I will use '[ ]$_F$' to mark out those parts of the sentence that are in focus. Now take the following question/answer pairs:

Who or what is wise? [Socrates]$_F$ is wise.
Who or what is wise? [Wisdom]$_F$ is exhibited by Socrates.

The first question/answer pair is acceptable, the second is not. Why? The question determines what can be in subject position, namely 'Socrates'. Given this question, 'Wisdom' can't be in subject position. This mismatch creates the incongruence. The existence of the mismatch is explained by the fact that an expression in subject position is in focus. This point will become important when we answer the exegetical question why Frege refers his readers in the above quotation to section 9 of the *Begriffsschrift*.

First we need to bring section 9 into the picture. Section 9 introduces the distinction between function and argument on which Frege's reform of logic rests. It is worth quoting the passage in full that Frege alludes to in his remark about the subject position:

> *The Function* §9. Let us suppose that the circumstance that hydrogen is lighter than carbon dioxide is expressed in our formula language. Then, in place of the symbol for hydrogen, we can insert the symbol for oxygen or nitrogen. By this means, the sense is altered in such a way that 'oxygen' or 'nitrogen' enters into the relations in which 'hydrogen' stood before. If we think of an expression as variable in this way, it divides into a constant component which represents the totality of the relations and the symbol which is replaceable by others and which denotes the object which stands in these relations. I will call the first component a function, the second its argument. This distinction [between argument and function] does not concern the conceptual content, *but is only a matter of apprehending it* [*Sache der Auffassung*]. Although, in the way of considering [*Betrachtungsweise*] just indicated, 'hydrogen' was the argument and 'being lighter than carbon dioxide' the function, we can also apprehend the same conceptual content in such a way that 'carbon dioxide' becomes the argument and 'being heavier than hydrogen' the function. In this case we need only think of 'carbon dioxide' as replaceable by other ideas like 'hydrogen chloride gas' or 'ammonia'.
>
> (CN: 126; BS: 15. In part my translation and emphasis.)

Sullivan says about the opening of section 9: 'I don't think that it would be too much of an exaggeration to hold that all of Frege's philosophy of logic should be traced to this passage' (Sullivan 2007: 101). Sullivan's assessment of the importance of this passage seems correct to me. Let us therefore work slowly through section 9. Take Frege's example sentence:

⊢ **Hydrogen** is lighter than carbon dioxide.

He asks us to vary some expressions in the sentence, while others are held fixed. Imagine that you vary or replace 'hydrogen' with other expressions:

├── **Hydrogen** is lighter than carbon dioxide.
├── **Oxygen** is lighter than carbon dioxide.
├── **Nitrogen** is lighter than carbon dioxide.

In this variation we hold part of the sentence constant. He calls the constant sentence part 'function(-expression)', the variable part 'argument(-expression)'. In the same sentence different parts can be varied:

├── Hydrogen is lighter than **carbon dioxide**.
├── Hydrogen is lighter than **hydrogen chloride gas**.
├── Hydrogen is lighter than **ammonia**.

Finally, both 'hydrogen' and 'carbon dioxide' can be varied simultaneously:

├── **Hydrogen** is lighter than **carbon dioxide**.
├── **Oxygen** is lighter than **hydrogen chloride gas**.
├── **Nitrogen** is lighter than **ammonia**.

The same sentence has different function- and argument-expressions. This is connected to Frege's view that under certain conditions the distinction between the function- and argument-expression is merely a matter of apprehending the same content. Roughly, how one divides a sentence into argument- and function-expressions does not affect what the sentence says.

The assumption that a sentence is composed of argument- and function-expressions allows Frege to describe how a sentence is composed of parts without being restricted by the traditional grammatical notions of subject and predicate. However, he has given us as yet no principles that guide us in varying sentence parts. For example, why can one not take 'is lighter than' as the argument-expression and 'Hydrogen ... carbon dioxide' as function-expression as in:

├── Hydrogen **is lighter than** carbon dioxide.
├── Hydrogen **is heavier than** carbon dioxide.
├── Hydrogen **is more radioactive than** carbon dioxide.

The expression 'is heavier than' can be argument, but not of 'Hydrogen ... carbon dioxide', it can be an argument of a higher-order function such as 'Nothing ... itself'.[10] In other words, why are only expressions that stand for particular objects considered to be arguments? The Cambridge philosopher Frank Ramsey (1903–1930) will later ask: '"aRb" does not naturally divide into "a" and "...Rb" and *we want to know why anyone should so divide it, and isolate the expression* "...Rb"' (Ramsey 1925: 409. My emphasis). Ramsey will go on to challenge the distinction between functions (properties) and objects (arguments). Assessing these arguments is not our topic here. However, I will try to answer Ramsey's question: what is the basis for dividing a sentence into variable and invariable parts?

WHY A BEGRIFFSSCHRIFT SENTENCE DIVIDES INTO ARGUMENT- AND FUNCTION-EXPRESSIONS

The *Begriffsschrift* does not contain an explicit answer to Ramsey's question. Only later Frege will state the principle that guides his use of the variation and the decomposition of a sentence into argument- and function-expressions. His considered view is that one decomposes sentences into argument- and corresponding function-expressions when one sees them as premises and conclusion in an inference from the general to the particular. Take:

$$a + b = b + a. \text{ (Law Statement)}$$
Therefore: $2 + 3 = 3 + 2.$ (Instance)
$$1 + 2 = 2 + 1.$$

Frege calls the particular sentences that can be inferred in this way from a general one the particular sentences that *belong to the general sentence* and goes on to comment:

> Here we have for the first time reason to decompose a sentence into parts none of which is a sentence. The general sentence has a part, to which congruent parts of the particular sentences correspond that belong to it, and another part – in the case under consideration it is the letter 'a' – to which correspond in the particular sentences non

congruent parts – the number signs '1', '2', '3'. The sentence parts are of different kind. The part in which the general sentence agrees with the particular sentences belonging to it, has gaps, namely in the place of the other sentence part, for example, '1'.

(PW: 201; NS: 217. In part my translation.)[11]

We decompose sentences into 'gappy' function-signs ('... + ... = ... + ...') and argument-signs when and because we infer what a particular sentence says from laws.[12] The gaps can be marked by Greek letters such as 'ξ' or particular kinds of brackets. The parts in which we decompose sentences in this way are different and they cannot be intersubstituted: the function-expression is the common constituent of the general sentence and the particular sentences belonging to it, insertion of a proper name or some proper names into the gap(s) of a function-expression turns it into a particular sentence, insertion of a letter into the gap of a function-expression turns it into a general sentence.

Frege's answer to the question why one distinguishes in a sentence variable and invariable parts seems to get the order of explanation wrong. For how can one bring a particular sentence under a general one if the particular one has not already a certain form, that is, it is decomposed into a function-expression and an argument-expression? Inference is sensitive to the form of the premises and conclusion; it does not determine the form of premises and conclusion. What is first, the decomposition of the thought or the inference we draw from it? The inference cannot be first, for we need to decompose a thought to infer something from it. But the decompositions of the sentence expressing a thought can also not be first, for according to Frege one has no reason to decompose a sentence apart from its role in inference.

Frege's official view is unsatisfactory. Fortunately, section 9 of BS hints at an alternative answer to the question why and according to which principles a sentence is decomposed into argument- and function-expressions. According to Frege, the division of a sentence into argument- and function-expression concerns only the apprehension of its content. How can one make sense of this idea? Let us go back to his comments on the grammatical subject of a sentence in section 3 of BS. The grammatical subject of a sentence is a position in a sentence 'in which one puts what one wishes the hearer to focus his attention on. (See also §9)' (CN: 113; BS: 3). Frege criticises the logical importance of the distinction between grammatical subject and predicate. He remarks that the subject position in a sentence highlights something for the attention of the audience. In this connection he asks his reader also to read section 9, the section in which he introduces the distinction between argument-expression and function-expression. Why?

Because being in subject position is just one way in which an expression can be in focus and thereby become the argument-expression in a sentence (CN: 128–9; BS: 18). *One starts to understand how a sentence can be decomposed in different ways in argument- and function-expressions without thereby affecting the content of the sentence if one generalises this phenomenon. And this is what Frege does in section 9: he finds further ways in which an expression can be in focus.* Frege makes the link between argument-expression and subject position in a sentence more explicit in the closing of section 9:

> In the mind of the speaker, the subject is usually the principal argument; the next in importance often appears as the object. Through the choice of forms or of words, for example,
>
> > active – passive
> > heavier – lighter
> > give – receive
>
> language has the freedom to make this or that sentence component to appear as the principal argument; however, this freedom is limited by the scarcity of words.
>
> (CN: 128–9; BS: 18)

We are free to single out certain expressions and put them into focus. Language enables us to do so by offering us different ways to express the same content. Putting an expression into subject position in a sentence is only one way among many to make it the principal argument-expression (variable part) of the sentence. The mistake of the tripartite analysis is that it takes this way of inducing structure into an assertoric sentence to be the only important one. A sentence constituent can be singled out as the argument-expression of a sentence in other ways. For example, even expressions that cannot occupy the position of the grammatical subject can be in focus. (In 'Hydrogen is [lighter than carbon dioxide]$_F$.' the grammatical predicate is in focus.) If the division of a sentence into argument- and function-expression are explained in terms of focus, it becomes obvious that different ways of dividing a sentence into argument- and function-expressions is only a matter of apprehending the same content. For instance, neither intonational focus nor syntactic focus can change what a sentence says, it just gives the sentence a background/foreground structure.

Let us explore the proposed answer in more detail. Consider an assertion of the sentence 'Hydrogen is lighter than carbon dioxide' as answering the question:

(Q1) Which substance is lighter than carbon dioxide?
(A1) [Hydrogen]$_F$ is lighter than carbon dioxide.

In (A1) 'Hydrogen' is in subject position and thereby put in focus. The intonational focus marks (1) the new information provided by (A1) and (2) contrasts hydrogen with a plurality of relevant alternative substances. If we shift the focus, we make a new set of contrasts relevant. The focus we are concerned with is therefore called *contrastive focus*. The importance of contrastive focus has been explored in the theory of explanation and knowledge.[13] Contrastive focus brings with it a range of alternatives that differ from the sentence under consideration in place of the item in focus. We can think of the sentence as an answer to a question that has outcompeted these alternatives.[14] Consider an example. Putting 'hydrogen' into focus makes a range of contrasting alternative answers to the question salient:

Ammonia is lighter than carbon dioxide.
Hydrogen chloride gas is lighter than carbon dioxide.

A competent speaker who understands how focus works will see (A1) as an element of a range of alternative contrasting answers.

Every answer of that range differs from (A1) in that a different expression occupies the subject position. It is natural (though metaphorical) to represent all these sentences as the results of filling a designated position in a sentence fragment:

( ) is lighter than carbon dioxide.

The expression in focus occupies a position that is filled in other sentences of the range of alternatives by other expressions.

Seeing a sentence as a member of a range of alternatives allows one to discern a common pattern in the range that is exemplified by the sentence uttered. One can discern in the sentence a constituent that it has in common with the other members of the range, the invariable part or function-expression in *Begriffsschrift* terminology (in Frege's later terminology *functional expression* or *concept-word*), and one constituent that distinguishes it from the other members of the range, the variable-part or argument-expression. The argument-expression is considered to be the variable or replaceable part because if it is in focus it is thereby contrasted with a range of other options.

Frege never considers something like 'Hydrogen ....' to be the function-expression in 'Hydrogen is lighter than carbon dioxide'. Why? A question that suggests the decomposition of 'Hydrogen is lighter than carbon dioxide' into the function-expression 'Hydrogen ...' plus remaining argument seems to be 'Hydrogen is what?' One is easily tempted to see 'Hydrogen ...' as the common part of the interrogative sentence and the assertoric one used in the answer. However, if we bring in question/answer congruence tests, we see that this is false. The congruent answer is:

Hydrogen is what? Hydrogen is [lighter than carbon dioxide]$_F$.

And not:

Hydrogen [is lighter than carbon dioxide]$_F$.

The general term is in focus, it provides the new information. Hence, the function-expression is 'Hydrogen is f', which stands for the concept under which all things fall that Hydrogen is (exemplifies).

WHY CONCEPTUAL CONTENTS ARE DECOMPOSED INTO ARGUMENTS AND FUNCTIONS

So far we have good reason to see the decomposition of a sentence into argument- and function-expression as only a matter of apprehending what it says. This strongly suggests that while Begriffsschrift sentences are divided into argument- and function-expressions, their contents are not so divided. Philosophers such as Dummett and Kenny have therefore argued that Frege proposed two different conceptions of a function.[15] In the *Begriffsschrift* functions are expressions, also called 'linguistic functions'. A linguistic function takes some complete expressions and returns for them as a value a sentence. After the split of conceptual content into sense and reference, functions will be located in the realm of reference, not in the realm of signs. This *two-phase interpretation* of Frege's theory of functions goes hand in hand with the two-phase interpretation of Frege's theory of generality as proposed by Stevenson.[16] Frege explains generality in 1879 by saying that a function sign that can be distinguished in a sentence yields for all argument-expressions a true sentence; later he explains generality differently: a general sentence is true if a part of it refers to a function, something in the realm of reference, that maps every argument, now also understood as a referent, to the True.

However, the two-phase reconstruction of Frege's theory of functions does not do justice to the Begriffsschrift.[17] He says, for instance: 'It is easy to see how regarding *a content* as a function of an argument leads to the formation of concepts' (CN: 107; BS: vii. My emphasis). Proponents of the two-phase interpretation have to explain remarks like these away, while their opponents take them to be central to Frege's understanding of functions. The proponents of the one-phase interpretation are, in turn, trying to explain away Frege's talk about functional signs. He wants to use functional signs when he actually mentions them in quotation marks.[18]

Resolving this exegetical dispute will help us to understand the Begriffsschrift better. The key to a resolution is the following passage:

For us, the different ways in which the same conceptual content can be apprehended as a function of this or that argument have no importance so long as function and argument are completely determined. But if the argument is *undetermined* as in the judgement 'You can take as argument for "being representable as the sum of four square numbers" any arbitrary positive number: the [resulting] sentence remains always correct', the distinction between function and argument attains relevance *for the content*. The reverse case is that the argument is determined, but not the function. In both cases will the opposition between *determinate* and *indeterminate* or *more* and *less* determinate decompose the whole into *function* and *argument* with respect to its content and not just with respect to the apprehension of the content.

(CN: 128; BS: 17. My translation.)[19]

Frege's main message is that one can, but need not, distinguish in the content of a sentence constituents corresponding to argument and function-expressions *if only sentences without generality such as '3 > 2' are concerned*. These sentences are decomposed in different ways into argument- and function-expressions, but there is no reason to take their content to be similarly structured. This changes when general sentences are under consideration. Hence, he acknowledges non-linguistic functions already in BS and keeps non-linguistic functions and linguistic functions apart.

Why does one need to acknowledge non-linguistic functions in addition to linguistic ones when one takes general sentences into account? Let us answer this question by considering Frege's explanation of generality:

In the expression of a judgement, the symbol to the right of ⊢ may always be regarded as a function of one of the symbols that occur in it. Let us replace this argument with a German letter, and insert a concavity into the content stroke, and make this same German letter stand over the concavity, e.g.

⊢─a──φ (a)

This signifies the judgement that the function is a fact whatever we may take its argument to be.

(CN: 130; BS: 19. My translation.)

Take as an example the judgeable content that John smokes. If we express the judgement by saying 'John smokes', we can regard the sentence as the value of the function-expression '… smokes' for the argument-expression 'John'. If we replace 'John' with a German letter, we attain a function-expression. With this function expression we can express the judgement that everyone smokes. In current symbolism: 'For all x, x smokes'. Which judgeable content do I take to be a fact when I make such a general judgement? Do I judge that each and every thing smokes, that is, does my judgement concern every thing? In his later work Frege will repeatedly answer that the conceptual content of a general judgement does not contain each individual of a totality. For example, in FA he agrees that 'All whales are mammals' looks like a general statement about whales. But 'if we ask which animal then we are speaking of, we are unable to point to anyone in particular. Even supposing that a whale is before us, our sentence still does not assert anything of it' (FA: 60. In part my translation).

Which circumstance do I then take to be a fact? The expression of a general judgement contains a function-expression. This suggests that the conceptual content contains a corresponding constituent: a function. When I judge that everyone smokes I take it to be a fact that the function x *smokes* yields a fact for every argument. A general judgement is a judgement about a function from objects to facts or a relation between functions. Frege calls such functions also 'concepts'. Concepts exist and stand in relations to each other whether there are things that are mapped by them to facts or not.

To sum up: when we make a general judgement we take circumstances that concern concepts to be facts. Not only expressions of conceptual content, but the contents themselves have argument/function structure. Frege makes this explicit when one year later he expands on the ideas of the *Begriffsschrift* in the following way:

If one takes the 2 in the content of a possible judgement

$$2^4 = 16$$

to be replaceable by something else, by −2 or by 3 say, which may be indicated by putting an x in the place of the 2:

$$x^4 = 16,$$

the content is thus split into a constant and variable part.

(PW: 16; NS: 17. My translation and emphasis.)

As a function-expression is distinguished in a sentence by varying some constituents and holding others fixed, a function is distinguished in a conceptual content by varying some of the contents constituents and holding others fixed. Consider, for instance, the following passage from *Foundations of Arithmetic*:

If from a judgeable content which deals with an object *a* and an object *b* we subtract *a* and *b*, we obtain as remainder a relation-concept ... If from the sentence

'the Earth is more massive than the Moon'

we subtract 'the Earth', we obtain the concept 'being more massive than the Moon'. If, alternatively, we subtract the object 'the Moon', we get the concept 'being less massive than the Earth' [...] instead of the Earth and Moon I can put, for example, Sun and Earth, and *eo ipso* effect the subtraction.

(FA: 82. In part my translation.)

The conceptual content of 'The Earth is more massive than the Moon' contains the Moon and the Earth. We can simultaneously subtract these planets from the circumstance and retain the remainder of the circumstance. Now you might ask 'How can I subtract the Moon and the Earth, *two planets*, from the fact that the Earth is more massive than the Moon?' The subtraction is effected in the imagination. If I imagine the Earth and the Moon replaced by other objects, say Venus and Mars, I have subtracted them from the circumstance. In my imagination I have put something else in their place. Thereby I have distinguished in the circumstance that the Earth is more massive than the Moon a constant and two variable parts. A constant part of a circumstance is what Frege calls in his early phase a *concept*.

To summarise: just as a Begriffsschrift sentence can be articulated in argument- and function-expressions, its conceptual content, the circumstance represented, can be articulated into argument and function. The articulation of a Begriffsschrift sentence into argument- and function-expression grounds an articulation of its conceptual content into argument and function if argument-expression and function-expression are not determined: 'For us, the different ways in which the same conceptual content can be apprehended as a function of this or that argument *have no importance so long as function and argument are completely determined*' (CN: 128; BS: 17).

Frege's symbolism reflects this division between Begriffsschrift sentences with and without logical generality. In the Begriffsschrift sentence '⊢ Socrates smokes' the predicate is '⊢ ...', the embedded sentence has no structure that is important for logical purposes. For example, judging that Socrates smokes and judging that smoking is something Socrates does are two descriptions of the same judgement; the same content is taken to be a fact. As we have seen, Frege expresses logical generality in BS by adding a concavity to the assertion sign: '⊢—*a*— F*a*'. What we judge by inscribing this Begriffsschrift sentence is that the function *F* combines with every argument to a fact (CN: 130; BS: 19). Here we have made in the conceptual content an argument/function (concept) distinction and marked it in the symbolism.

These observations shed light on the problem we have encountered on page 72 of the last chapter: how can Frege start with judgeable contents and arrive at concepts by decomposing judgeable contents if judgeable contents need to be structured to be decomposable in the first place? The *Begriffsschrift* suggests the following answer: the judgeable contents of Begriffsschrift sentences contain concepts and objects in combination. But for sentences without logical generality, there is no need to distinguish in their content arguments and functions. Hence, their judgeable contents need not be decomposed into concepts and arguments. One can start with these contents and proceed to distinguish concepts in conceptual contents only when one discusses logical generality. However, it is misleading to speak about concept *formation* as Frege does. Some of the concepts will not be formed, rather one will uncover concepts which one had no need to distinguish before thinking about logical generality.

MULTIPLE DECOMPOSABILITY OF CONTENTS

If conceptual contents are combinations of arguments and concepts, we face new questions. The same sentence can be divided in different ways into argument- and function-expressions. Can a conceptual content be similarly divided in different ways into different arguments and functions? Frege proposed an answer in a letter to Stumpf:

> I do not believe that for any judgeable content there is only one way in which it can be decomposed, or that one of these possible ways can always claim objective pre-eminence. In the inequality 3 > 2 we can regard either 2 or 3 as the subject. In the former case we have the concept 'smaller than 3', in the latter, 'greater than 2'. We can also regard '3 and 2' as a complex subject. As a predicate we then have the concept of the relation of the greater to the smaller.
>
> (PMC: 101; BW: 164)

How can the same conceptual content be decomposable in different ways into different objects and functions?

One answer is that the conceptual content is itself the value of a function, the concept, for an argument. A mathematical function maps an argument to a value. Frege has this mathematical notion in mind when he writes about functions. Different functions can return the same value for different arguments (3 is the value of the function '$x + 1$' for the argument 2. But neither 2 nor the function '$x + 1$' are parts of the number 3). Hence, different functions from objects into conceptual contents can return the same conceptual content for different objects.

However, this account of the composition of a conceptual content does not sit well with Frege's view that judgemental contents are composed out of the conceptual contents of the words composing the sentence that voices the judgement. The argument and the function are not contained in the value of the function for the argument. Precisely because different functions can return the same value for different arguments, arguments and functions cannot be recovered from the value of the function for the argument.[20]

One way to avoid the problem is to argue that there are different incomplete decompositions, but only one complete decomposition of a judgeable content into argument and functions. The decompositions of the content that 3 > 2 are:

Argument: 3; Function: $\xi > 2$
Argument: 2; Function: $\xi < 3$
Arguments: 2, 3; Two-Place Function: $\xi < \zeta$

The last decomposition is the complete decomposition; the concepts and objects it uncovers cannot be decomposed further. When it comes to explain what a general statement says and what can be inferred from it, all decompositions 'are created equal'. However, we can only make sense of the idea that a conceptual content contains argument and functions as variable constituents by assuming that there is a complete decomposition.[21]

CONCEPTS AND UNSATURATEDNESS

While Frege speaks in BS only about variable or replaceable and invariable or non-replaceable constituents of sentences and circumstances, he changes tack shortly afterwards. The variable/invariable terminology is superseded by the saturated (complete)/unsaturated (incomplete) metaphor. This change is evident in Frege's letter to Stumpf from 1882 in which concepts are characterised as unsaturated (see PMC: 101; BW: 164). If I take '... > 2' to be an expression that is held fixed and not replaced in a sentence, I make no substantial assumptions about it. I have characterised it via a particular role, namely to be held fixed in a process of variation. In contrast, the unsaturatedness metaphor suggests that it is part of the nature of certain expression to be incomplete. Consider Frege's analogy with the division of a line to get a grip on his notion of unsaturatedness (FC: 141, 7). If we divide a line by a point without remainder, the dividing point can only belong to one segment. This segment is complete, the other incomplete. Frege uses this analogy to 'to show that the argument does not belong with the function, but goes together with the function to make a complete whole [...]' (FC: 140, 6). Just as the line without an endpoint is incomplete, the function is incomplete. This is manifest in the expression that refers to the function. In '$2 \times x^3 + x$'

> x must not be considered as belonging to the function; this letter serves only to indicate the kind of supplementation that is needed; it enables one to recognise the places where the sign for the argument must go in.
>
> (FC: 141, 7–8)

Frege's unsaturatedness or incompleteness metaphor is central in his theory of concepts and function-expressions, but it is difficult to spell out. The function-expression '$\xi > 2$' is unsaturated because it has a gap marked by 'ξ'. However, if function-words really are nothing but sentence-remainders with gaps, they carry no information about the particular kind of completion that will turn them into a sentence. For instance, the sentence-remainder '... > 0' can be completed in numerous ways to a true sentence. Consider the following examples:

> 'John believes that 7' completes '... > 0' to 'John believes that 7 > 0'.
> 'Either 1 < 0 or 1' completes '... > 0' to 'Either 1 < 0 or 1> 0'.

Frege wants to say that some function-expressions refer to concepts and that concepts require completion by objects. But if the gap in ' ... > 0' can be filled by expressions that do not refer to objects, why should one take it to refer to such a concept? The notion of a function-expression supports Frege's view only if the 'hole' in the sentence-remainder is like a key-hole in which only some things fit. However, since according to him the hole is a mere absence, it is difficult to see what can effect the required restrictions on the argument-expressions. For these reasons function-expressions must be more than mere sentence-remainders.[22]

A similar problem arises for concepts themselves. As the incompleteness of a function-expression should not be understood in terms of a mere absence, the incompleteness of the concepts cannot consist in a concept having a gap. Russell, for example, argues against the view that concepts are incomplete remainders of circumstances as follows:

> [I]n general it is impossible to define or isolate the constant element in a propositional function, since what remains, when a certain term, wherever it occurs, is left out of a proposition, is in general no discoverable kind of entity. Thus the term in question must not simply be omitted, but replaced by a variable.
>
> (Russell 1905: 107)

Although unsaturatedness is a problematic notion, it plays a crucial role in Frege's work. What distinguishes the list whose members are the number 2, the number 3 and the relation of being greater than from the circumstance that 3 is greater than 2? The circumstance seems to have a different kind of unity than the list. In what does this difference consist? Frege brings unsaturatedness to bear on this question:

> Just as it itself [the concept-word] appears unsaturated, there is also something unsaturated in the realm of reference corresponding to it: we call this concept. *This unsaturatedness of one of the components is necessary, since otherwise the parts do not hold together.* Of course two complete wholes can stand in a relation to one another; but then this relation is a third element – and one that is doubly unsaturated!
>
> (PW: 177; BW: 192. My emphasis.)

Something can only be a circumstance if it contains at least one unsaturated concept. But this gives us only a necessary condition for the unity of a circumstance. As far as I know Frege never completed this proposal. In his later work he will dispense with circumstances and the problem of the unity of circumstances disappears. However, similar problems will resurface.

To sum up: we have now seen

- how a Begriffsschrift sentence expresses a content;
- that and why function- and argument-expressions can be distinguished in such a sentence; and

- that the content of a Begriffsschrift sentence, at least if it is general, can similarly be split up into argument and function.

In the next section I will reconstruct Frege's reason for changing this picture.

4

SPLITTING CONCEPTUAL CONTENT INTO SENSE AND REFERENCE

In Chapter 3 we motivated and discussed the *Begriffsschrift* theory of content. Frege will work with this theory of content from 1879 onwards and use it in *The Foundations of Arithmetic*. In 1891 Frege outlines in his talk 'Function and Concept' 'some supplementations and new conceptions, whose necessity has occurred to me since [writing *Begriffsschrift*]' (FC: 136, 1). In the introduction to the *Basic Laws of Arithmetic* he identifies the main changes:

> Earlier I had distinguished two things in that whose outward form is an assertoric sentence: 1) the acknowledgment of truth, 2) the content, which is acknowledged as true. The content I called judgeable content. This content is now split up into what I call thought and what I call truth-value. This is the consequence of the distinction between the sense and reference of a sign. [...] This has been argued for in more depth in my previously mentioned paper on sense and reference.
>
> (GGA I: x. My translation.)

The trilogy 'Function and Concept' (1891), 'On Sense and Reference' (1892) and 'On Concept and Object' (1893), aims to motivate, expound and explore these changes in the theory of conceptual content and its expression. The most important change is the split of conceptual content into sense and reference. In this chapter I will reconstruct Frege's argument for the split.

BACKGROUND: CONTENT-IDENTITY IN THE *BEGRIFFSSCHRIFT*

Frege's argument in 'On Sense and Reference' is driven by a problem of the *Begriffsschrift* theory of content that concerns the conceptual content of identity judgements. He argues that a Begriffsschrift needs a sign for content-identity, that is, for the relation that obtains between two signs if, and only if, they have the same conceptual content. He will go on to use the sign '≡' to stand for the relation of *content-identity*.

Why do we need a sign for content-identity in a Begriffsschrift?[1] A Begriffsschrift is a formula language made for inferential thinking. Hence, one should expect that one only needs a sign for content-identity if judgements of content-identity are of importance for inference. Are there inferences one could not make if one did not have a sign of content-identity at one's disposal?

Yes, argues Frege. A Begriffsschrift can and should contain different signs for the same content. He considers examples like the following (see CN: 124–5; BS: 14. See also PMC: 80; BW: 128). I notice an object a in the evening sky, which I would like to observe further. In order to observe a on different evenings I need to know a property that distinguishes it from all other objects. I see that a is the brightest star in the evening sky. This knowledge enables me to keep track of a in the evening sky; I have now a mode of determining a. If I possess such a mode of determination, I can introduce a name for the object determined. To make things simple, I will call the brightest star in the evening sky, 'the evening star'. Modes of determination will figure in Frege's work from the *Begriffsschrift* onwards. Later they will be called 'modes of presentation'. He trusts that his readers will acquire an intuitive understanding of what a mode of determination is by attending to his examples. Many modes of determination are specifiable by complex descriptions, in this case 'the brightest star in the evening sky'.

Let us spin out the example a bit more. An object, *b*, in the morning sky might also catch my interest. I can distinguish *b* from other objects as the brightest star in the morning sky. The modes of determination of *a* and *b* are intuitively different. For one needs to know different things to apply the different names correctly to an object. Now if you have two different modes of determination that both determine in fact one and the same object, and you want to introduce names for the object(s) you have singled out, how many names should you introduce; one or two? If you don't know that the modes of determination determine the same object, Frege's answer is: '[O]ne *must* give the object determined by the two modes of determination different names each name corresponding to one of the modes' (CN: 125; BS: 14. My emphasis).

Frege's 'must' in the quotation above is deontic (as in 'One must not sleep during lectures'). To see why this is so, imagine that you have a mode of determination of the brightest star in the evening sky and one for the brightest star in the morning sky. You can distinguish one object in the evening sky and one in the morning sky, but you don't know whether they are the same or different. If you introduce the name 'Sunev' for the brightest star in the evening sky and the brightest star in the morning sky, you will make a mistake. If you use 'Sunev' as a proper name intending to refer to one and the same object throughout, your assertions will be unwarranted by your evidence. For example, if you say 'Sunev shines in the evening and Sunev shines in the morning', you at least suggest that the same star shines in the evening and the morning. But you have no evidence for the truth of the suggested or even presupposed thought. Hence, you should not use one name corresponding to the two different modes of presentation. If you use 'Sunev' without intending to refer to the same object, you have introduced an ambiguous name. This is a violation of the rule of non-ambiguity which Frege takes the most important rule logic imposes on language (see Chapter 2, p. 52). Again your acts of name-giving deserve criticism. Provided one has no further knowledge, one ought to introduce different names corresponding to different modes of presentation. Frege will stick to this maxim in subsequent work. For instance, he writes to Jourdain:

> An object can be determined in different ways, and every one of these ways of determining it can give rise to a distinct name, and these distinct names then have different senses; for it is not self-evident that it is the same object which is determined in different ways.
>
> (PMC: 80; BW: 128)

The different ways of determining the star can give rise to the introduction of different names if the star captures our attention for long enough. If they indeed give rise to the introduction of names, these names must be distinct.

If one has introduced designators according to the prescriptions expounded above, one will sometimes have the need to acknowledge that different names stand for the same object. For the fact that different modes of determination determine the same object can be recognised in a judgement of content-identity. Frege takes such judgements to be expressed by statements of content-identity. Take again our example. You determine the content of 'the evening star' as the brightest star in the evening sky and the content of 'the morning star' as the brightest star in the morning sky. In this situation the statement 'The evening star is the same as the morning star' will contain new information for you. You can come to learn a new fact when you accept this statement. Could you gain this new information without a sign that has the same import as 'is the same as'? Frege argues that you can't:

> Thus, the need of a symbol for content-identity rests upon the following fact: the same content can be fully determined in different ways; but, that the *same content*, in a particular case, is indeed given by two modes of determination is the content of a judgement. Before this judgement is made, we must give the object determined by the two modes of determination different names, each name corresponding to one of the modes. The judgement requires for its expression a symbol for identity of content which connects the two names. It follows from this that different names for the same content are not always merely an indifferent

matter of form; but rather, that they concern the heart of the matter if they are associated with different modes of determination.

(CN: 125–6; BS: 14–15. In part my translation.)

Can one do without a sign for identity in a Begriffsschrift? If a Begriffsschrift contained just one name for each object, there would be no need for such a sign. Frege considers this option for the design of a Begriffsschrift and rejects it:

[T]he name B has in this case the same content as the name A; and yet one could not have used only *ONE* name from the beginning since the justification for doing so is first given by our answer [to the question 'Is the point A the same point as B?'].

(CN: 125; BS: 14. The emphasis is Frege's, it is not picked up in CN.)

Imagine that you try to translate the language of astronomy into a Begriffsschrift designed according to the same-object-same-name-convention. In order to do so, one will first need to recognise that 'the evening star' and 'the morning star' have the same content; stand for the same object. This relevant recognition will take the form of a straightforward identity judgement. We come to know that the evening star is the same planet as the morning star. From this we learn that the content of 'the evening star' is the same object as the content of 'the morning star'. How can such a recognition of an identity, whether conceived of as relation between signs or not, make an extension of a Begriffsschrift possible, while this very recognition cannot be stated in the extended Begriffsschrift itself? The recognition that the evening star is the same planet as the morning star is a valuable scientific insight. Such insights should be expressible in a Begriffsschrift. By taking the sign of content-identity to be part of a Begriffsschrift Frege makes room for the expression of such insights.

A Begriffsschrift needs to contain a sign that allows one to state that an object is the same as another. But if one assumes the *Begriffschrift* theory of content, and takes sentences such as 'The evening star is (the same object as) the morning star' at face value, one faces a new problem. We have already seen in Chapter 3 (p. 82) that, *provided we take '≡' to stand for the identity-relation*, Frege's criterion for content difference delivers the result that the sentence (1) 'The evening star ≡ the evening star' and (2) 'The evening star ≡ the morning star' differ in conceptual content. If one exchanges (2) with (1) in Inference 1, the result, Inference?, no longer allows one to come to know the conclusion on the basis of one's knowledge of the premises:

Inference 1	*Inference?*
The evening star is a planet.	The evening star is a planet.
The evening star ≡ the morning star.	The evening star ≡ the evening star
Therefore: The morning star is a planet.	Therefore: The morning star is a planet.

Hence, (1) and (2) differ in their inferential potential and therefore in conceptual content. But if circumstances are conceptual contents of Begriffsschrift sentences, (1) has the same content as (2). The content of (2) is the circumstance consisting of the content of 'the evening star', the planet Venus, the content of '≡', the relation of content-identity, and the content of 'the morning star', the planet Venus again. Since the evening star is the morning star (1) has exactly the same content as (2).

The sentences (1) and (2) represent the same circumstance, yet differ in inferential potential. Hence, we have a conflict between, first, the identification of the conceptual content of a sentence *s* with a circumstance consisting of the contents of the parts of *s* and, second, the individuation of conceptual content in terms of inferential potential.[2]

How can Frege respond to this problem? Sentences such as 'The evening star is the same planet as the morning star' seem to say of the evening star and the morning star that they are the same. Their conceptual content consists of the relation of identity and an object. (I follow Frege in taking relations to be a kind of concept. We attain a relation if we vary more than one constituent in a circumstance.) The relation combines with objects to circumstances, some of which are facts.

To avoid the inconsistency in his theory Frege can give up either

1   that identity statements involve objects and the relation of
     (content-)identity; or
2   that conceptual contents are individuated by their inferential
     potential; or
3   the identification of conceptual content with a complex that
     contains objects and functions.

In BS Frege gives up (1): the conceptual content of the sentence
'The evening star ≡ the morning star' does not contain the planet
Venus and the relation of identity, a relation between objects. He
takes the problem under consideration to show that identity is not
a relation between contents:

> Identity of content differs from conditionality and negation by relating
> to names, not to contents. Although symbols are usually only repre-
> sentatives of their contents—so that each combination [of symbols
> usually] expresses only a relation between contents—they at once
> appear in *propria persona* as soon as they are combined by the symbol
> of identity of content, for this signifies the circumstance that the two
> names have the same content. Thus, with the introduction of a symbol
> for identity of content, a bifurcation is necessarily introduced into the
> meaning of every symbol, the same symbols standing at times for their
> contents, at times for themselves.
>
> (CN: 124; BS: 13–14)

The idea that the signs to the left and the right of '≡' refer to themselves in some contexts is supposed to explain the difference in
inferential potential between 'The evening star ≡ the morning star'
and 'The evening star ≡ the evening star'. For example, it can be
news to learn that 'the evening star' stands for the same object as
'the morning star'. Hence, if one can interpret the judgement that
the evening star is the same as the morning star as a judgement
about the expressions 'the evening star' and 'the morning star', its
difference in inferential potential from the judgement that the
evening star is the same object as the evening star is readily
explained.

Treating statements of content-identity as the exception to the
rule that every expression just stands for an object allows Frege to

retain (2) and (3). But this solution comes at a price, which he will find too high in SR. After an important clarification in the next section, I will turn in the following section to the argument with which Frege opens SR to reconstruct his criticism of the *Begriffsschrift* view.

A CLARIFICATION: FREGE ON COMPLEX AND SIMPLE PROPER NAMES

Frege's argument for distinguishing between sense and reference starts by observing that '*a = a*' and '*a = b*' are sentences that differ in what he will call 'cognitive value'. What are '*a*' and '*b*' short for; what does he mean when speaks of signs in the context of the argument he proposes? After Frege has reached the conclusion of the argument he says:

> It is clear from the context that by 'sign' and 'name' I have here under-stood any designation that can stand in for a proper name, whose reference is thus a definite object (this word taken in the widest range), but not a concept or relation, which shall be discussed in another article. The designation of a single object can also consist of several words or other signs. For brevity, let every such designation be called a proper name.

> (SR: 158, 27. In part my translation.)

It seems to me that it is better to get clear about 'sign' and 'name' before working through the argument. Every expression that purports to refer to a *single* object is in Frege's broad understand-ing of the term a 'proper name'. Later, he will distinguish between a complex proper name ('*Einzelname*', '*zusammengeset-zter Eigenname*') and a simple proper name ('*eigentlicher Eigenname*'). A complex proper name can be a proxy for a simple proper name (see N: 387, 156). Examples for complex proper names are 'the negation of the thought that 2 + 2 = 5' or 'the Victor of Austerlitz'. According to Frege, both complex and simple proper names purport to designate a *single determinate object* ('*ein bestimmtes Einzelnes*', N: 387, 156). What does it take for a sign to purport to designate a single determinate object? In preparing a crucial argumentative move in FA Frege gives the following answer: 'If the symbol a shall designate an object, we must have a criterion for deciding in all cases whether b is the same as a, even if it is not always in our power to apply this criterion' (FA: 73. In part my translation).

In more familiar terminology: '(Singularity) "a" can only refer to *one object x* if mastery of "a" consists in part in knowledge of a criterion of re-identifying x.' Why is (Singularity) plausible? If 'Hesperus' purports to designate *one* object x, an application of 'Hesperus' to y can only be correct if $x = y$. One uses 'Hesperus' only as a sign that purports to designate one object if one is sensitive to the fact that 'Hesperus' can only be correctly applied to x and y if $x = y$. In most cases one will not be able to state the conditions under which $x = y$, but we are able to defer to experts who are aware of them. If one can understand an expression completely without knowing that it applies to the *same* object in different uses, the expression is not a sign that refers to an object. Nothing more than the satisfaction of (Singularity) seems to be required for a sign to be a proper name.

(Singularity) is important for three reasons. First, it helps one to understand modes of determination better. Possessing a mode of determination for an object a may give rise to the introduction of a designation 'N' for it. 'N' can only designate *one object*, if the mode of determination enables one to determine for different potential referents whether they are the same as a. If we look back at Frege's example, the modes of determination mentioned in them satisfy this condition.

Second, Frege takes complex expression such as 'the negative square root of 4' to be a 'complex proper name constructed from a concept expression with the help of a singular definite article' (SR: 170, 40. See also PMC: 96; BW: 154). A concept expression or *nomen appellativum* is a general term that can be true of many objects such as '(a) square root of 4'. Russell will call expressions that consist of the singular definite article followed by a general term 'definite descriptions'. It is controversial to say that complex expressions such as 'the Victor of Austerlitz' are proper names. Napoleon might not have won the battle of Austerlitz, Tzar Alexander I might have won in his stead. The alternate possibility in which Tzar Alexander I won is correctly described by saying that he might have been the Victor of Austerlitz. Hence, 'the Victor of Austerlitz' can correctly apply to Napoleon and to Tzar Alexander I even if they are numerically different. Definite descriptions are satisfied by at most one object, but under different circumstances they can be satisfied by different objects. This is one reason to distinguish between definite descriptions and proper names. If a definite description designates, it designates at most one object. If a proper name designates something, it designates one and the same object. For example, in different possibilities 'Napoleon' will refer to one and the same object and not to different ones. Frege does not consider examples that suggest that what a definite description designates can vary. This is one reason why he sees no important difference between definite descriptions and proper names.

Third, (Singularity) will become important in Chapter 7 (p. 247). Frege holds that concept-words don't refer to objects. (Singularity) is the key to understand this thesis.

If Frege's argument for distinguishing between sense and reference goes through, it will show that proper names, either simple or complex, have sense and reference. Whether sentences and concept-words also have sense and reference is left open by the argument. Questions about the sense and reference of sentences and concept-words will be discussed in Chapters 6 and 7.

FREGE'S ARGUMENT FOR SPLITTING CONCEPTUAL CONTENT INTO SENSE AND REFERENCE

The first paragraph of SR lays out Frege's reasons for splitting up conceptual content into sense and reference.[3] Below I have quoted the whole paragraph and inserted headings that divide up Frege's reasoning into five parts:

Introduction

> Equality [Footnote: I use this word in the sense of identity and take '$a = b$' to have the sense of 'a is the same as b' or 'a and b coincide'] gives rise to challenging questions which are not altogether easy to answer.

Is it a relation? A relation between objects, or between names or signs for objects? In my *Begriffsschrift* I assumed the latter.

Motivating the Begriffsschrift view

The reasons which seemed to favour this are the following: $a = a$ and $a = b$ are obviously statements of differing cognitive value ('Erkenntniswert'); $a = a$ holds a priori and, according to Kant, is to be labelled analytic, while statements of the form $a = b$ often contain very valuable extensions of our knowledge. The discovery that the rising sun is not new every morning, but always the same, was of very great consequence for astronomy. Even today the re-identification of a small planet or comet is not always a matter of course. Now if we were to regard identity as a relation between that which the names 'a' and 'b' designate, it would seem that $a = b$ cannot differ from $a = a$ (i.e., provided that $a = b$ is true). A relation would thereby be expressed of a thing to itself, and indeed one in which everything stands to itself and to no other thing. What is intended to be said by $a = b$ is that the signs 'a' and 'b' designate the same thing, so that those signs would be under discussion, a relation between them would be asserted.

Criticising the Begriffsschrift view

But this relation would hold between the signs or names only insofar as they designate something. It would be mediated by the connection of each of the two signs with the same designated thing. But this is arbitrary. Nobody can be forbidden to use any arbitrary producible event or object as a sign for something. In that case the sentence $a = b$ would no longer refer to the subject-matter, but only to its mode of designation; we would not express any proper knowledge by its means. But in many cases this is just what we want to do.

The main critical point and the constructive suggestion

If the sign 'a' is distinguished from the sign 'b' only as object (here, by means of its shape), not as sign (i.e. not by the manner in which it designates something), the cognitive value of $a = a$ becomes essentially equal to that of $a = b$, provided $a = b$ is true. A difference can arise only if the difference between the sign corresponds to a difference in the mode of presentation of the thing designated. ...

It now suggests itself to think of there being connected with a sign (name, combination of words, letter), besides that to which the sign refers, which may be called the referent of the sign, also what I would like to call the *sense* of the sign, wherein the mode of presentation is contained.

> (SR: 157–8, 25–7. I have used parts of Geach and Black's 1948 translation.)

Summary and conclusion (at the very end of SR)

If we found, in general, '$a = a$' and '$a = b$' to have different cognitive values, the explanation is that for the cognitive value of the sentence, its sense, namely the thought it expresses, is no less relevant than its reference, that is its truth-value. If $a = b$, the reference of 'b' is the same as 'a' and therefore the truth-value of '$a = a$' is the same as that of '$a = b$'. In spite of this, the sense of 'b' may differ from that of 'a', and thereby the thought expressed in '$a = b$' may differ from the one expressed in '$a = a$'. In this case the two sentences don't have the same cognitive value. If we understand by 'judgement' the advance from the thought to its truth-value, as in the above paper, we can also say that the judgements are different.

> (SR: 176–7, 50. I have changed the translation.)

I will now work step by step through the argument.

Introduction

Frege's introduction will surprise a reader of the *Begriffsschrift*. Frege's Begriffsschrift contains a sign for content-identity: '≡', and it is used in reconstructing mathematical reasoning that contains the distinct sign '=' (see CN: 205; BS: 89–90). In SR Frege uses only '='. He explains the change in the Introduction to *Grundgesetze I*:[4]

Instead of three parallel lines I have adopted the ordinary sign of equality, since I have persuaded myself that it has in arithmetic precisely the meaning that I wish to symbolise. That is, I use the word 'equal' to

mean the same as 'coinciding with' or 'identical with' and the sign of
equality is actually used in arithmetic in this way.

(GGA I: ix. My translation.)

In BS, content-identity is explained as a relation between two
expressions:

$a \equiv b$ if, and only if, 'a' has the same content as 'b' if, and only if, the content of 'a' can be exchanged for the content of 'b' in all conceptual contents salva veritate.

In FA Frege traces this definition back to Leibniz:

Now Leibniz's definition is as follows:
'Eadem sunt, quorum unum potest substitui alteri salva veritate.'
[Things are the same as each other, of which one can be substituted for
the other without loss of truth.]
This I propose to adopt as my own definition of equality. [...] Now it is
actually the case that in universal substitutability all the laws of identity
are contained.

(FA: 76–7)

There are several problems for the Leibnizian definition of identity that lead to Frege's rejection of it in later work. First, it rests
on a conception of conceptual contents as states of affairs in
which objects can be substituted for each other. As we have seen,
this conception is incompatible with the individuation of conceptual contents in terms of inferential potential. Hence, it will turn
out that for mature Frege conceptual contents are not available to
define equality (identity).

Second, definitions that analyse a concept can be seen as equations. (Being a bachelor is the *same* thing as being an unmarried
eligible man.) Frege concludes from this that identity cannot be
defined: 'Since any definition is an identification, identity itself
cannot be defined' (CP: 200, 320).

Now a definition of truth should be true, a definition of
necessity should be necessarily true. Are the concepts of truth or
necessity therefore undefinable? Drawing this conclusion

would be too quick. So far we only have reason to say that the conditions uncovered in the definition must apply to these definition themselves.

Motivating the Begriffsschrift view

Earlier in this chapter we have seen that in section 8 of BS Frege took content-sameness to be an equivalence relation between *signs* in order to solve a tension between his metaphysics of conceptual contents and their individuation. The sentences 'The evening star is the evening star' and 'The evening star is the morning star' differ in inferential potential. In SR he expands on this point. What 'The evening star is the evening star' says is analytic and a priori because it can be inferred immediately from the law of identity, what the 'The evening star is the morning star' says not. He presupposes that every constituent of a sentence that is either true or false has a referent.[5] Given this presupposition, the inference

$(\forall x)\ (x = x)$. Therefore, the evening star is the same as the evening star

is correct. Please recall that an inference is a judgement made in the light of justifying reasons. By contrast, the inference

$(\forall x)\ (x = x)$. Therefore, the evening star is the same as the morning star

is incorrect. The truth of what 'The evening star is the same as the morning star' says cannot be inferred from the law of identity *without further premises*. The difference is now described by saying that the sentences differ in cognitive value.

Frege illustrates the difference in cognitive value by pairs of identity sentences, one element of which is analytic and a priori, the other synthetic and a posteriori. But the difference in cognitive value does not consist in the difference between analyticity and syntheticity etc. Take Frege's letter to Russell:

> The words 'morning star' and 'evening star' designate the same planet, Venus; but to recognise this, a special act of recognition [*Erkenntnisthat*] is required; it cannot simply be inferred from the principle of

identity. Wherever the coincidence in reference is not self-evident, we have a difference in sense. Thus the sense of '$2^3 + 1$' is also different from the sense of '3^2' even though a special act of recognition is required in order to see this. Thus the equations '$3^2 = 3^2$' and '$2^3 + 1 = 3^2$' do not have the same value for cognition [*sind nicht für die Erkenntnis gleichwerthig*], although the truth-value is the same.

(PMC: 152; BW: 234–5. In part my translation.)[6]

Both equations '$3^2 = 3^2$' and '$2^3 + 1 = 3^2$' say something that is analytic and a priori. For the truth of their contents can both inferred from logical laws and definitions alone. However, they differ in cognitive value. Why? Because the content of the first equation can be inferred from the law of identity alone, the second one can't. My justification for judging that $3^2 = 3^2$ is that everything is self-identical; no further reason is needed to entitle me to make the judgement (if one works like Frege with the assumption that in scientific discourse singular terms are non-empty). By contrast, knowing that everything is self-identical does not give me a reason to judge that $2^3 + 1 = 3^2$; I need further reasons to hold that $2^3 + 1 = 3^2$ is true.[7]

If the true sentence '$a = a$' can, while the true sentence '$a = b$' can't be inferred directly from the law of identity, the sentences differ in cognitive value. They have different value for inferential knowledge acquisition. If the content of a sentence is to determine its inferential potential (cognitive value) completely, the sentences '$a = a$' and '$a = b$' must differ in content. If identity is a relation between expressions, '$a = a$' and '$a = b$' differ in content: the first says that 'a' refers to the same object as 'a', the second says that 'a' refers to the same object as 'b'. In BS Frege held therefore that identity statements are about signs. This move allowed him to hold that the content of an identity statement determines its inferential potential. In the next part of the argument he will argue against this solution.

Criticising the Begriffsschrift view (1)

By accepting an identity sentence such as 'The evening star = the morning star' I can come to learn an astronomical fact. However, argues Frege, if such a sentence states a relation between 'a' and 'b', the sentence can't express *proper* knowledge, in this case astronomical knowledge. We can clarify his point with an example. Imagine the following situation: I have frequently seen a and know that it is the brightest star in the evening sky. I decide that it would be good to have two names for a, so that I can use them as stylistic alternatives in my poems about the sky. Seeing a I therefore introduce two names in one act of naming 'I name this planet "Hesperus" and also "Lucifer"'. No one can be forbidden from giving *one* object *two* names if s/he so desires. I will apply 'Hesperus' as well as 'Lucifer' to an object if, and only if, it is the brightest star in the evening sky. Here we have two designators that differ in shape (geometrical properties). Now take the true statements 'Lucifer is Hesperus' and 'Lucifer is Lucifer'. For myself and everyone who accepts my explanations of these names, these statements have the same cognitive value, although they contain names that differ in shape. One can exchange in the inference below the second premise with 'Lucifer is Lucifer' and still be justified in accepting the conclusion:

> Hesperus is a planet. Hesperus = Lucifer. Therefore: Lucifer is a planet.

Why? Because as I have introduced these names one needs to possess the same knowledge about heavenly objects to apply them correctly; 'Hesperus' and 'Lucifer' are mere stylistic variants. If we now transcribe the identity statement into meta-linguistic form ('"Lucifer" refers to the same planet as "Hesperus"' and '"Lucifer" refers to the same planet as "Lucifer"'), the statements will have the same cognitive value, *although they concern different signs*. There is a difference in sign, but no difference in cognitive value. The only thing one can learn from 'Lucifer is Hesperus' is that 'Lucifer' and 'Hesperus' are different signs for the same object, but in coming to know this we can't extend our knowledge of astronomy. We only come to know that two signs are stylistic variants. If the meta-linguistic theory is true, we learn a fact about my use of the names, not an astronomical fact. But accepting 'The evening star is the morning star' can extend one's astronomical knowledge. The question is how is this possible. So much is clear; the fact that signs of different shape are contained in the sentence does not explain what needs explaining.

THE MAIN CRITICAL POINT AND THE CONSTRUCTIVE SUGGESTION

Frege goes on to make the general point that $a = a$ can only differ from $a = b$ if 'a' and 'b' differ in mode of presentation. The 'Lucifer'/'Hesperus' example shows that 'Lucifer is Hesperus' and 'Lucifer is Lucifer' and 'Hesperus is Hesperus' can only differ in cognitive value if 'Lucifer' and 'Hesperus' differ in the manner in which they designate something. If 'Lucifer' and 'Hesperus' are mere stylistic variants, the sentence might differ in aesthetic, but not in cognitive value.

Under which conditions do sentences of the form '$a = a$' and '$a = b$' differ in cognitive value? They only differ in cognitive value if signs of different shape also differ in *mode of presentation* (see also FA: 79). Modes of presentation are close relatives of the modes of determination of the *Begriffsschrift*. If there is a difference between a mode of presentation and a mode of determination, it is not relevant for Frege's argument at this point. He has argued in BS that a rational person ought to introduce distinct names if s/he has distinct mode of determination. Imagine again that I know that a is the brightest star in the evening sky and I also know that b is the brightest star in the morning sky. If I don't know whether the brightest star in the evening sky is the same object as the brightest star in the morning sky, I should introduce two different names, say 'the evening star' and 'the morning star' corresponding to the different modes of determination or presentation. If the name producers conform to the norm for name introduction, they have chosen names that differ in shape and the difference in shape corresponds to a difference in mode of presentation. As Frege said in the letter to Jourdain previously quoted, different modes of presentation can give rise to different names, which will differ in sense. The different names differ in sense because each is connected to the mode of presentation that gave rise to it. If different modes of presentation of the same object have given rise to the introduction of names that differ in shape, there is an interesting fact that can be discovered.

In SR Frege packages this idea as an insight about what a *sign* is. An inscription has geometrical and chemical properties. Frege calls the inscription also a 'figure' (see CP: 115, 97). But we can produce a figure with the intention to designate something. In this case the figure is a sign (ibid.). One cannot designate something by producing a figure without designating it in some particular way. This suggests a way of collecting sign-tokens into types:

a is a token of the same sign as *b* if, and only if,

a and *b* have the same shape, and

a and b are used with the intention to designate an object determined in the same way.

If '"*a*" is distinguished from "b" *as a sign*' and not just as a physical object, the distinction concerns *the way 'a' ('b') designates something*. Two physical objects differ as signs if they purport to designate something in different ways.

Frege's examples show that the cognitive value of '*a* = *b*' depends on the modes of presentation that, in part, individuate '*a*' and '*b*'. When we take 'The evening star is the same as the morning star' to have a cognitive value, we must take 'the morning star' and 'the evening star' to be distinct signs *that express distinct modes of presentation*.

Frege's assumption that '*a* = *a*' can *only* differ in cognitive value from '*a* = *b*' and both be true, if '*a*' and '*b*' express different modes of presentation of the same object seems so plausible that it is seldom discussed. Recently, however, it has come under pressure. Here is a representative counter-example due to Kit Fine. Envisage a universe that is completely symmetric around a person's centre of vision:

Whatever she sees to her left *is* and *looks* qualitatively identical to something she sees to her right (not that she conceptualises the two sides as 'left' and 'right' since that would introduce an asymmetry). She is now introduced to two identical twins, one to her left and the other to her right, and she simultaneously names each of them 'Bruce'; using a left token of 'Bruce' for the left twin and a right token of 'Bruce' for the right twin. The two tokens of 'Bruce' are then always used in tandem so as not to disturb the symmetry. [...] It seems intuitively clear that she has the use of two names or, at least, the ambiguous use of a single name: and this is something that the Fregean should in any case accept since the names or name can be used to state an informative identity. But what, then, is the difference in sense?

(Fine 2007: 36)

'Bruce$_{\text{Left}}$ = Bruce$_{\text{Left}}$' differs in cognitive value from 'Bruce$_{\text{Left}}$ = Bruce$_{\text{Right}}$'. But what can the difference in mode of presentation be?

Frege himself suggests that the names differ in how the speaker originally distinguished the object when s/he introduced the names. The distinct names express the distinct mode of presentations that gave rise to them. This suggestion makes the mode of presentation that led to the introduction of the name the main ingredient of its sense.

However, Fine has a good reply to this point. The modes of presentation that gave rise to the different names may be distinct but they are not important for the use of the name. Often we forget how we distinguished an object in the first place when we introduced a name for it. In general, it is plausible to say that understanding a proper name is not tied to one mode of presentation (or a distinctive bundle of modes of presentation), a fortiori it is not tied to the mode of presentation that gave rise to its introduction.

This suggests that there need not be *one* mode of presentation of the proper name bearer that is the main ingredient of the constant sense of a proper name. Different modes of presentation are the main ingredient of sense at different times. Frege can therefore uphold his assumption that the difference in cognitive value between '$a = a$' and '$a = b$' is due to the fact that 'a' and 'b' differ in mode of presentation. But the difference in cognitive value is constituted by 'a' and 'b' expressing different pairs of modes of presentations of the same object at different times. The counter-example poses a question for Frege: if the mode of presentation of a proper name can vary and change, shall we say that the proper name changes its senses? If so, what accounts for the intuition that a name such as 'Hesperus' is unambiguous and has an unshifting sense? I will come back to this point in Chapter 5 (p. 174).

Another well-known criticism of the assumption that '$a = a$' can only differ in cognitive value from '$a = b$' if, 'a' and 'b' express different modes of presentation proposes a different explanation of the observed difference in cognitive value. Putnam has argued that 'The evening star is the evening star' and 'The evening star is the morning star' differ in logical form.[8] The two sentences would be translated differently into the language of first-order logic with identity: as '$a = a$' and '$a = b$'. Why not say that the difference in logical form is responsible for the difference in cognitive value? But how can we determine the logical form of a statement independently of a method of individuating signs? If 'b' is a mere stylistic alternative for 'a' (the difference in form indicates no difference in mode of presentation), the logical form of '$a = b$' is $a = a$. If differences of cognitive value between sentences are to depend on differences of logical form, logical form cannot be solely determined by the geometrical properties of signs. Logical form must also depend on the sense expressed by the signs. Properly speaking, thoughts have logical form. The appeal to logical form can therefore not make the notion of sense superfluous.

We can sum up Frege's argument so far as follows:

(P1) '$a = a$' and '$a = b$' are true statements that differ in cognitive value.

(P2) If 'a' and 'b' differ only in shape, '$a = a$' and '$a = b$' cannot differ in cognitive value.

Therefore: (C1) 'a' and 'b' differ not only in shape.

(P3) If different modes of determination (presentation) give rise to the introduction of designators 'a' and 'b' that differ in shape, but not in content (reference), the identity sentences '$a = a$' and '$a = b$' can be both true and differ in cognitive value.

Therefore: (C2) 'a' and 'b' have the same content (reference), but differ in shape *and* mode of presentation.

Criticising the Begriffsschrift view (2)

So far Frege has argued convincingly that we need *signs* and cannot make do with *figures*. But he already held in his *Begriffschrift* that one only needs a sign of content-identity if the same object can be determined in different ways. A judgement of content-identity registers that two modes of determination determine the same object. He already appealed to *signs* in this sense when expounding the *Begriffsschrift* view of content-identity: the judgement that '*a*' has the same content as '*b*' is synthetic (can extend our knowledge) if, and only if, '*a*' and '*b*' are connected with different modes of determination, that is, if they are different signs (see CN: 126; BS: 15). So far Frege has not refuted, but merely expounded the *Begriffsschrift* view in a new way. No wonder then that some exegets take him not to have given up on this view.[9]

But although Frege does not refute the *Begriffsschrift* view of identity statements in SR, he has provided all the materials to do so.[10] The main problem for the meta-linguistic view of identity is the treatment of general identity statements expressed by means of quantifiers and variables. Take Leibniz's Law:

$$(\forall x)\,(\forall y)\,((x = y) \leftrightarrow (\forall F)\,(Fx \leftrightarrow Fy))$$

Non-symbolically and somewhat misleadingly: 'Two' things are the same if, and only if, they share all their properties. Now x and y might indeed share all their properties, among them the property of *having never been referred to*. (Just imagine that the domain over which the variables range includes such uninteresting and ephemeral things as raindrops.) Since x and y have never been referred to, there are no expressions referring to them. Consequently, there are no 'meta-linguistic' statements that contain terms referring to x and y and that say that such terms refer to the same object. Hence, the identity of x and y cannot consist in such meta-linguistic facts. Yet, according to the law of identity x and y are identical. But do the variables 'x' and 'y' not refer to the objects supposed to be nameless and never referred to? No, variables don't refer at all; they range over a domain without referring to any object in the domain.

For similar reasons, we cannot read the law of identity as saying that 'x' designates the same object as 'x' in the same manner. The sign 'x' does not designate an object at all. Consider in addition an inference from the law of identity:

$(\forall x)\ (x = x)$
Therefore: The evening star = the evening star.

Inferences like this yield knowledge of particular logical truths on the basis of a logical law. But if 'The evening star = the evening star' says that the both sign-tokens designate the same object in the same manner, the inference is not valid. One cannot infer from the law that everything is self-identical that tokens of 'the evening star' designate something in the same manner. That they do so is a presupposition of a correct inference from the law of identity, but cannot itself be inferred from the law. These are strong reasons to conclude that identity is not a relation between signs.

Conclusion and summary

If we can't find a plausible way to turn identity statements into statements about signs, we should be content that they are statements about objects. Identity sentences are not about modes of presentation, but in referring to an object we always refer to it in a particular way. Two singular terms refer in different ways if, and only if, different modes of presentations have given rise to their introduction. Frege's talk of *ways* of referring is an important ingredient of his proposal. An expression that refers to an object in a particular way still refers to an object. As a picture of some sunflowers painted in a particular way is still a picture of some sunflowers, a sign that refers to Venus in a particular way is still a sign that refers to *Venus*. Therefore one can extend one's *astronomical* knowledge by accepting the sentence 'The evening star is the same planet as the morning star'. For the same reason, the sentence 'The evening star is the same planet as the evening star' is about an object and can directly be inferred from the law of identity. The mode in which an object is referred to in a sentence and the object referred to determine jointly the cognitive value of a sentence.

A look at a footnote in 'On Sense and Reference' indirectly clarifies the relation between signs and mode of presentation further. Frege writes:

> In the case of an actual proper name (*'eigentlichen Eigennamen'*) such as 'Aristotle' opinions as to the sense may differ. It might, for instance, be taken to be the following: the pupil of Plato and teacher of Alexander the Great. Anybody who does this will attach another sense to the sentence 'Aristotle was born in Stagira' than will a man who takes as the sense of the name: the teacher of Alexander the Great who was born in Stagira.
>
> (SR: 158, 27 fn)

Frege seems to suggest that the sense of 'Aristotle' might be taken to be the pupil of Plato and teacher of Alexander the Great. But the pupil of Plato and teacher of Alexander the Great is Aristotle, the famous philosopher, not a sense. Well, isn't that a slip that should be corrected? Should one correct the slip to: 'The sense of "Aristotle" might be taken to be the following: the sense of "the pupil of Plato and teacher of Alexander the Great"'?

No, that would not say what the sense of 'Aristotle' is. For I can know that two expressions have the same sense without knowing the sense of either. If a competent speaker of German informs a monolingual speaker of English that *'Füllen'* has the same sense as *'junges Pferd'*, s/he will not come to know what sense *'Füllen'* has.

According to a more charitable reading, Frege makes no mistake at all, but specifies the sense of 'Aristotle' by saying in a particular way what its reference is. When we state what the referent of an expression is, we can do this in different ways. Here are some of them:

> The referent of 'Aristotle' is Aristotle.
> The referent of 'Aristotle' is the inventor of formal logic.
> The referent of 'Aristotle' is the philosopher I heard of in my last lecture.

One such sentence will say which thing the referent of 'Aristotle' is and in doing this it will put one in the position to understand 'Aristotle ...' utterances. This reference-sentence will show the sense of the proper name: '[F]or Frege, we say what the referent of a word is, and thereby show what its sense is' (Dummett 1981a: 227).

Frege's critics often pointed out that he has said very little about modes of presentation. But indirectly he says under which mode of presentation a proper name refers to an object by explaining for which object a name stands or purports to stand.[11]

Frege will develop this idea further in his *Basic Laws of Arithmetic*.[12] For each atomic sign of his Begriffsschrift, he stipulates that it refers to something under such-and-such conditions. For example, he makes the following semantic stipulation for "=": '"$\Gamma = \Delta$" refers to the True if, and only if, Γ is the same as Δ' (GGA I: 11).

Let us call such conditions *reference-conditions*. The sense of a complex truth-value name, a sentence of the language of *Basic Laws of Arithmetic*, is given by the conditions under which it stands for the True, which are derived from the reference-conditions for its atomic constituents:

> Every name that has correctly been built up from our signs has not only a reference, but also a sense. Every such name of a truth-value expresses a sense, a thought. For our stipulations determine under which conditions it stands for the True.
>
> (GGA I: 50. My translation.)

For example, someone who knows Frege's stipulations for '=' and '1' can derive from them the sentence:

> '1 = 1' refers to the True if and only if the number of the concept [equals 0] is the same as the number of the concept [equals 0].

A speaker who knows that the sentence '1 = 1' is true under these conditions grasps the thought expressed.

With this idea in place, we can say that '$a = b$' and '$a = a$' are both about the same object. The informativity of '$a = b$' and the triviality of '$a = a$' is explained by saying that 'a' and 'b' refer to the same thing *in different ways or modes*. If a sign always refers to an object in a particular way, namely via a mode of presentation, we have all the ingredients to explain the differences and commonalities between '$a = b$' and '$a = a$'. These sentences differ in cognitive value if the signs refer in different ways, but the sentences have necessarily the same truth-value, because the signs refer to the same object.

THE RESULT OF THE SPLIT

Let us now see how Frege's argument splits, as he himself puts it, conceptual content into sense and reference. In the *Begriffsschrift* the conceptual content of a judgement or Begriffsschrift sentence determined (1) the truth of the judgement and (2) its inferential potential. Frege's argument showed that the conceptual content of identity sentences cannot do both (1) and (2) if it is composed out of the contents of the sentence constituents. For sentences whose conceptual content is composed out of the same things can differ in inferential potential.

Frege realised that conceptual content cannot do the *two* jobs it was supposed to do. Therefore he splits up conceptual content into sense and reference, each of which fulfils one function of conceptual content. The inferential role of a sentence is determined by the mode of presentation; the truth by the reference. Both sense and reference must be employed in order to describe how an inference can lead from acknowledgment of one truth to the justified acknowledgement of another truth.

From Frege's argument we can extract the following information about the reference of complex proper names (definite descriptions) and simple proper names. Frege holds, in general, that the reference of a word is the object one wants to speak about when one uses the expression normally. (More in the next section.) Applied to proper names this yields the more specific thesis:

> (R1) The reference of a simple proper name is its bearer; the reference of a complex proper name is the object that falls under the concept mentioned in the name.

Later Frege will add (R2):

> (R2) Exchanging signs with the same reference in a complex sign does not change its reference.

For the sense of (simple or complex) proper names we get:

> (S1) The main constituent of the sense of a proper name is a mode of presentation.

(S2) Differences in cognitive value are based on differences in sense.

(S3) The mode of presentation of a proper name is distinct from its reference.[13]

(S4) If two proper names have the same sense, they have the same reference; if two proper names have the same reference, they can differ in sense.

(S5) Proper names are individuated partly in terms of mode of presentation: two tokens of the same shape are only the same proper name if they express the same mode of presentation.

The result of the split is encoded in a new terminology:

> To make short and exact expressions possible, let the following set phrases be established:
> A proper name (word, sign, sign complex, expression), expresses its sense, *stands for or designates* its reference. By means of a sign we express its sense and designate its reference.
>
> (SR: 161, 31. In part my translation.)

So far Frege has not told us very much about mode of presentation (that is, roughly sense). The premises of the argument are compatible with every assumption about the nature of sense that allows the sense of a proper name to differ from its reference and that makes sense-sameness entail reference-sameness. In the following sections I will therefore clarify the notion of sense and reference further by paying close attention to the use Frege makes of these notions.

THE GENERAL NOTION OF REFERENCE

So far Frege has taught us what reference is by giving us an example: the reference of a simple proper name is its bearer; the reference of a complex proper name the object that falls under the concept mentioned in the name. However, he will need a general notion of reference when he wants to argue that sentences and concept-words refer. SR contains hints that direct us to such a general notion of reference.

Frege connects the notion of reference with the non-technical notion of what-one-wants-to-speak-of: 'If words are used in a normal way, that of which one wants to speak is their reference' (SR: 159, 28. My translation). Please note that Frege speaks here of *words*, not of signs. This suggests that he has not only proper names in mind when he makes this remark. Let us assume we have an intuitive understanding of what it is to use words normally. The words are not used in quotation marks, scare quotes, they do not occur in indirect speech etc. Then we can use our grip on 'normal use' and 'what one intends to speak of' to determine what the reference of some words is:

(R) The reference of a word or some words = that of which one wants to speak when one uses the word or words normally.

Frege uses (R) to justify ascriptions of reference to signs, i.e. proper names: '[I]n order to justify talk of the reference of a sign it is sufficient to point out what our intention in speaking and thinking is, although we have to add the reservation: provided that such a reference exists' (SR: 162, 32. My translation). But the general notion of reference is not restricted to proper names or singular terms.[14]

Our intention in speaking and thinking when using 'the Moon' normally is to speak of the Moon and not of its sense or an idea. Hence, the Moon is the reference of 'the Moon' (provided there is such a thing), argues Frege. He uses the connection between reference and what one wants to speak about with one's words suggested by (R) also to argue against views of concept-word reference. Does the concept-word 'a man' refer to each man, that is, does it refer to Socrates, chief Akpanya etc? No, he says: 'It should be clear that someone who utters the sentence "All men are mortal" does not want to state something about chief Akpanya whom he may never have heard of' (CP: 205, 327). What I want to talk about with 'men' is the factor that determines whether and what this word refers to. I will come back to this point in Chapter 7 (p. 234). To anticipate, when I call Hans a man I apply the concept-word 'a man' to him. With the concept-word 'a man' I then *want to speak about a concept* that subsumes Hans.

The general notion of reference as 'what one wants to talk about' is different from the notion of reference, which Frege's exegets often ascribe to him. Dummett takes Fregean reference to have two ingredients: the name/bearer relation and the semantic role of an expression (see, for example, Dummett 1981b: 148ff.).[15] The relation between a (simple) proper name and its bearer is, argues Dummett, the paradigm of the relation of reference. The point of the relation of reference is, however, more general. We need to ascribe something to an expression '*a*' that determines the truth of sentences that contain '*a*'; the semantic role of '*a*'. Take a simple proper name such as 'Hesperus'. If one uses 'Hesperus' normally, the truth/falsity of sentences in which the name occurs depends on how things are with Hesperus. Hence, one can specify the semantic role of 'Hesperus' by assigning Hesperus to it. All expressions that have only been assigned Hesperus to specify their semantic role have the same semantic role. Such expressions can therefore be exchanged for each other *salva veritate* in all sentences in which their semantic role is unchanged. For example, 'Hesperus' and 'Phosphorus' have the same semantic role. If one uses 'Hesperus' or 'Phosphorus' normally in a sentence, the truth of the sentence depends on how things are with the planet Hesperus. Exchanging 'Phosphorus for 'Hesperus' in 'Hesperus is a planet' can therefore not change the truth-value of this sentence. For proper names, both ingredients of the notion of reference march in step: Hesperus is the bearer of the name 'Hesperus' and assigned to the name to specify its semantic role. But the name/bearer relation and the semantic role will come apart for other expressions such as assertoric sentences and concept-words to which Frege also ascribes reference. How can the name/bearer relation be extended to concept-words etc. if they have reference?

If we look at Frege's remarks on reference in SR, it is difficult to find evidence that the name/bearer relation is 'an ingredient' of the notion of reference. In the first part of SR he used the sense and reference of proper names as examples. But he neither said nor suggested that that the name/bearer relation is an ingredient of the general notion of reference. If Frege's notion of reference lacks this ingredient, the reference and semantic role of sentences and concept-words can march in step. Or, more precisely, there is no need to distinguish between them. For example, in one decomposition of 'Hans is a man', one wants to speak about a concept with the concept-word 'a man'. Under this decomposition, the truth of what I say with 'Hans is a man' depends in part on what I speak about with 'a man', i.e. on the concept *man* and what it subsumes. It is then not surprising that Frege never distinguished two ingredients in the notion of reference.

SENSE WITHOUT REFERENCE

We now have an initial understanding of reference. The most convincing way to demonstrate that sense and reference differ is to point to signs that have sense, but no reference. Hence, directly after the introduction of the sense/reference distinction Frege discusses empty complex proper names:

> It may perhaps be granted that every grammatically well-formed expression standing in for a proper name [*der für einen Eigennamen steht*] always has a sense. But this is not to say that to the sense there also corresponds a referent. The words 'the celestial body most distant from the Earth' have a sense, but it is very doubtful if they also have a referent. [...] In grasping a sense, one is not certainly assured of a referent.
> (SR: 159, 28. In part my translation.)

Later Frege will argue that the existence of empty proper names is a defect of the language that contains them (see SR: 168–9, 41). Why? Take 'The celestial body most distant from the Earth is a planet' and assume with Frege that 'ξ is a planet' refers to a concept. If 'The celestial body most distant from the Earth' does not refer to an object, there is no object that can be mapped by the concept *being a planet* to a truth-value. The concept cannot return the value True or False. The sentence falls into a truth-value gap. A sentence that is neither true nor false has no place in a language designed for thinking. One can neither infer something from the thought expressed by such a sentence nor can this thought be inferred from already recognised truths.

Natural language does not satisfy the demands that Frege imposes on a language designed for inferential thinking. It contains empty singular terms. He reflects on them to deepen his understanding of the distinction between sense and reference. He proposes a sufficient condition for having a sense:

> (S6) If x is a grammatically well-formed expression that goes proxy for a proper name, x has a sense.

Take a grammatically well-formed expression that purports to refer to a single object such as 'the King of France'. If it is a grammatically correct combination of parts that have a sense, such an expression has a sense. What secures a sense for a complex proper name is that it is grammatically correct composition of parts that have a sense. But an expression can satisfy (S6) and yet have no reference. The difference between sense and reference is manifest in the difference between the conditions for having a sense and having a reference.

Frege's sufficient condition for having a sense is incomplete. A simple proper name such as 'Aristotle' does not or at least need not consist of parts that have a sense on their own. When does such a proper name have a sense? Frege answers this question in 'Comments on Sense and Reference' that was written between 1892 and 1895:

> The passage [in Homer's *Odyssey* X, 305] cited need not lack a sense, any more than other passages in which the name 'Nausicaa', which probably does not refer to or name anything, occurs. But it behaves as if it names a girl, and it is thus assured of a sense.
>
> (PW: 122; NS: 133. In part my translation.)

Frege will have had passages like the following from the *Odyssey* in mind: 'The mighty Alcinous had a young daughter called Nausicaa, tall and beautiful as a goddess' (Homer 1946: 77). It is unclear whether Homer actually introduces 'Nausicaa' to refer to a real person or whether he only purports to do so to tell a story. But as one can do something *in different ways* one can *purport* to do something in different ways. Similarly, as a name can refer to something in a particular way a name can also behave as if it refers to something in a particular way. Now 'behaves as if it names something' is in need of further elucidation. When does an expression behave as if it names something?

Answer: if it behaves as if it designates a single object. For example, Homer's introduction of 'Nausicaa' tells us what it takes for an object to be referred to by 'Nausicaa'. For any object x, x is the reference of 'Nausicaa' if and only if, x is the daughter of mighty Alcinous and is tall and beautiful as a Goddess. (Let us assume for ease of exposition that the Gods give a mortal at most one daughter of such beauty.) This reference-condition for 'Nausicaa' is also a criterion for deciding whether the same object is referred to in different uses of 'Nausicaa'. Now an expression can be introduced in such a way that it has such a reference-condition, although there is no object that satisfies the condition. To sum up: if one needs to know a criterion of re-identification of the type discussed in order to master an expression, it behaves as if it is a name. A proper name can behave as if it names something, although there is nothing that it in fact names. Moreover, it can purport to refer to an object in a particular way. The particular way is specified by the reference-condition that gave rise to the introduction or acquisition of the name. Hence, we end up with (S6*):

(S6*) If an expression behaves as if it refers to a single object, it has a sense.

An expression behaves as if it refers to a single object if it either combines concept-words and the singular definite article in a grammatically correct way or one's mastery of the expression requires knowledge of a criterion of re-identification of one object.

Now proper names can satisfy the condition for expressing a sense without having a reference. There can be sense without reference:

Sense without reference: A proper name can have a sense, although there is no object to which it refers.

If *sense without reference* is true, talking of modes of presentation is misleading. For there can be no mode of presentation without something that is presented. Some Fregeans take the notion of a mode of presentation to be so central that they reject *sense without reference*. For example, Evans says: 'If sense is a mode of presentation of semantic value, we should hardly expect to be introduced to the sense of an expression save in the course of being given, or being presented with, its semantic value' (Evans 1982: 26).

We have seen in the reconstruction of Frege's argument that sense is a manner of referring. How can there be a manner in which, for instance, a name refers to something, if there is nothing to which the name refers? Answer: it is of course true that there cannot be such a manner of referring to something. But Frege's 'Nausicaa' example points us to a weaker condition for possessing a sense. 'Nausicaa' purports to refer to something and it cannot purport to refer without purporting to refer in a particular way. Hence, purporting to refer is sufficient for having a sense. Modes of presentation should better be called 'modes of purported presentation'.

Evans argues further that it is of the essence of a thought that if it is not true, it is false.[16] But if a sentence contains an empty singular term, it is neither true nor false. Whatever the sentence 'says' is not governed by the law of excluded middle. But why is satisfaction of the law of excluded middle essential for thoughts? Frege holds that imperative sentences such as 'Destroy Carthago!' express a sense, but this sense is not a thought: 'We should not wish to deny sense to an imperative sentence, but this sense is not such that the question of truth could arise for it. Therefore I shall not call the sense of an imperative sentence a thought' (T: 62, 355). If Frege is right, there are sentential senses, which are not thoughts. (More about such senses in Chapter 5, p. 189.) A sentence containing an empty proper name can express such a sense.

The arguments pro and contra sense without reference are based on existence conditions for thoughts. According to Evans, a thought only exists if it obeys the laws of excluded middle. Frege is less demanding:

> The being of a thought may also be taken to lie in the possibility of different thinkers' grasping the same thought as one and the same thought. In that case the fact that a thought has no being would consist in several thinkers' each associating with the sentence a sense of his

own, this sense would in that case be the content of his particular consciousness, so that there would be no *common* sense that could be
grasped by several people.

(N: 376, 146)

He provides the following existence condition for thoughts:

(E!) The thought that *p* exists if different thinkers can grasp it as the
same.

He expands on (E!) in a helpful way. A thought is the sense of a
complete propositional question. One grasps the thought
expressed by a propositional question if, and only if, one knows
when the question deserves the answer 'yes' and when it deserves
the answer 'no'. In 'Negation', Frege envisages a group of scientists raising and investigating a propositional question (N: 376,
146). This practice, he argues, presupposes that each scientist
grasps the same thought. There is a mere illusion of a thought, if
different thinkers cannot rationally engage with the same question. We have no reason to believe that the scientists suffer from
such an illusion. Hence, (E!) is satisfied. On the basis of (E!), Frege
rejects the view that false thoughts aren't thoughts. It was rational
to ask whether the circle can be squared and different thinkers
could rationally engage with this question. Hence, there is a
thought and not merely a thought illusion, although the thought
is necessarily false.

Now one can imagine a group of scientists investigating
whether there is such a substance as phlogiston. The fact that they
can raise and rationally investigate this question is a good reason
to assume that the interrogative sentence 'Is there such a substance as phlogiston?' expresses a thought. In fact, in answering
this question they will draw on their knowledge of the sense of
'phlogiston'. Hence, we have good reason to suppose that 'There
is such a substance as phlogiston' expresses a thought, although
'phlogiston' is empty. Imagine that the scientists reach the right
conclusion that there is no such substance. How should they
report their findings? It seems natural that they will say 'It is not
the case that there is a substance identical with phlogiston' or 'It

turned out to be false that there is a substance identical with phlogiston'. Since Frege argues that sentences with empty proper
names are neither true nor false, he must treat these answers as
misguided. If one finds this counter-intuitive one must engage
with his arguments for the view that no sentence with an empty
proper name is true (see SR: 168–9, 40–1).

Evans gives a further argument, the argument from diversity,
that concludes that one cannot understand an utterance with an
empty proper name (Evans 1982: 336). Different people count as
understanding an utterance of 'Aristotle was fond of dogs',
although each thinks of Aristotle under a different mode of presentation. All that is required is that they think of the right object:
Aristotle, the philosopher. However, this condition for understanding can by definition not be satisfied by an utterance with an
empty proper name. Now it would be ad hoc to require that in the
case of an empty proper name such as 'Nausicaa' one needs to
grasp a special mode of presentation to count as understanding an
utterance containing it. Hence, there are no conditions under
which one counts as understanding a 'Nausicaa ...' utterance. If
there are no such conditions, the utterance is unintelligible and
therefore does not express a sense.

Evans's modus ponendo ponens is Frege's modus tollendo tollens. It is less controversial to assume that we understand
'Nausicaa ...' utterances than to follow Evans in his further
assumptions. Hence, we should continue looking for a condition
on understanding a proper name that holds, *whether the name is
empty or not*. One proposal is that a speaker A understands
another speaker B's utterance of a proper name if A is justified in
taking co-reference between his and B's uses of the name for
granted. Since only justification, and not knowledge is required,
this condition holds in the empty as well as in the successful case.[17]

SAMENESS OF SENSE IS TRANSPARENT AND MAKES
SAMENESS OF REFERENCE TRANSPARENT

We can deepen our understanding of the distinction between
sense and reference further by considering a distinctive epistemic
property of sense. My acknowledging the truth of

Premise 1: Hesperus is a planet

and

Premise 2: Hesperus shines in the evening

entitles me to judge:

Therefore, there is at least one thing that is a planet and shines in the evening.

A necessary condition for this inference to enable me to come to know the conclusion on the basis of my knowledge of the premises is:

Transparency of sense sameness: Necessarily, the sense ('*a*') = the sense ('*b*') →
(T grasps the sense ('*a*') and T grasps the sense ('*b*') → T knows that the sense ('*a*') = sense ('*b*')).[18]

Assume for *reductio* that sameness of sense is not transparent in the inference above. Then you might understand and accept 'Hesperus is a planet' (first premise) and understand and accept 'Hesperus shines brightly' (second premise), but fail to recognise that the two 'Hesperus' tokens have the same sense. Hence, your understanding of the premises does not entitle you to give them the form 'Fa', and 'Ga'. Consequently you cannot discern the logical form that ensures the formal validity of the inference. As a result you may know the premises and exercise your knowledge of logic and yet you cannot come to know the conclusion from the premises alone. The inference would be incomplete. In order to infer the conclusion one would need to add a further premise:

Hesperus mentioned in premise 1 is the same thing as Hesperus mentioned in premise 2.

Since we take some inferences such as the one above to be complete and knowledge-transmitting, sameness of sense must be transparent.[19]

Transparency of sameness of sense is important in Frege's theory. For instance, he argues in SR that only senses can be constituents of the sense of a sentence: 'A truth-value cannot be a part of a thought, any more than, say, the Sun can, for it is not a sense, but an object' (SR: 164, 35). Frege endorses the *Homogeneity Principle*: 'The sense of a sentence (the thought) can only have other senses as constituents'. Russell disputes the principle in a letter to Frege:

> I believe that in spite of all its snowfields Mont Blanc itself is a component part of what is actually asserted in the proposition 'Mont Blanc is more than 4,000 metres high'. We do not assert the thought, for this is a private psychological matter: we assert the object of the thought, and this is, to my mind, a certain complex (an objective proposition, one might say) in which Mont Blanc itself is a component part. If we do not admit this, then we get the conclusion that we do not know anything about Mont Blanc itself.
>
> (PMC: 169; BW: 250–1)

Why should one believe the Homogenity Principle? Frege argues that if the mountain Etna is part of the sense of 'Etna is a mountain', every piece of solidified lava that is part of Etna is part of the sense: 'But it seems to me absurd that pieces of lava, even pieces of which I have no knowledge, should be parts of my thought' (PMC: 79; BW: 127). He concludes that Etna is not part of the thought that Etna is a mountain.

There are various ways in which one might attempt to block this argument. Frege assumes that thoughts are mereological complexes in the following sense: if s is a part of the thought that p, then every part of s is a part of the thought that p. Russell can defend his position that Etna can be part of a thought by pointing out that a thought, or more generally, a proposition, is not a mereological complex, if it is complex at all. Consider the extensionality principle of mereology (wholes with the same parts are the same). Take a world in which Romeo, Juliet and the relation Love exist. In that world there is just one mereological whole that contains Romeo, Juliet and Love as parts. However, propositions can 'contain' the same things and yet differ: *that Juliet loves Romeo* is a different proposition from *that Romeo loves Juliet*, although they have the same constituents. A proposition is more like an ordered sequence of things. There is no reason to assume that every part of an element of the sequence <Juliet, Loves, Romeo> is an element of the sequence. The same goes for thoughts.

However, even if we reject the mereological conception of thought composition, a problem remains. Frege thinks that we cannot know an object that is not a sense completely; it is always given to us partially, say, from a certain perspective (see SR: 158, 27). If Etna is a part of the thought that Etna is a mountain in a non-mereological sense, I could not know whether the thought expressed by my utterance of 'Etna is a mountain' yesterday and my utterance of 'Etna is a mountain' today is the same just by grasping the senses expressed. For Etna could be given to me differently on different days. I would have to do research in order to find out whether the thoughts are the same/different. Hence, Frege cannot allow Etna to be a constituent of the thought that Etna is a mountain if thought-identity shall be transparent.

Now to a further dimension of transparency:

If
(1) the sense ('a') determines a and the sense ('b') determines b and
(2) the sense ('a') = the sense ('b') and
(iii) S grasps the sense ('a') and S grasps the sense ('b'), then
S knows immediately that $a = b$.

Frege's relies on this principle in his discussion of the sense of the first-person pronoun and proper names in 'The Thought'. For instance, he uses the assumption:

If two sentences s and s* with a proper name (indexical) express the same thought, everyone who grasps the sense of s and s*, immediately knows that the same thing is represented in s and s*.[20]

Knowledge is factive: if one knows that $a = b$, then $a = b$. According to Frege, the self-evidence of $a = b$ must entail that $a = b$. Hence, the above principle implies a further principle which is often referred to as 'Sense-determines-Reference':

(S7) ($\forall x$) ('*a*' has the same sense as '*b*' → ('*a*' refers to x ↔ '*b*' refers to x'))

(S7) ensures that one is justified in moving from the premises of argument 1 to its conclusion without being justified in an additional identity judgement. Only if (S7) holds are inferences of the form 'F*a*, G*a*, Therefore: ($\exists x$) (F*x* and G*x*)' complete.[21]

In these principles we cannot easily equate *grasping the sense of (a natural language singular term)* '*a*' with *understanding* '*a*'. You and I may master the proper name 'Robert Schmidt' perfectly; we are both competent and fluent in our use of the name etc. The name in fact refers to one and the same person in your and in my mouth. Nonetheless, it may come to us as a surprise that we refer to the same person with this name. If understanding were knowledge of the sense of the name and sameness of sense makes sameness of reference obvious, such a surprise would be impossible. Frege maintains the transparency of sense and that sameness of sense makes sameness of reference obvious. When it comes to proper names, knowledge of meaning is not grasping a particular sense. His warning remark indicates this: 'But knowledge of the language is a special thing when proper names are involved' (T: 358, 65). I will come back to this and similar problems in Chapter 5 (p. 170).

SENSE-IDENTITY

Frege's basic insight is that two signs can differ in sense and yet have the same reference. This insight has been made plausible by providing examples. But in order to develop his insight in a systematic way, we need a general answer to the question 'When is the sense of one expression the same (different) from the sense of another expression?' As Frege puts it in a letter to Husserl in 1906: 'It seems to me that an objective criterion is necessary for a recognising a thought again as the same, for without it logical analysis is impossible' (PMC: 70; BW: 105).

We have seen in Chapter 3 (p. 82) that the criterion for content-identity in *Begriffsschrift* gave rise to various problems. No wonder then that Frege proposes a different criterion when he writes to Husserl:

Now it seems to me that the only possible means of deciding whether sentence A expresses the same thought as sentence B is the following, and here I assume that neither of the two sentences contains a logically self-evident component part in its sense. If *both* the assumption that the content of A is false and that of B true *and* the assumption that the content of A is true and that of B false lead to a logical contradiction, and if this can be established without knowing whether the content of A or B is true or false, and without requiring other than purely logical laws for this purpose, then [...] what is capable of being judged true or false in the contents of A and B is identical, and this alone is of concern to logic, and this is what I call the thought expressed by both A and B.

(PMC: 70–1; BW: 105–6)

It is for a good reason this proposal does not find its way into Frege's manuscripts or published work.[22] I can establish that the sentence 'It is raining' and the sentence 'If it is not the case that (it is raining and it is not the case that it is snowing), then it is not the case that (it is snowing if it is not the case that it is raining)' are both true (false) without knowing whether they are true of false. I just have to work out that they cannot take different truth-value on the basis of the rules of propositional logic. But to say that these sentences have the same sense goes against the point of Frege's notion of sense. His introduction of the notion of sense connects sameness of sense with triviality and difference of sense with informativity. I can extend my knowledge by finding out that, necessarily, it is raining if, and only if, if it is not the case that (it is raining and it is not the case that it is snowing), then it is not the case that (it is snowing if it is not the case that is raining). Hence, the sentences should express different thoughts.

In 1906 Frege opens the paper 'A Short Survey of My Logical Doctrines' with a proposal for a criterion of sense-identity:

Now two sentences A and B can stand in such a relation that anyone who acknowledges the content of A as true must thereby acknowledge the content of B as true and, conversely, that anyone who acknowledges the content of B must straightaway acknowledge that of A.

(*Equipollence*). [1] It is here being assumed that there is no difficulty in grasping the content of *A* and *B*. [2] The sentences need not be equivalent in all respects. For instance, one may have what we may call a poetic aura, and this may be absent from the other. Such a poetic aura will belong to the content of the sentence, but not to that which we acknowledge as true or reject as false. [3] I assume there is nothing in the content of either of the two equipollent sentences *A* and *B* that would have to be immediately acknowledged as true by anyone who grasped the sentence properly.

(PW: 197; NS: 213. In part my translation.)

Frege's explanation of sense identity via equipollence is carefully hedged. To see why let us start with the basic idea stripped of the caveats:

(Sense identity 1) Sentence *A* expresses the same sense (thought) as sentence *B* if, and only if, everyone *x* who grasps the sense of *A* and the sense of *B* must (straight away) acknowledge the truth of the sense of *B* if *x* acknowledges the truth of the sense of *A* (and vice versa).

Why 'straight away acknowledge'? The identity-criterion Frege expounded in the letter to Husserl allowed one *to work out* that the thoughts expressed by *A* and *B* must have the same truth-value one the basis of one's knowledge of logic. This feature was responsible for the counter-systematic consequences of the criterion. Now he requires that one must immediately acknowledge the thought expressed by *A* as true if one acknowledges the thought expressed by *B* as true (and vice versa) and thereby excludes the problematic examples.

In which sense of 'must' must one immediately acknowledge the sense of *A* as true if one acknowledges the content of *B* as true? Take an example: if I acknowledge what 'John is a bachelor' says, but reject (doubt) what 'John is an unmarried eligible male' says, I make a mistake. Either I don't understand what my words say and should consequently be criticised for speaking without understanding or I understand what I say but I am criticisable for manifestly contradicting myself. The best explanation for this manifest contradiction is that I take the same content to be true and false.

Now to Frege's qualifications. I will start with (3) that excludes obviously true sentences from the criterion.[23] Everyone who understands 'Every natural number has a successor' must assent to it. The same goes for every other obvious truth. But then everyone who assents to 'Every natural number has a successor' must also immediately assent to 'No one is his own father' (and vice versa). Hence, Frege's criterion makes them express the same sense. For example, if we accept the criterion for sense identity, arithmetic is grounded in only one axiom and not five. All sentences used by Dedekind would express the same thought. Frege responds by excluding obvious truths from the range of sentences to which his criterion applies. This is an unattractive consequence. Don't we need to know whether two sentences express the same obvious truth or not?

One response is to say first when individual words express the same sense and then go on to say that sentences express the same thought if, and only if, they are built up from words that express the same sense in the same way. However, this is opposed to the spirit of Frege's *Begriffsschrift*. He wants to start with judgeable contents and provide a criterion for their identity that does not require a decomposition of such contents. This approach is not changed in his later work. Let's see whether we can solve the problem in the spirit of his approach.

Frege's criterion assumes that the contents of A and B are simultaneously entertained. Under this condition, one must immediately acknowledge what A says as true, if one acknowledges what B says as true and vice versa given that the thoughts expressed are obvious truths. This is compatible with the possibility that one can extend one's knowledge by acknowledging what B says as true, although one already has acknowledged what A says as true. Frege considers obvious truths in 'Compound Thoughts':

> In such a case the questions arise: 'Does this sentence express a thought? Does it not lack content? Do we learn anything new upon hearing it?' Now it may happen that before hearing it someone did not know this truth at all, and had therefore not acknowledged it. To that extent one could, under certain circumstance, learn something from it.
> (CT: 405, 50)

I may already know a lot of things, among them that no one is his own father. It can be true to say of me that I know that no one is his own father, but that I don't know that if London is bigger than Glasgow, London is bigger than Glasgow. I have never considered the question whether if London is bigger than Glasgow, London is bigger than Glasgow is true. Hence, learning this obvious truth will extend my knowledge. If I can *extend* my knowledge in this way, the truth that if London is bigger than Glasgow, London is bigger than Glasgow is a new truth, different from the ones I have already recognised. Inspired by Frege's example, we can propose the following modification of his criterion:

> (Sense identity 2) Sentence A has the same sense as sentence B if, and only if,
>
> (a) everyone x who grasps the sense of A and the sense of B must (straight away) acknowledge the truth of the sense of B if x acknowledges the truth of the sense of A (and *vice versa*) and
>
> (b) if x has already acknowledged or rejected the truth of the sense of A, x cannot extend x's knowledge by acknowledging or rejecting the truth of the sense of B (and vice versa).

Rejection is introduced to take care of contents that are obviously false like the thought that something is not self-identical: everyone who grasps them must take them to be false.

Frege will argue in SR that a sentence in indirect discourse ('believes that', 'says that') is a complex name of the sense it usually expresses and that sentences with the same content can be exchanged in indirect discourse without changing the truth-value of the complex sentence in which they are embedded. Take:

> Dedekind already knew that no one is his own father; later he learned that no one is his own father.

This is false and should remain false if we replace one of the embedded sentences with a sentence referring to the thought to which 'No one is his own father' refers in (single embedded) indirect discourse. But

> Dedekind already knew that no one is his own father; later he learned
> that if London is bigger than Glasgow, London is bigger than Glasgow,

can be true. Therefore, 'If London is bigger than Glasgow, London is bigger than Glasgow' and 'No one is his own father' must express different thoughts. The new criterion allows Frege to say this.

Now I move on to the second qualification about poetic aura. Frege wants to say that 'Fido is a dog' and 'Fido is a cur' express the same thought, although they differ in what he calls 'colouring' or 'tone'. Different words can have the same sense, but invoke different ideas and feelings. According to him, the difference between 'Fido is a dog' and 'Fido is a cur' does not matter for scientific discourse; it matters only for style. A scientist can use 'Fido is a dog' as well as 'Fido is a cur' to describe Fido, but a poet can't. However, there seems to be more than a difference in colouring here. When one says that Fido is a cur, one commits oneself to the truth that Fido is shabby etc.

Frege will not accept this. Near the end of SR he gives examples of sentences that express a main thought as well as subsidiary thoughts (see Chapter 2, pp. 52–3). He writes about the example 'Napoleon, who recognised the danger to his right flank, himself led his guards against the enemy position':

> One may in fact doubt whether this thought [that Napoleon himself led his guards against the enemy position because he recognised the danger to his right flank] is merely lightly suggested or really expressed. Let the question be considered whether or sentence should be false if Napoleon's decision had already been made before he recognised the danger. If our sentence could be true in spite of this, the subsidiary thought should not be understood as part of the sense.

(SR: 174, 49)

A thought is only suggested by a sentence if the sentence can still be true if the thought is false. In this sense, he can argue that 'Fido is a cur' expresses the thought that Fido is a dog and suggests that he is shabby etc. He in effect discovers the idea that sentences often suggest or convey more than they literally and strictly say.

The distinction between literally saying and merely suggesting has been explored in detail by Grice.[24]

Now two sentences *s* and *s** may have the same sense, but someone may acknowledge what *s* says as true, while s/he doubts what *s** says. I may agree that Fido is a dog, but dispute that he is a cur. Frege can argue that I mistakenly take what 'Fido is a cur' merely suggests into account when considering whether to acknowledge what it literally says. This recommends that we should add to (sense identity 2) a further condition:

> (Sense identity 3) Sentence A has the same sense as sentence B if, and only if,
>
> (a) everyone *x* who grasps the sense of A and the sense of B must (straight away) acknowledge the truth of the sense of B if *x* acknowledges the truth of the sense of A (and vice versa) OR the impression that the senses of A and B can differ in truth-value can be explained away by appealing to non-truth related reason for uttering A instead of B (and vice versa) and
>
> (b) if *x* has already acknowledged or rejected the truth of the sense of A, *x* cannot extend *x*'s knowledge by acknowledging or rejecting the truth of the sense of B (and vice versa).

I am unsure whether this last move will allow Frege to say all he wants to say. For my assertion that 'Fido is a cur' seems to be false if we take it to be false that Fido is shabby etc. But modifying the criterion in this way will help with further examples.

Finally, onto Frege's first simplifying assumption that there is no difficulty in grasping the sense of A and B. What is an example of a word whose sense is difficult to grasp? He discusses in 'Logic in Mathematics' the example of 'integral':

> We simply do not have the mental capacity to hold before our minds a very complex logical structure so that it is equally clear to us in every detail. For instance, what man, when he uses the word 'integral' in proof, ever has clearly before him everything that appertains to the sense of the word! And yet we can still draw correct inferences, even though in doing so there is always a part of the sense in penumbra. Weierstrass has a sound inkling [*Ahnung*] of what number is and

working from this he constantly revises and adds to what should really
follow from his official definitions.

(PW: 222; NS: 240. In part my translation.)

Our partial grasp of some senses is manifest, argues Frege, in the
knowledge-extending character of definitions that aim to capture
the sense of words already in use. For example, it is informative to
come to know that the number 0 is the extension of the concept
equinumerous with the concept $\xi \neq \xi$. But if this showed that the
sense of '0' differed from 'the extension of the concept *equinumerous with the concept* $\xi \neq \xi$' he would not have explained the
sense of '0', but re-defined it.

We grasp the sense of 'integral' without grasping every part of
this sense. How is it possible that some parts of a sense are not
grasped when one grasps *this sense*? Frege had argued previously
that we often use words without grasping their sense. What we are
conscious of when we reason is not the sense of, say, 'integral', but
the word itself.[25] We use the word relying on our ability to recall
its sense when necessary. This view that reasoning, especially
mathematical reasoning, is conducted by mentally manipulating
signs while 'ignoring' their meaning is part of the motivation of
the introduction of a calculus. Whitehead, for example, distinguishes between the expressive signs of ordinary language and the
substitutive signs of algebra: '[A] word is an instrument for thinking about the meaning which it expresses; a substitute sign is a
means of not thinking about the meaning which it symbolises'
(Whitehead 1898: 3–4). I take it that Frege has these phenomena
in mind when he talks about difficulties in grasping a sense.

Frege's criterion of sense-identity is not applicable to words,
whose sense we only grasp unclearly: if there are two sentences
and one of them contains a word whose sense I only partially
grasp, I can understand both and rationally take different attitudes to them although they have the same sense because of my
partial grasp of their sense. For the same reason two words that
express the same sense may not be exchangeable *salva veritate* in
indirect speech. It may be correct to assent to 'Dedekind believes
that 0 is 0', while it is incorrect to assent to 'Dedekind believes that
0 is the extension of the concept *equinumerous with the concept* ξ

$\neq \xi$', although '0' and 'the extension of the concept *equinumerous with the concept* $\xi \neq \xi$' are synonymous. If Dedekind has only a partial grasp of the sense expressed by '1' he might not assent to '1 is the extension of the concept *equinumerous with the concept* $\xi \neq \xi$'. Finally, if one can only partially grasp the sense of a word, then the fact that two synonymous words have the same sense will not be obvious to everyone who grasps them.

Frege's simplifying assumptions make the criterion difficult to apply. For now we need to know whether the sense of the sentences under consideration has been completely grasped or not. How do we know whether we have a complete grasp of a sense? If Frege's psychological explanation of partially grasping a sense is correct, we should rely on our memory of the sense. However, it seems hard to believe that arriving at a correct analytic definition is a matter of remembering something one already knew.

Often we will credit someone with an incomplete grasp of a sense if his or her explanation and application of the words fall short of the explanations and applications of the same word offered by a designated group of people ('the experts'). It is, however, unclear whether this explanation of incompletely grasping a sense allows Frege to sustain his view that attaining a proper grasp of a concept may require centuries of intellectual work even by the dedicated experts:[26]

> What is known as the history of concepts is a history either of our knowledge of concepts or of the meanings of words. Often it is only through great intellectual labour, which can continue over centuries, that a concept is known in its purity, and stripped of foreign covering that hid it from the eye of the intellect.
>
> (FA: vii. In part my translation.)

To conclude: Frege's remarks about incompletely grasping a sense threaten the applicability of the concept of sense. If senses can be incompletely grasped, they are no longer transparent and transparent senses cannot do the work he wants sense to do: to make sameness of reference obvious. Fregeans therefore seems to face a choice between giving up the theory of partially grasping a sense and the theory of sense and reference itself.

5

THE SENSE AND REFERENCE
OF NATURAL LANGUAGE
SINGULAR TERMS

THE REGULAR AND THE RELAXED CONNECTION
BETWEEN SIGN, SENSE AND REFERENCE

Frege has presented in SR a good argument that singular terms express a mode of presentation that determines at most one reference. The assumptions of the argument are compatible with different ways in which a sign, a mode of presentation and a reference are related. For example, the argument does not exclude that a sign expresses different modes of presentation, each of which determines a different reference. Frege goes beyond the argument presented when he introduces in SR 'the regular connection' (*regelmäßige Verknüpfung*) between sign, sense and reference:

> The regular connection between a sign, its sense, and its reference is of such a kind that to the sign there corresponds a definite sense and to that in turn a definite reference, while to a given reference (an object) there does not belong only a single sign.
>
> (SR: 159, 27–8. In part my translation. See also PW: 118; NS: 128)

In a letter to Husserl he uses a diagram to illustrate the regular connections between signs of different kinds and their senses and references:

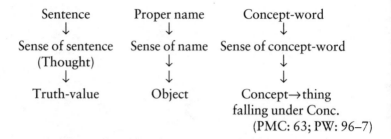

Sentence	Proper name	Concept-word
↓	↓	↓
Sense of sentence	Sense of name	Sense of concept-word
(Thought)	↓	↓
↓	↓	↓
Truth-value	Object	Concept→thing
		falling under Conc.
		(PMC: 63; PW: 96–7)

In this diagram, every sign has exactly one sense and signs that differ in shape have different senses. Importantly, Frege adds in SR the following comment:

> To be sure, exceptions to this regular behaviour occur. To every expression belonging to a perfect totality of signs [*Ganzes von Bezeichnungen*], there should certainly correspond a definite sense; but natural languages often do not satisfy this demand [*Forderung*], and one must be content if the same word has the same sense in the same connection [*Zusammenhang*].
>
> (SR: 159, 28–9. My translation.)¹

The regular connection between sign, mode of presentation is not a statistical regularity. 'Regular' translates '*regelmäßig*'. The relevant meaning of 'regular' is *characterised by the presence or operation of a definite rule or set of rules*. The regular connection is a connection between sign, mode of presentation and reference that conforms to a rule. Which rule and why is this rule in operation?

A language that can be used to conduct proofs must be unambiguous, that is, its signs must express one and only one sense. A proof is an inference. An inference is a mediated judgement justified by other judgements. It can be expressed in words and beings like us must express inferences in words to make them at all. Assume now that '2 + 2 = 4' has different senses. What does a proof whose conclusion is expressed by the words: 'Therefore:

2 + 2 = 4' establish? One wants to say that 2 + 2 = 4. But one can't, for '2 + 2 = 4' does not identify *one* content. According to Frege, 'the most important rule that logic must impose on written and spoken language' is therefore the requirement that words have only one sense.[2] A Begriffsschrift is designed to make gapless proofs possible. Hence, each of its signs must have exactly one sense that determines at most one referent (see Chapter 2, p. 52). In other words, the regular connection between sign, sense and reference must hold.

Natural language is not designed to make gapless proofs possible. Hence the regular connection between sign, sense and reference need not obtain. Signs that are similar in shape may have more than one sense ('Bank') or change their sense from one utterance to another ('Aristotle' in my mouth and your mouth). Even the language of mathematics contains complex signs with more than one referent ('$\sqrt{2}$'). Natural language is not designed to conduct gapless proofs. So, why should it conform to the requirements imposed by logic? Frege makes the crucial point himself in a letter to Peano when he discusses the conditions for defining a concept-word:

> The fallacy known by the name of 'Acervus' rests on this, that words like 'heap' are treated as if they referred to a sharply delimited concept whereas this is not the case. Just as it would be impossible for geometry to set up precise laws if it tried to acknowledge threads as lines and knots in threads as points, so logic must demand sharp limits of what it will acknowledge as a concept unless it wants to renounce all precision and certainty. Thus a sign for a concept whose content does not satisfy this requirement is to be regarded as without reference from the logical point of view. *It can be objected that such words are used thousands of times in the language of life. Yes: but our vernacular languages are also not made for conducting proofs. The task of vernacular languages is essentially fulfilled if people engaged in communication with one another connect the same thought, or approximately the same thought, with the same sentence. For this it is not at all necessary that the individual words should have a sense and reference of their own, provided that only the whole sentence has a sense.*
>
> (PMC: 114–15; BW: 182–3. In part my translation and emphasis.)[3]

If we take our logical laws to apply to thoughts expressed with vague concept-words such as 'ξ is a heap', we will commit logical fallacies. For instance, the *Acervus* or *Sorites* fallacy takes us from the true premises (1) that 10,000 grains are a heap and (2) that the removal of one grain does not turn a heap into a non-heap via repeated application of modus ponendo ponens to the false thought that one grain is a heap. Frege does not try to illuminate the reasons that lead to such paradoxes or to find ways to dissolve them.[4] His main concern is to eliminate vague and incompletely defined concept-words in a Begriffsschrift, a language made for conducting (gapless) proofs. Every concept-word of a Begriffsschrift must be sharply defined. Frege restricts this so-called *sharpness requirement* to the concept-words of a *scientific* language.

In contrast to a Begriffsschrift, a language whose main use is communicative and not inferential can contain vague and incompletely defined concept-words. The concept-word 'ξ is a natural number' is only defined for numbers, the sense of the word does not determine its application to flowers; 'ξ is a heap' is vague; it is neither true nor false of some collections of grains. Even if the concept-word 'ξ is a heap' will engender a paradox, we can perfectly well impart information by using 'ξ is a heap' about heaps. When I say 'Many collections of grains of sand are heaps' you can understand what I am saying and assess its truth. Many assertions containing 'ξ is a heap' and similar vague concept-words strike us as true. Although Frege never endorses this proposal, it seems natural from his perspective to adopt the idea that vague concept-words refer to partial functions, that is, functions that return no values for some arguments. After all, we take many sentences with such concept-words to be true (false). Concept-words that refer to partial functions will not meet the demands of logic, but they will suffice for communication.

These examples show that a Begriffsschrift is designed to satisfy demands that are not motivated for natural language. The 'regular connection' between sign, sense and reference is relaxed in natural language. For example, Frege points out in the last quotation that we have no reason to take individual words in natural language sentence to have sense and reference of their own.

If the regular connection between sign, sense and reference is relaxed, the sense and reference of a natural language expression cannot play the same explanatory role as the sense and reference of a Begriffsschrift expression. Consider an example. Frege says in SR: 'The sense of a proper name is grasped by everybody who is sufficiently familiar with the language or totality of designations to which it belongs' (SR: 158, 27).

Let us first set an influential interpretation of this sentence aside. Evans writes in his *Varieties of Reference*:

> Frege's idea was that it may be a property of a singular term as an element of a public language that, in order to understand utterances containing it, one must not only think of a particular object, its Meaning [Reference], but one must think of that object in a particular way: *that is, every competent user of the language who understands the utterance will think of the object in the same way.* 'The sense of a proper name is grasped by everybody who is sufficiently familiar with the language or totality of designations to which it belongs.'
>
> (Evans 1982: 16. My emphasis.)

But 'totality of designations' is Frege's description of his Begriffsschrift (see FC: 137, 1). Every sign of the Begriffsschrift has exactly one sense. The (primitive) proper names are introduced only by semantic stipulations that specify conditions under which the names refer. Someone who does not know these conditions does not understand the proper names. If you have mastered the Begriffschrift, you will grasp the sense of its proper names. Moreover, since having a particular sense is an objective property of proper names in Begriffsschrift, you will know which sense a proper name has when someone else uses it, provided you know that s/he writes in Begriffsschrift. This is different for natural language proper names. For example, one cannot say that the sense of 'Hesperus' is grasped by everybody who is sufficiently familiar with English. Consequently, one cannot say that understanding a sentence containing a proper name consists in grasping the sense (thought) expressed by this sentence. Sense seems no longer to play a central role in describing natural language communication. The general question that arises from these considerations is clearly expounded by Dummett:

> The extent to which it must be conceded even by Frege that the expressions of natural language fail to have a unique, determinate, objective sense represents a gap which an adherent of Frege's theory of meaning has to fill with excuses, reasons why it is nevertheless profitable to think in terms of the situation Frege provides as an ideal.
>
> (Dummett 1981a: 585)

Although it is misleading to say that the Begriffsschrift is an ideal – Frege argues that it is a single-purpose language designed to capture all and only the inferential potential of a judgeable content – Dummett's main point is correct. Even if the distinction between sense and reference can be independently motivated, the question arises how one can justify applying Frege's theory of sense and reference to natural language if the regular connection between sign, sense and reference does not obtain. Answering this question is the general challenge everyone faces who takes the theory of sense and reference to be the foundation of a theory of meaning and understanding for natural language.

In this chapter I will investigate whether Frege's theory of sense and reference can be applied to natural language singular terms and if it can, how it needs to be modified to take distinctive features of natural language into account. In the second section I will discuss the problem posed by context-dependent expressions for the application of the theory of sense and reference to natural language. In the third section I will turn to proper names as expressions whose sense varies while their reference remains the same. The chapter closes with a discussion of Frege's theory of indirect discourse in the fourth section.

APPARENT SHIFTS OF SENSE AND REFERENCE

The problem of the essential indexical

Natural language contains unambiguous signs, tokens of which stand for different things in different utterances *because the sign means what it does*. Here are some examples:

- Personal pronouns: 'I', 'you', 'my', 'he', 'she', 'it'.
- Demonstrative pronouns: 'that' and 'this'.
- Adverbs: 'here', 'now', 'today', 'yesterday', 'tomorrow'.

The reference of such expressions is determined by their context of utterance. What is a context of utterance? The fact that an utterance is an action performed by an agent at a time and place gives us an initial notion of context of utterance (see Lewis 1980: 79). The context of utterance includes at least the agent, time and place of the utterance.[5] The context of utterance for demonstratives may contain further elements. Which object the utterance of an indexical or demonstrative refers to is determined by features of the context of this utterance. For example, the reference of an utterance of the first-person pronoun 'I' is the agent of the utterance. The role (Perry) or character (Kaplan) is a rule that governs the correct use of an indexical (demonstrative). This rule encodes how reference depends on context of utterance. For instance, in most dictionaries one can find entries such as:

> Now: the time of utterance
> I: the speaker

Before moving on, a note of caution: the English personal pronoun 'he' can be used, for instance, as a demonstrative ('He is hungry'), as a natural language surrogate for a bound variable ('If someone is hungry, he will look for food') and as a quasi-indicator ('Peter believes that he (himself) is hungry', roughly: 'Peter believes what he would express by saying "I am hungry"'). So we better say that an expression has a use as a context-dependent expression. It is so used if its meaning determines the referent of an utterance of the expression depending on features of the context of utterance (the time, place or producers of the utterance).

Perry has argued in his influential paper 'Frege on Demonstratives' (1977) that context-dependent expressions pose a major problem for Frege's theory of sense and reference. A discussion of this problem will help us to understand Frege's position better.

Let us take the temporal adverb 'now' as the representative example of an indexical. According to Frege, the sense expressed by a token of 'now' at t in the sentence '… now …' must combine with the sense of the other words in the sentence to a thought. A thought is true full-stop: 'The thought we express by the Pythagorean theorem is surely timeless, eternal, unvarying'

(CP: 370, 76). The thought expressed by the Pythagorean theorem is atemporally true. In fact all thoughts are either true or false absolutely:

> But are there not thoughts which are true today but false in six months' time? The thought, for example, that the tree there is covered with green leaves, will surely be false in six months' time? No, for it is not the same thought at all. The words 'This tree is covered with green leaves' are not sufficient by themselves to constitute the expression of thought, for the time of utterance is involved as well. Without the time-specification thus given we have not a complete thought, i.e. we have no thought at all. Only a sentence with the time-specification filled out, a sentence complete in every respect, expresses a thought.
>
> (T: 370, 76)

If thoughts are true absolutely, the thought that I express at t with, for example, 'The meeting starts now' cannot be the same thought as the thought that I express a minute later by the same words. If they were the same, a thought could be true at one time, false at another. Now the words 'The meeting starts ...' seem to have the same sense at both times. Hence, we arrive at the conclusion that tokens of the English word 'now' that are produced at different times differ in sense.

What is the sense of a token of 'now' at t that determines this time as its reference? Is it the sense as of a definite description of the time t at which 'now' is uttered? No, take any definite description d of the time t that does not itself contain 'now' or a synonym of 'now'. No statement of the form 'd is now' is trivial. Take as a representative example 'The start of my graduation ceremony is now'. Surely, it is not self-evident that the start of my graduation ceremony is now.

Hence, Perry takes Frege to be settled with the following unattractive conclusion:

> Frege will have to have, for each time, a primitive and particular way in which it is presented to us at that time, which gives rise to thoughts accessible only at that time, and expressible, at it, with 'now'. This strikes me as very implausible.
>
> (Perry 1977: 491)

Every token of 'now' that is produced at time t differs in sense from all other tokens of 'now' produced at other times. Since this token is not synonymous with any non-indexical expression, the thought expressed by my utterance of 'The meeting starts now' cannot be expressed again at a different time in different words.

Frege himself presents in 'Thoughts' an argument that extends this conclusion to proper names and the first-person pronoun:

> Consider the following case. Dr. Gustav Lauben says, 'I was wounded'. Leo Peter hears this and remarks some days later, 'Dr. Gustav Lauben was wounded'. Does this sentence express the same thought as the one Dr. Lauben uttered himself? Suppose that Rudolph Lingens was present when Dr. Lauben spoke and now hears what is related by Leo Peter. If the same thought was uttered by Dr. Lauben and Leo Peter, then Rudolph Lingens, who is fully master of the language and remembers what Dr. Lauben said in his presence, must now know at once from Leo Peter's report that he is speaking of the same thing. But knowledge of the language is a special thing when proper names are involved.
>
> (T: 358, 65)

Frege's last remark will be discussed further in the third section of this chapter. Let us assume here for the sake of the argument that the sense of 'Gustav Lauben' is shared by Leo Peter and Rudolph Lingens. Even then Rudolph Lingens will not know immediately that the same person is the topic of the 'I ...' and 'Gustav Lauben ...' utterance. Frege concludes: 'I say, therefore, in this case: the thought which Leo Peter expresses is not the same as that which Dr. Lauben uttered' (T: 359, 65).

Why is the conclusion that there are primitive and time, place or person-bound senses unattractive? If every token of 'now' expresses a new primitive sense, grasping the sense of one of them does not help one to understand the others. But it seems implausible to say that one needs to know something new to understand different tokens of 'now' uttered as times passes. The result generalises to other context-dependent words. Hence, Frege's view of context-dependent expressions seems implausible.

Thoughts that are true at a time etc.

Perry offers Frege the following response to the problem: Give up the view that a sentence such as 'I am making a mess' ('The meeting starts now') expresses a thought that is true (false) absolutely:

> [W]hy not think of it as completely identifying a new-fangled proposition that is true or false only at a person? More precisely, one that is true or false at a time and a person, since though true, when I said it, it has since occasionally been false.
>
> (Perry 1979: 13)

This response allows us to hold that non-simultaneous utterances of 'now' can express the same sense, although they refer to different times.

Why can't Frege accept this proposal?[6] So far he has not given us any reason to believe that truth is an absolute property. To my knowledge, he never provides the needed argument; he takes it to be obvious that truth is not a relation between a thought and something else. But why should thinking about context-dependence not make us revise the view that truth is absolute? While Frege himself does not address this question, others have outlined arguments that help his cause.[7] Let us have a look at these arguments.

The basic point of these arguments is that the contents of assertion cannot be true relative to a time. Since thoughts are supposed to be the contents of assertions, this point is supposed to show that thoughts are true full-stop.

Evans has argued for this point in the following way.[8] Your knowledge of when a sentence is true should assist you in making assertions by means of it. If truth is relative to a time, should you utter 'It is raining now' with assertoric force if, and only if, it is currently raining? Well, the same sentence will be false tomorrow, true in two weeks, etc. Should I utter the sentence when it is true at the time of utterance or when it is true at some other time or at all times? These questions are better avoided and the view that the truth of what one asserts is absolute avoids them.

Evans's argument makes the controversial assumption that assertion is a speech act performed with the aim to put forth a truth. Philosophers who take truth to be a relation between a truth-value bearer and some parameters can resist this argument by exploiting the communicative nature of assertions. When I utter an indexical sentence with assertoric force, I aim to let others know what I believe. In addition, my audience may arrive at true beliefs when they take me to believe truly and trust me. If the aim of assertion is communicative, the success of assertions does not depend on their truth. Hence, Evans's argument does not get going.[9]

Fair enough. But Frege has characterised his distinctive approach to logic by saying that he starts with *judgements* and their contents. In judgement one acknowledges the truth of a thought. It seems therefore more promising to argue that thoughts are absolutely true in virtue of being the contents of judgements. Judgement aims, if it aims at all, at truth. When applied to judgement Evans's point can be resurrected. Assume that the thought expressed by 'The meeting starts now' is true relative to a time. When do I have judged successfully that the meeting starts now? Do I aim to judge that the meeting starts now if the thought that the meeting starts now is true at all times? At some times? At the current time? If at the current time, why does the fact that the same thought is false at a later time not make my judgement incorrect? The relativism under consideration raises these difficulties, Frege's truth absolutism avoids them. This speaks in favour of his view.

Evans's line of thought is supplemented by considerations about knowledge and inference. Assume again that an English indexical sentence expresses the same thought in all contexts of utterance and that the truth-value of the thought varies from one context to another. For example, the sentence 'It is raining here' expresses in all context the same thought named by '(the thought) that it is raining here'. Under this assumption, inferences such as the following one should be good inferences:[10]

John knows that it is raining here (said truly yesterday).
Peter knows that it is raining here (said truly today).
Therefore, there is one thing that both John and Peter know.

But they are not good inferences. John did not know yesterday that it is raining today. The fact that he knew yesterday that it was raining then is perfectly compatible with ignorance about future rain.

We can use a similar argument to argue against the view that the same first-person mode of presentation is contained in the first-person thoughts of different thinkers. Assume that the phrase 'that I am hungry' is the name of a thought that different people grasp when they all think that they themselves are hungry. This thought can vary in truth-value from thinker to thinker and time to time. The following inference should then be a good inference:

> I know that I have blood-type A (said by John).
> I know that I have blood-type A (said on by Peter).
> Therefore, there is one thing that both John and Peter know.

Again the conclusion does not follow: John's knowledge of his blood-type does not constitute knowledge of other peoples' blood-type. The knowledge differs because John's first-person thought contains a first-person mode of presentation that presents him and no one else. The thought that is the content of John's self-knowledge is true absolutely as is the thought that is the content of Peter's self-knowledge.

Hence, we have an argument that the possible contents of judgement and knowledge are absolutely true and contain modes of presentation that determine a reference once and for all. Fregean thoughts cannot vary in truth from one situation to another. Therefore the same words will express in different contexts of utterance different thoughts.

Sentences of English and complete sentences

If thoughts are true (false) full-stop, they are not completely expressed by English sentences. Take 'This tree is covered with green leaves'. The sentence says something true when uttered in spring 2009 pointing to the tree in my garden, false when uttered in winter 2009 when uttered pointing to the same tree. Hence, it expresses only partially a thought; it expresses a sense that can be completed to a thought if something is added to it. If the English sentence 'This tree is covered with green leaves' does not express a complete thought, what does? Let us look at some recent proposals before turning to Frege's own.

Quine calls a sentence *eternal* 'whose truth-value stays fixed through time and from speaker to speaker' (Quine 1960: 193). 'Any casual statement of inconsequential fact can be filled out into an eternal sentence by supplying names and dates and cancelling the tenses of verbs' (Quine 1970: 13). So if one fills out 'This tree is covered with green leaves' to 'The tree in MT's garden on the 15 March 2009 is covered with green leaves', we produce an eternal sentence. However, the thought I express with an utterance of 'This tree is covered with green leaves' on the 15 March 2009 pointing to the tree in my garden is not the thought expressed by the eternal sentence 'The tree in MT's garden on the 15 March 2009 is covered with green leaves'. In order to understand the eternal sentence, one needs to master the proper name 'MT' etc.; in order to understand my utterance one doesn't. Eternal sentences have a fixed truth-value, but they don't express the thoughts context-dependent sentences express on specific occasions of utterance.

Quine himself toys with the idea to use sentence-tokens as alternatives to eternal sentences. But sentence-tokens don't have fixed truth-values either. The same token-inscription of 'I am ill' may be used in different utterances to say different things.

A further candidate for the expression of Fregan thoughts are utterances. A particular utterance made by an agent at a particular time and place seems to express one thought completely. But consider this case: you address two different people (one in person, one over the phone) by uttering 'You are not ill, believe me'. Given the right setting you will have put forth two thoughts with one utterance. Hence, the utterance does not express a complete thought independently of context; it expresses relative to a context one thought, relative to another context another thought. Some utterances don't identify a thought uniquely.

What does, then, express a complete thought uniquely? Frege

argues that what expresses a thought in natural language is not a sentence, a string of words that can be written down:

> [T]he mere wording, as it can be written down, is not the complete expression of the thought; the knowledge of certain [circumstances] accompanying the utterance, which are used as means of expressing the thought, is needed for us to grasp the thought correctly. Pointing the finger, hand gestures, glances, may belong here too.
>
> (T: 358, 64)

The object that expresses the thought completely is a sentence plus the circumstances of utterance.[11] Frege goes on to generalise this idea. For example, he adds the following footnote to an example in his late paper 'Negation':

> Here we must suppose that these words by themselves do not contain the thought in its entirety; that we must gather from the circumstances in which they are uttered how to complete them so as to get a complete thought.
>
> (N: 375, 145. See also PMC: 191 fn 69; BW: 121)

He gives a striking illustration how a wording can be completed to a thought expression: '[I]t is [...] *the whole consisting of the concept-word together with the demonstrative pronoun and accompanying circumstances* which has to be understood as a proper name' (PW: 213; NS: 230. My emphasis). What has to be understood as a proper name contains the English expression 'that dog' *plus* certain circumstances of utterance: finger pointings, glances of the eye, times etc. These circumstances are often called 'demonstrations'.[12]

In a Begriffsschrift signs with the same shape have the same sense. This is different in natural language: signs of the same shape can differ in sense (and reference). When we reason in natural language, we cannot reason with shape-individuated type-sentences, but we can create the equivalent to a Begriffsschrift sentence 'on the fly' by adding to a natural language sentence the circumstances that determine together with the sense of the sentence its cognitive value. A complete sentence is a complex of a type-sentence and certain features of the context of utterance. For example, the English type-sentence 'This tree is covered with green leaves' is completed by the time of utterance to a complete expression of a thought. The complete sentence is, like the thought it expresses, true *full-stop*. The complete sentence has a content from which we can draw inferences etc.

If we acknowledge complete sentences as the bearers of sense and reference, Perry's case against Frege's doctrine of sense and reference breaks down right at the start. Perry asks what needs to be added to the sense of a predicate such that a sentence consisting of it and an indexical expresses a complete thought. He goes on to search in vain for a missing conceptual ingredient. No wonder, there is no missing conceptual ingredient if the object expressing the thought is a grammatical string of words plus the relevant features of the context of utterance. Perry has built part of his case against Frege on a wrong assumption about the bearer of sense and reference.

Limited accessibility

Is Frege settled with the unattractive view that thoughts expressed by indexical sentences are of limited accessibility? For example, can the thought you express by saying now 'The meeting starts now' only be grasped now and never again? He himself does not think that thoughts are of limited accessibility:

> If someone wants to say today what he expressed yesterday using the word 'today', he must replace this word with 'yesterday'. Although the thought is the same its verbal expression must be different in order that the change in sense which would otherwise be effected by the differing times of utterance may be cancelled out. The case is the same with words like 'here' and 'there'.
>
> (T: 358, 64)

Perry misinterprets this passage when he writes: 'But this cannot have been Frege's view. This criterion actually introduces a new kind of thought, corresponding to informationally equivalent classes of the old kind' (Perry 1977: 483). Perry takes Frege to argued that *any* replacement of a token of, for example, 'today' as uttered on a day d with a designator of d, say 'the day that NN reads page 147 of *The GuideBook to Frege on Sense and Reference*' would preserve the thought expressed by uttering the original token on d. Imagine that you make an utterance of 'The meeting is today' on the day you read this page. Perry settles Frege with the view that 'The meeting is today' and 'The meeting is on the day that NN reads page 147 of *The GuideBook to Frege on Sense and Reference*' express the same thought.[13] It is, as Perry correctly remarks, difficult to see which theoretical purpose thoughts should satisfy if they were individuated in this way. In effect, thoughts would be individuated in the same way as states of affairs. Perry conceives of a state of affairs as a class of thoughts that contains all and only those thoughts which are about the same things and ascribe the same properties to them.

However, Frege's view is not that you can replace a token of 'today' uttered on a day d with every other designation of d and still express the same thought as the original utterance. He holds that there are restrictions on the replacements of the indexicals by other indexicals that correspond to changes in context. A thought expressed by a sentence with a certain indexical i in context c can be re-expressed by a related indexical i^* in a related context c^*. The *same* thought can be expressed in *different* context of utterance by using *different* indexicals.

Which indexicals are appropriately related to express the same thought in different contexts of utterance? Frege points us to pairs of indexicals, 'today'/'yesterday', 'here'/'there'. Frege's view needs to be developed further. For instance, if the sense of 'today' is a mode of presentation the day d, how can 'yesterday' express the same mode of presentation? For, intuitively, on the one hand, the modes of presentation differ: one includes the aspect of being present, the other of being in the past. On the other hand there is a good sense to holding that someone who asserts on d 'It will rain today' and on $d + 1$ 'It was raining yesterday' that he voices one and the same belief.

The first problem gives us a reason to be wary of the notion of a mode of presentation. But we can use the idea that sameness of sense makes sameness of reference obvious to argue for Frege's view of indexicals. Consider the following temporally extended inference:

Argument A:
If it will be raining tomorrow, I will stay home tomorrow (said on d).
Today it is raining (said on $d + 1$).
Therefore: I stay home today (said on $d + 1$).

This is a good inference: I can come to know the conclusion if I know the premises and retain this knowledge from yesterday to today. If we could not make such temporally extended inferences, planning for the future would be difficult. Now the inference can only be a good one that takes me from something I know to further knowledge, if 'tomorrow' and 'today' have the same sense. Otherwise we would need to add to the inference the further premise that the same day is under consideration in both premises. It does of course not follow that every token of 'tomorrow' and 'today' have the same sense, but the relevant tokens in the argument have the same sense. Similar things hold for the Argument B:

Argument B:
It is cold here (said at point A and time t).
It is snowing over there (said at point B and time t while pointing to A).
Therefore, it was cold and snowing sometime somewhere.

Frege's 'Thoughts' contains the well-known claim that the 'I' of thinking has a different sense than the 'I' of communication. If you say 'I am ill', I can grasp the thought you expressed. Indeed, different people trade on identity in the following argument:

Argument C:
Jim addressing John: I am ill.
John addressing Jim: If you are ill, you should go to the doctor.
Jim addressing John: So I should go to the doctor.
John addressing Jim: So you should go.

There is therefore a good reason to assume that words with different linguistic meanings can express the same thought in different contexts of utterance. In temporally extended reasoning our premises and conclusion may be expressed by different indexical sentences in different contexts. This does not prevent one from producing good inferences. Hence, we must be able to express the same sense with different indexicals in different contexts of utterance.

One may object that arguments A to C rely on tacitly made background premises. For example, John and Jim may suppose (and it may be common knowledge between them) that John's 'I' utterances refer to the same thing as Jim's 'you' utterances. But then the question arises what justifies this supposition. A prima facie plausible answer is that John and Jim know the rules for the English first- and second-pronoun and can apply them correctly in the context of utterance. It is, however, difficult to develop this suggestion in a plausible way. How does one apply the semantic rules to the context of utterance? John can reason as follows:

> If someone addresses x with 'you', he refers with 'you' to x.
> I am now addressing Jim with 'you'.
> Therefore: I am now referring with 'you' to Jim.

In his reasoning John either takes for granted that his tokens of 'Jim' and 'I' co-refer without further reason. Hence, the same question as before arises.

This suggests that we must have room for identities that are taken for granted without further reason. For example, simple reasoning of the form 'p, if p, then q, therefore: q' takes it for granted that 'p' has the same semantic value in the first and second premise. Frege allows us to take such identities for granted without further justifying reasons if the co-referring terms (or utterances there of) express the same sense. He can therefore avoid an unwelcome regress of reasons for identity-beliefs or presumptions that would ensue if we assumed that the above arguments were enthymematic.

Kaplan's objection

We have reason to believe that there are verbal adjustments that allow one to express the same thought in different contexts of utterance. This idea takes the sting out of the problem of the essential indexical. Not so, argues Kaplan:

> Suppose that yesterday you said, and believed it, 'It is a nice day today'. What does it mean to say, today, that you have retained that belief? ... Is there some obvious standard adjustment to be made to the character, for example replacing *today* with *yesterday*? If so, then a person like Rip van Winkle, who loses track of time, can't retain such beliefs. This seems strange.
>
> (Kaplan 1989: 538)

Nothing so far has committed Frege to hold that there are 'obvious standard adjustments', only that the same thought can be expressed in different contexts of utterance differently. But to understand Frege's view it will be helpful to work through Kaplan's objection.

Rip van Winkle slept many years without realising that he did; when he awoke from his sleep he believed that he slept only one night. In this situation it will seem to Rip that he can re-express what he said many years in the past by uttering 'Today is fine' with an utterance of 'Yesterday was fine'. But the second utterance must express indirectly a belief Rip did not hold before. Consider a situation in which Rip's utterances would form parts of an argument extended over what is in fact a very long time:

Argument D:
If it will be raining tomorrow, I will stay home tomorrow (said on 1 May 1789).
Today it is raining (said on 2 May 1800).
Therefore: I stay home today (said on 2 May 1800).

This argument is a bad one, but it may seem to be a good one if one has lost track of time.

If we accept that some inferences may appear to be legitimate to a subject that completely grasps the thoughts expressed, while the inferences are fallacious, we must give up on the transparency of sameness of sense. If Rip van Winkle has completely grasped the thoughts his two utterances of different indexicals express, he fails to recognise that they differ in sense. Hence, the example shows that for indexicals sameness (difference) of sense is not transparent.

However, there is a different response to the example. Rip van Winkle has failed to grasp the sense of the 'today' or the 'tomorrow' tokens. Difficulties in grasping the sense of indexicals can arise because tokens of these words don't express senses completely, only the words plus 'certain circumstances accompanying the utterance, which are used as means of expressing the thought' express a thought (T: 358, 64). For instance, in order to grasp the thought expressed by an utterance of 'Tomorrow it will be raining' one needs to know when the utterance was made; in order to know that utterances of 'Tomorrow it will be raining' and 'Today it is raining' are co-referential one needs to keep track of the passage of time, measured in days. Natural language communication and inference rely on the shared ability to make right guesses about the circumstances of utterance; to know and remember when and where one said something. One can fail to make the right guess and therefore fail to grasp the thought expressed. If we make the wrong guesses, it can seem to us as if we have grasped a thought, while in fact we have failed to do so. Hence, sameness of mode of presentation is transparent, but we can be under the illusion to have grasped a sense, while we have failed to do so. Rip van Winkle's mistake is a case in point. Mere knowledge of the invariant linguistic meaning of an indexical is not sufficient to grasp the thought expressed by an utterance containing the indexical. In contrast, in a Begriffsschrift whose signs (1) express *all and only* conceptual content (sense) and (2) signs of the same shape have the same sense in all contexts, one's mastery of the script is sufficient to grasp the sense of the signs.

Sense/reference and character/content

Perry's critique that Frege's theory of sense and reference cannot be applied to context-dependent expressions has led to a new orthodoxy in the philosophy of language. Perry and Kaplan have argued that one should replace Frege's distinction between sense and reference with the distinction between character and content.

Consider one of Perry's examples for illustration. You say 'I am about to be attacked by a bear' and I point to you saying 'He is about to be attacked by a bear'. Your utterance and mine are about the same person ascribing the same property to it; they both represent the same fact. If you and I successfully communicate, we think of the same fact. If we both represent the same fact, why do I act differently from you (I role up into a ball, while you run to get help)? Because you and I represent the same fact, but under different characters. Now vary the example. You and I say 'I am about to be attacked by a bear'. We both behave similarly (we both role up into a ball), yet our utterances are made true by different facts. Yours by the fact that you are about to be attacked by a bear, mine by the fact that I am about to be attacked by a bear.

These observations suggest to Perry and Kaplan that we must distinguish between the propositional attitudes we express by means of utterances of indexical sentences and what they are about (see Perry 1979: 181f.). My belief that I am about to be attacked by a bear is individuated by its psychological role, its connection with other propositional attitudes and actions. What it is about is the fact that must obtain for the propositional attitude to be correct. The psychological role of the attitude corresponds to the character of the sentence that one uses to express it in a context of utterance. Hence, utterances of different indexical sentences in different context of utterance correspond to different propositional attitudes. The different attitudes can have something in common: they can be made true by the same fact.

Can the duo character/content (fact) do the same work as Frege's duo sense and reference? The fact believed under a character is a replacement of Fregean reference. In the Perry/Kaplan picture, the cognitive value of a sentence is determined by the character under which the fact is believed or entertained. Now consider the 'context-hopping' argument A again:

Argument A:
If it will be raining tomorrow, I will stay home tomorrow (said on day d).
Today it is raining (said on $d + 1$).
Therefore: I stay home today (said on $d + 1$).

If this is a good inference, the indexicals 'tomorrow' as uttered on *d* and 'today' on *d* + 1, must have the same sense. We have seen that Frege makes room for sameness of sense across different contexts of utterance. The cross-contextual sameness of sense cannot consist in a sameness of character or role. For the characters of 'today' and 'tomorrow' are different. However, the different characters determine in different contexts of utterance the same day as their content. Hence, if the premises of argument A are true, so is the conclusion. Isn't that sufficient for argument A to be a piece of good reasoning? No, compare

Hesperus is a planet.
Phosphorus shines in the evening sky.
Therefore: There is something that is a planet and shines in the evening sky.

Since Hesperus is Phosphorus, if the premises of the argument are true, so is the conclusion. If one accepts the necessity of identity, it is not possible that the premises are true and the conclusion isn't. However, this does not make the argument a good inference. It clearly isn't, one cannot come to know the conclusion if one knows the premises. The same goes for argument A: the mere co-reference of 'tomorrow' and 'today' is too weak to make it a good inference.

The Kaplan/Perry theory has so far provided no theoretical posit that makes sameness of reference across contexts obvious. In contrast, Fregean sense makes sameness of reference obvious. Frege, I assume, would therefore take recent treatments of indexicals to be incomplete. But he himself has work to do. The theory of complete sentences needs defence and development. I hope to have convinced the reader that it merits such development.

UNSYSTEMATIC SHIFTS OF SENSE: FOOTNOTE 2 OF 'ON SENSE AND REFERENCE'

In Chapter 4 (pp. 105–6) we have seen that Frege assumes that modes of presentations are independent of and prior to proper names. For this reason they can play a part in individuating proper names. The assumption that modes of presentations are prior to proper names still animates the so-called *description theory of proper names*. 'How do you learn a proper name?' asks the proponent of this theory. A prima facie plausible answer goes as follows: first your attention is drawn to an object of which you come to know some facts that distinguishes it from others. (It is over there, it is the thing that currently fascinates you, the person who discovered the incompleteness theorems etc.) Among these facts is that it is called *N*. Knowing these facts suffices to be able to use the name with understanding. If this is so, how can saying '*N* is ...' express a thought that outstrips the known facts? Surely if it did, no assertion of a sentence containing the name would be warranted?[14]

We may have ways of determining objects before we have names for them. But most people determine the same object in different ways. You will distinguish your mother from other things in a different way than I do.

This provides the background for Frege's often discussed footnote 2 in 'On Sense and Reference'. The footnote is a comment on the following sentence: 'The sense of a proper name is grasped by everybody who is sufficiently familiar with the language or totality of designations to which it belongs' (SR: 158, 27). Frege's footnote makes clear that this is not how things are in natural language for genuine proper names:

> In the case of an actual proper name such as 'Aristotle' opinions as to its sense may differ. It might, for instance, be taken to be the following: the pupil of Plato and teacher of Alexander the Great. Anybody who does this will attach a different sense to 'Aristotle was born in Stagira' than will a man who takes as the sense of the name: the teacher of Alexander the Great who was born in Stagira. So long as the reference remains the same, such variation of sense may be tolerated, although they are to be avoided in the theoretical structure of a demonstrative science [*beweisende Wissenschaft*] and ought not occur in a perfect language.
>
> (SR: 158, 27 fn 2)

Frege suggests that the sense of a proper name (in the idiolect of a speaker) is given by a definite description that the speaker would use to distinguish the proper name bearer from all other things. For example, *my* sense of 'Aristotle' might be given by the definite description 'the inventor of formal logic'. Kripke takes Frege to argue against the naive version of this description theory of proper names in footnote 2 (Kripke 1980: 30). An improved version of the theory is available: the name 'Aristotle' is roughly synonymous with a cluster of definite descriptions. The referent of the proper name is the object that fits the majority of the important descriptions in the cluster. Although Frege does not endorse the view Kripke ascribes to him, Kripke's criticism has been important for recent developments in the philosophy of language. I will therefore devote the next section to it.

Kripke's criticism of Frege

Kripke presents two main objections against the view that the sense of a proper name is given by a definite description that determines the reference of the name. First, the modal objection:[15]

(1) Proper names are rigid designators.

(2) The descriptions commonly associated with proper names by speakers are non-rigid.

(3) A rigid designator and a non-rigid one do not have the same sense. Therefore: (4) No proper name has the same sense as a definite description commonly associated with it.

(Kripke 1980: 57f. and 61f.)

A singular term is a rigid designator of an object x if, and only if, it refers to x in every possible world *in which x exists* (Kripke 1980: 48–9). One can make sense of rigid designation without invoking a plurality of possible worlds. If the sentence that results from uniform substitution of singular terms for the ellipses in the schema

... might not have been ...

expresses a proposition that we intuitively take to be false, then the substituted term is a rigid designator, if not, not.

Why accept premise (3)? If 'Aristotle' had the same sense as 'the inventor of formal logic', we should be able to substitute 'the inventor of formal logic' in all sentences without altering the truth-value (*salva veritate*). But 'Aristotle might not have been the inventor of formal logic' strikes us as true, while 'Aristotle might not have been Aristotle' doesn't. How can substituting 'Aristotle' for 'the inventor of formal logic' change the truth-value of the sentence? Kripke's answer is: even if everyone would agree that Aristotle is the inventor of formal logic, the description 'the inventor of formal logic' is not synonymous with 'Aristotle'. The description is only used to *fix the reference of the proper name*. If someone answers the question 'Who is Aristotle?' by using the description, s/he gives no information about the sense of 'Aristotle'. S/he just gives you advice how to pick out the right object.

The modal argument is controversial for several reasons. Can the difference between sentences with (non-rigid) descriptions and proper names not be explained without positing a difference in sense? A good first-stab reply is that the argument shows that the sense of a proper name can only be given by a definite description that is itself a rigid designator such as 'the inventor of formal logic *in the actual world*' (see, for example, Jackson 2005). Another reply starts from the observation that sentences in which definite descriptions and modal expressions occur (for instance, 'The inventor of formal logic might not have been the inventor of formal logic') are structurally ambiguous. The two readings can be distinguished as follows:

1 The inventor of formal logic might not have been the inventor formal logic. (True!)
2 It might not have been the case that the inventor of formal logic is the inventor of formal logic. (False!)

Our intuition that

3 Aristotle might not have been the inventor of formal logic.

is true does not contradict the assumption that 'Aristotle' is a disguised definite description if we add the further assumption that descriptions so disguised always force the first reading upon us.[16]

Second, the epistemic objection: most people associate with proper names only indefinite descriptions that are not satisfied by only one thing ('Aristotle is a famous Greek philosopher') or by the wrong object ('Peano is the mathematician who first proposed the axioms for arithmetic'. The 'Peano' axioms were first proposed by Dedekind (see Kripke 1980: 84)).

Again friends of the definite description theory of proper names have responded to Kripke by modifying the theory. Kripke's second argument shows that the sense of a proper name such as 'Peano' is not given by 'famous deeds' descriptions such as the one mentioned above.[17] But there are other ways to distinguish an object in order to name it. For example, one might distinguish by important relations it stands or stood to oneself (Betty Miller is *my first wife*).

Kripke's argument can be met by modifying the definite description theory of proper names. Surprisingly, Frege himself points us into the direction of a strong argument against the definite description theory of proper names ascribed to him by Kripke and others.

Frege on the variability of the sense of simple proper names

The basic observation of footnote 2 is that different speakers connect different modes of presentation with an equiform proper name of the same object. Hence, argues Frege, tokens of the same equiform proper name of the same object vary in sense from one speaker to another. Frege holds that proper names are individuated by mode of presentation and shape. In natural language tokens of a proper name referring to one and the same thing often have the same shape but differ in mode of presentation expressed. If these two factors come apart, what shall one say? Do we have different proper names or not? In 'Thoughts' Frege seems to be inclined to say that, *strictly speaking*, a proper name such as 'Gustav Lauben' belongs to different languages if it expresses different senses (T: 359, 65).

Frege's conclusion is unappealing. Often I am entitled to disquote your words. You utter assertorically 'Aristotle was born in

Stagira', I disquote 'He asserted that Aristotle was born in Stagira'. If you and I indeed used different proper names or spoke different languages, such disquotational reports would be mistakes similar to a fallacy of equivocation.

One can try to block the argument that leads to this unattractive conclusion right at the start. 'Aristotle' has the same sense when you and I use it, but we both have only a partial grasp of this sense and the parts we grasp are different. This seems to be independently plausible. People disagree about how a concept they already possess is to be defined. How could they if there was no partial grasping of the same sense?[18]

However, appealing to partial grasp of sense does not help Frege. For now we have to ask: 'How can it be correct for me to disquote your words "Aristotle was born in Stagira", if I grasp a different part of the sense of "Aristotle" than you?' One avoids the consequence that 'Aristotle' belongs to many different languages, but the substantial problem remains.

Frege himself simply accepts that the sense of genuine proper names varies. And why not accept this as a feature of *natural language* expressions? Sense variation is tolerable outside demonstrative sciences. Natural language's main purpose is the transmission of thoughts: 'The task of vernacular languages is essentially fulfilled if people engaged in communication with one another connect the same thought, or approximately the same thought, with the same sentence' (PMC: 115; BW: 183). If you and I connect with 'Aristotle was born in Stagira' approximately the same thought, we have communicated successfully. What does 'approximately the same' amount to? What is the common factor that links together uses of 'Aristotle' and makes them all tokens of the proper name 'Aristotle' referring to Aristotle, the philosopher? Frege's answer on the first pages of 'On Sense and Reference' was that 'Aristotle' tokens that express the same mode of presentation are tokens of the same sign, the same proper name. But in his footnote he backtracks. His remark 'So long as the reference remains the same, such variation of sense may be tolerated' suggests that he is happy to say that, *when it comes to natural language proper names*, sameness of reference is sufficient to make different tokens of, for example, 'Aristotle' tokens of the same name. I will understand your utterance of 'Aristotle was born in Stagira' if you and I refer to the same object and predicate the same concept of it, even if the modes of presentations under which we think of the object and concept differ. A proper name contributes therefore only its bearer to what is understood.[19]

The result is that, by Frege's own lights, sense plays no role in the description of the use of natural language proper names in communication. Russell draws this conclusion when he writes to Frege:

> In the case of a simple proper name like 'Socrates' I cannot distinguish between sense and reference; I see only the idea, which is psychological, and the object. Or better: I don't acknowledge the sense at all, but only the idea and the reference.
>
> (Letter to Frege 12 December 1904. PMC: 169; BW: 251)

Surprisingly, then, Frege himself emerges as a source of a strong argument against the application of sense and reference to shared natural language proper names. Many philosophers working on these problems have accepted this argument from sense-variation and moved to the so-called *Hybrid View*.[20] The Hybrid View has it that 'Hesperus is a planet' and 'Phosphorus is a planet' *literally say* the same, while '*S* believes that Phosphorus is a planet' and '*S* believes that Hesperus is a planet' attribute *different beliefs* to *S*. One grasps what an assertoric utterance of an atomic sentence with a proper name literally says if one latches on to the right object(s) and ascribes to it the right properties. The mode in which object and property are presented does not matter. If a theory of meaning is a theory of understanding, sense is no ingredient of meaning.

Responses to the variability challenge

A convincing response to the challenge from sense-variability requires an answer to the question Dummett asked at the beginning of this chapter: *Why is it profitable to think of natural language in terms of the Fregean ideal in which every expression has exactly one sense that determines at most one referent?* Dummett himself answered that

> the ideal picture is of importance, not because we ought to purge our language so as to correspond completely to it, but because, in particular problematic situations, we need to impose a new practice, which approximates to the ideal picture, on the employment of some or other fragment of our language, in order to resolve the problem with which we are faced.
>
> (Dummett 1981a: 106)

Whenever we face, for example, an existence question (some of Napoleon's unbelievable feats may make one ask 'Did Napoleon really exist?') we must come to an agreement about what would answer the question. In coming to such an agreement, we fix the sense of our words.

But it seems implausible to holds that the applicability of the notion of sense depends on the existence of such 'problematic situations'. If, for instance, in a group of speakers such questions about the existence of a particular object never arose, their words would have no sense, only reference. This is a counter-intuitive consequence. We need an argument that secures the applicability of the notion of sense independently of such contingent circumstances.

Evans made a further strong critical point against Dummett's attempt to close the gap between the ideal and the normal case: '[I]t is the actual practice of using the name "a", not some ideal substitute, that interests us [...]' (Evans 1982: 40). The semanticist studies English, not a future language that will be closer to the Fregean ideal.

Heck has given another answer that is immune to the objection that the Fregean theory is not a theory for a language anyone (already) speaks. Assume that communication is essentially a mode of knowledge transmission (see Evans 1982: 310). If understanding your utterance of 'George Orwell wrote *1984*' consists at least in part in coming to *know* of George Orwell that the utterance is about him, one will only understand the utterance if one grasps a particular mode of presentation of George Orwell. The speaker will assume that his audience can come to know what he is talking about on the basis of his utterance and features of the context. If the audience method of finding out who is talked about does not draw on these reasons, they still might get it right. But it might easily have been the case that the beliefs they actually acquired were false. In this situation they would not *know* who I am talking about with 'George Orwell':

> There are thus limits upon how one may think of George Orwell if one is to understand the utterance. If one does not know that George Orwell is Eric Blair, one cannot think of George Orwell as Eric Blair and yet understand an utterance containing 'Eric Blair'. That is to say, there will be a (more or less) vague collection of ways in which one may think of George Orwell if one is to understand such an utterance [...].
>
> (Heck 1995: 102)

If this argument for the application of the sense/reference distinction to natural language is along the right lines, the bearers of sense and reference are no longer signs, in part distinguished by their shape. The argument shows that the constraints on understanding an *utterance* are more demanding than getting the references of the uttered words and their mode of combination right. In order to understand the utterance of a proper name one must think of its referent in a particular way, but audience and speaker need not think of the same object in the same way. The important requirement is that they all know what they are referring to.

Heck's argument uses as its central premise a controversial assumption about the point of communication: communication is essentially a mode of knowledge transmission. This may be right, but we can argue the same point on the basis of Frege's own assumptions.

In 'Negation' Frege expounds the theory of sense and reference by starting from propositional questions, that is, question whose sense is a thought. What do I need to know in order to answer such a question? He says:

> A propositional question contains a demand that we should either acknowledge the truth of a thought, or reject it as false. In order to meet

this demand correctly, two things are requisite: first, *the wording of the question must enable us to recognise without any doubt the thought under discussion.* [...].

(CP: 373, 143. My emphasis.)

To ask for knowledge 'beyond a doubt' which thought your question expresses seems unmotivated. Let us bring out the plausible core of Frege's idea by considering a simple example. Consider the mini-conversation:

You: Is Hesperus a planet?
Me: Yes, Hesperus is a planet.

I indeed answer to your question if you and I use a name and we are both entitled to take for granted that the name in your mouth refers to the same object as in my mouth. Now compare my answer to an answer in which I have exchanged 'Hesperus' with the co-referential proper name 'Phosphorus':

You: Is Hesperus a planet?
Me: Yes, Phosphorus is a planet.

If you and I do not already presuppose in the conversation that Hesperus is Phosphorus, my assertion is no answer to your question at all, although 'Hesperus' and 'Phosphorus' have the same referent. In order to answer your propositional question, it is not sufficient that I assert a thought whose parts presents the same objects and functions as the thought you expressed. I must, as Frege puts it, come to think the *same thought* as you and present it as true or false. Such examples can easily be multiplied.

In line with this observation is another one. Frege argues that one only needs to avoid sense variation in languages 'designed' for gapless proof. In a Begriffsschrift, signs of the same shape have always the same sense and therefore the same reference. We also make inferences in natural languages; communication in natural language is often *joint* reasoning. These inferences in natural language can leave something to guesswork; we aim to share knowledge, not to give gapless proofs. Therefore the sense of the same (shape-individuated) sign can vary from one context to another. But within one inference the sense of the involved proper names should not vary. Consider the following joint inference:

> You: Mick Jagger is famous.
> Me: And Mick Jagger has been knighted.
> We: Therefore, someone is famous and has been knighted.

Neither I nor you know independently of each other both premises; each person knows one premise and transmits to the other person knowledge of this premise via testimony. Together we can come to know the conclusion by deduction from the premises. But our joint inference can only be a good one if you and I are entitled to take for granted that 'Mick Jagger' in the first premise names the same person as 'Mick Jagger' in the second premise without further justification. Otherwise the argument would be incomplete, its rational force would rests on implicit background premises. According to Frege, sameness of sense makes sameness of reference obvious; if the sense of 'a' and 'b' is the same, we are entitled to take for granted that $a = b$ without requiring a further justifying reason.[21] A number of simple inferences only work if we can take sameness of reference for granted. Hence, we have a good reason to assume that utterances of singular terms have sense and reference.

This argument shows that we need to ascribe more than reference to our words to do justice to all aspects of communication. But it is still unclear whether we need Fregean sense to make co-reference obvious. Consider again the main points of Frege's original proposal:

First, we acquire a mode of presentation of an object x prior to and independently of the introduction of a singular term for x. If we have such a mode of presentation, we can introduce, for example, a proper name for x. The proper name will then express this mode of presentation.

Second, the mode of presentation expressed by a name 'NN' guides our application of the name and it determines, at least in part, the cognitive value of sentences containing it.

Let us grant Frege the assumption that the introduction of a proper name is based on the possession of mode of presentation that purports to represent an object. But if different people express with 'NN' different modes of presentation, modes of presentation lose explanatory power. Consider an example. Why can you and I trade on the fact that your and my tokens of 'Mick Jagger' are co-referential? Not because we both connect the same mode of presentation to the name and this fact is common knowledge between us. Even if the name expresses different modes of presentation in your and my utterances, we can often enough trade on co-reference.

Now we know already that the mere fact that my and your 'Mick Jagger' tokens are co-referential is insufficient to ensure that we can take this fact for granted. Something must entitle us to take the co-reference for granted, but this extra factor need not be a shared mode of presentation expressed both by my and your 'Mick Jagger' tokens. What can the extra factor be?

An analogy points to a prima facie plausible answer: natural language communication is like a collective jazz improvisation while Begriffsschrift 'writing' is like playing from a mutually known score.[22] Let us expand on this analogy: each member of the Takács Quartet knows what each other member will play because each member knows that each other member has learned the same score for a music piece. Frege's Begriffsschrift works according to this 'classical model of meaning' (see also Evans 1982: 21–2). Writers of a Begriffsschrift know that they designate the same thing with the same sign because they have learned the same axioms for the primitive signs. These axioms determine the references of the signs. Hence, Begriffsschrift 'writers' know which modes of presentation are expressed by which signs. If a Begriffsschrift writer and his audience know that each has the intention to write in Begriffsschrift, this knowledge grounds their ability for joint reasoning.

Jazz musician don't learn a score before a performance and then play according to it. Yet, they still manage to produce a joint performance by improvising together. How? They are trained in making reliable guesses which motif the other wants to develop and they respond adequately to it.

Our ability for joint reasoning, more generally, our ability to grasp what others have said, has a similar basis. Like jazz musicians we make educated guesses about what a speaker wants to refer to with 'Mick Jagger' or that he wants to co-refer with us. Such educated guesses are out of place in understanding Begriffsschrift inscriptions, yet we cannot do without them when we communicate in natural language. And they are easily made:

> For instance, the mere fact that the speaker is addressing you with familiar words and grammatical structures is strong evidence that she intends to invoke common referential practices English speakers have built around those expressions. Speakers wear their co-referential intentions on their sleeves.

> (Bigelow and Schroeter 2009: 103)

Sometimes we will need draw on joint background knowledge about Mick Jagger to ensure that we are still talking about the same person. But it is implausible that the features are encoded in the sense of the proper name. For example, in different situations different features might be relevant. But the sense of the proper name should be constant from one situation of use to another.

This picture sits well with the observation that much of what we know about particular objects we know because we first acquired their names and mastery of the name has put us into a position to acquire knowledge about them.[23] Our use of proper names is, in general, not based on the possession of independently available modes of presentations of their bearers.

I don't think that the issue between Frege and his critics is settled by the considerations of this section. But the 'jazz model of communication' is a competitor of Frege's view. It merits further development.

SYSTEMATIC SHIFTS OF SENSE AND REFERENCE: SENTENCES AS NAMES OF THOUGHTS ETC.

In Chapter 6 we will work through Frege's theory of the sense and reference of assertoric sentences. According to Frege, the regular connection between sentence, thought and truth-value is that a *complete* assertoric sentence expresses exactly one thought which in turn determines a truth-value. Again there are exceptions from the regular connection:

> In indirect speech one talks about the sense, e.g. of another person's remarks. It is quite clear that in this way of speaking words do not have their customary reference but designate what is usually their sense. In order to have a short expression, we will say: In reported speech, words are used *indirectly* or have their *indirect* reference. We distinguish accordingly the *customary* reference from the *indirect* reference of a word; and its *customary* sense from its *indirect* sense. The indirect reference of a word is accordingly its customary sense. Such exceptions must always be borne in mind if the mode of connection between sign, sense, and reference in particular cases is to be correctly understood.
>
> (SR: 159, 28)

In this section I will be concerned with the exceptions, in the next chapter with the rule. Let us start by illustrating the exceptions of Frege mentions:

> Gottlob: The evening star shines brightly in the evening sky.
> Direct speech: Gottlob said 'The evening star shines brightly in the evening sky.'
> Indirect speech: Gottlob said (believes) that the evening star shines brightly in the evening sky.

If Frege is right, the sentence 'The evening star shines brightly in the evening sky' refers to the True. Its reference remains unchanged when we exchange in the sentence terms with the same reference. For instance, if 'The evening star shines brightly in the evening sky' refers to the True, and 'the evening star' refers to the same planet as 'the morning star', 'The morning star shines brightly in the evening sky' refers also to the True.

In direct speech one quotes the words uttered. In my utterance of 'Gottlob said "The evening star shines brightly in the evening sky"' the words in quotation marks name the type-sentence they are a token of. In direct speech 'the evening star' has not its usual reference: these words refer to the type-expression 'the evening star'. Hence, one cannot exchange terms with the same normal or usual reference for each other in direct speech without risking changing the truth-value of the sentence. If one replaces 'the evening star' with 'the morning star', the resulting sentence 'Gottlob said "The morning star shines brightly in the evening sky"' differs in truth-value from the original sentence. However, one can exchange 'the evening star' with a term that has the same reference in direct speech. The quotation name '*the evening star*' refers to the same type-word as 'the evening star', hence, they are exchangeable *salva veritate* in direct speech.

Whether 'Gottlob said (believes) that the evening star shines brightly in the evening sky' is true or false depends on what Gottlob said, not on the truth-value of what he said. The sentences 'The evening star shines brightly in the evening sky' and 'The morning star shines brightly in the evening sky' are both names of the True, but exchanging them in indirect speech can change the truth-value of the indirect speech report. For example, although 'Gottlob said that the evening star shines brightly in the evening sky' is true, 'Gottlob said that the morning star shines brightly in the evening sky' is false.

One might argue against Frege that the latter indirect speech report is true if the former is and vice versa. Imagine that your audience does not command the name 'the evening star'. Hence, you use 'the morning star' to make the point in conversation that Gottlob made by using 'the evening star'. Your utterance of 'Gottlob said that the morning star shines brightly in the evening sky' seems true. Depending on conversational context, we apparently change the conditions for the truth of indirect speech reports. Burge defends Frege by arguing that 'Frege was interested in an ideal language for attributing attitudes *in order to specify what the attitudes are*. This involves specifying the representational perspective of the individual with the attitudes' (Burge 2005: 198). Speech and propositional attitude reports that do not respect the perspective of the thinker seem indeed inadequate. You will backtrack from your assertion 'Gottlob said that the morning star shines brightly in the evening sky' if challenged. An attitude that reveals what Gottlob said or believed is what we aim for, but often we have to settle for the second-best option. Frege's theory applies to the case in which we actually achieve our aim.

Frege points out that indirect speech is not *yet* introduced in *Begriffsschrift* (PMC: 149; BW: 232). The Begriffsschrift is a formal tool for mathematical reasoning, but it is supposed to be extendable to further reasoning. If one wants to express, for example, the laws of psychology (if there are such laws) in Begriffsschrift one can hardly avoid introducing indirect speech. Since he had yet no reason to develop a systematic semantics for indirect speech, one finds in SR only an outline of such a view.[24]

The starting point of Frege's outline is that in indirect speech a sentence-nominalisation is the name of a thought. In the sentence 'It is true that the evening star shines brightly in the evening sky' the sentence-nominalisation 'that the evening star shines brightly in the evening sky' refers to the True. The same words have another reference in 'Gottlob said that the evening star shines brightly in the evening sky'; now they name the mode of presentation of the True that they express in the first sentence. The reference of a sentence is sometimes, but not always its truth-value. The reference of a sentence varies with its linguistic surroundings.

He proposes in a letter to Russell a linguistic reform to bring natural language closer to the Begriffschrift in which sense and reference are constant: '[W]e ought really to have special signs in indirect speech, though their connection with the corresponding signs in direct speech should be easy to recognize' (PMC: 153; BW: 236). Let us implement Frege's reform of indirect speech by introducing indices that indicate sense types. The index 0 stands for the customary sense expressed by an unembedded occurrence of a sign, 1 for the sense the sign expresses when embedded under one indirect speech operator such as 'S said ...' . By iterating 'S said ...' we can generate an infinite hierarchy of senses:

- Direct speech: The-evening-star$_0$ shines$_0$ brightly$_0$ in$_0$ the-evening-sky$_0$.
- Indirect speech: Gottlob$_0$ believes$_0$ that the-evening-star$_1$ shines$_1$ brightly$_1$ in$_1$ the-evening-sky$_1$.
- Doubly indirect speech: Bertrand$_0$ believes$_0$ that Gottlob$_1$ believes$_1$ that the-evening-star$_2$ shines$_2$ brightly$_2$ in$_2$ the-evening-sky$_2$.

- Triply indirect speech: $Ludwig_0$ $believes_0$ that $Bertrand_1$ $believes_1$ that $Gottlob_2$ $believes_2$ that the-evening-$star_3$ $shines_3$ $brightly_3$ in_3 the-evening-sky_3.
- And so on.

The expression 'the-evening-$star_0$' refers to Venus and expresses a mode of presentation of it; 'the-evening-$star_1$' refers to the customary sense of the expression 'the-evening-$star_0$', a mode of presentation of Venus; 'the-evening-$star_2$' refers to a mode of presentation of the mode of presentation of Venus and expresses a mode of presentation of a mode of presentation of a mode of presentation of Venus.

Before discussing this complication of the theory of sense and reference further, let us first attend to a point that requires a conservative modification of Frege's theory. It seems natural to say that the name of a thought ('that the evening star shines brightly in the evening sky') is composed of the nominaliser 'that' and the names of the thought constituents in an order ('that' + 'the evening star' + 'shines' …). If 'the evening star' names a sense in 'Gottlob said that the evening star shines brightly in the evening sky', 'Gottlob said that the evening star shines brightly in the evening sky and it does shine brightly in the evening sky' should be false. For 'it' refers back to the reference of 'the evening star'. Since the words have now their indirect reference, they refer to a sense. But the sense of 'the evening star' does not shine brightly. How can the sentence then be true?

Does this refute Frege's reference shift thesis? No, for can't one designator refer to two things? The designator 'the evening $star_1$' refers to the sense of 'the evening $star_0$' *and* to the evening star. Since such anaphoric back-reference seems always possible, we have no reference shift, but 'the evening star' 'gains' new referents.[25] The minimal view is that 'the-evening-$star_n$' refers to Venus and the sense of 'the-evening-$star_{n-1}$'. More refined versions of this thesis are possible. Their plausibility depends on further observations about anaphoric back-reference etc.

Frege himself should be sympathetic to this suggestion. He gives in SR the following example:

John is under the false impression that *London is the biggest city in the world*.

According to him, the italicised sentence is to be taken twice (*'ist doppelt zu nehmen'* (SR: 175, 48)). What is taking a sentence twice? Consider 'John is under the false impression that London is the biggest city in the world'. When we want to say when the sentence is true we need to use the nominalisation of the sentence 'London is the biggest city in the world' twice, once with its shifted reference referring to a thought, once with it normal reference referring to a truth-value:

> 'John is under the false impression that London is the biggest city in the world' is true if, and only if,
> John is under the impression *that London is the biggest city in the world*
> AND
> It is not the case *that London is the biggest city in the world*.

Instead of doubly counting the same sentence-nominalisation, we can let it refer to a truth-value as well as to a thought that determines the truth-value. Reference increase seems more adequate than reference shift.

Philosophers have been sceptical of Frege's sense hierarchy. Carnap's theory of intension and extension is at least partly motivated by a rejection of Frege's hierarchy. Carnap rejects Frege's theory of sense and reference because it ascribes to an expression infinitely many senses and references and sometimes to the same expression more than one reference. He recommends his 'method' of extension and intension because every expression has one intension and extension in all contexts.

We have already seen that there are plausible cases of one expression having multiple referents. This leaves the second point. What is so bad about an infinite hierarchy of senses and references? Davidson has argued that on Frege's reference shifting theory of indirect discourse every word is infinitely ambiguous.[26] On one reading of Frege's proposal, for instance, 'London' has infinitely many senses. It expresses one sense in 'John believes that London is in the UK', it expresses another sense in 'Peter believes that John believes that London is in the UK' and so on. Because of this finite beings like us cannot learn the language of indirect discourse. There is no finite body of knowledge possession of that enables us to understand 'London' in all its occurrences in indirect discourse. For the same reason we cannot understand indirect discourse that we have not heard before.

I will not try to respond to Davidson's argument here.[27] For the more basic question whether we have reason to believe in a hierarchy of senses needs to be addressed first. We get an infinite hierarchy of senses on the following assumptions:

(P1) Indirect reference of w in n embeddings = sense of w in $n-1$ embeddings.

(P2) Indirect sense of w in n embeddings $\neq$ sense of w in n embeddings.

(P3) Indirect sense of w in n embeddings $\neq$ indirect sense of w in m embeddings, if $n \neq m$.

But why accept (P1) to (P3)? If the two occurrences of 'bachelor' in

(1) John believes that all bachelors are dirty; and
(2) John believes that Peter believes that all bachelors are dirty;

differ in sense and reference, one should expect that in (2) 'bachelor' cannot be substituted for a word that has the same sense as 'bachelor' in (1), say, 'unmarried eligible male'. However, if we substitute 'unmarried eligible male' in (2) for 'bachelor', the truth-value remains the same. There are two explanations for this: either the sense and reference of 'unmarried eligible male' also changes when substituted for 'bachelor' in (2) or neither 'bachelor' and 'unmarried eligible male' change their sense in (2). Dummett goes for the second explanation when he writes:

[T]he replacements of an expression in double *oratio obliqua* which will leave the truth-value of the whole sentence unaltered are – just as in single *oratio obliqua* – those which have the same sense. The view that doubly indirect sense and reference must be distinguished from simply indirect sense and reference was a mechanical deduction from a slightly faulty theory.

(Dummett 1981a: 269)

Frege, in turn, will accept the first explanation. The problem with this situation is that there is nothing that singles out one of the explanations as the correct one: we have no means to determine whether the sense changes systematically or has never shifted. In view of lack of direct arguments one should remain agnostic about the question whether there is an infinite hierarchy of senses.[28]

Frege will work in SR through further exceptions from the thesis that an assertoric sentence is a truth-value name. Interesting further exceptions are inference reports: 'Columbus inferred from the roundness of the earth that he could reach India by travelling to the west' (SR: 167, 38). Although we don't try to capture the content of what another person said in such reports, the words specifying the premise and the conclusion of the inference have their indirect reference. For instance, it seems plainly false to say: 'Columbus inferred from the roundness of the solar systems' only inhabited planet that he could reach India by travelling to the west' (SR: 167, 39). The Columbus example helps one to see a point Frege himself neglects. He takes his discussion to show that abstract noun-clauses (that-clauses) are noun phrases (*Nennworte*) that refer to thoughts in certain contexts. However, 'the roundness of the earth' is no abstract noun-clause, yet it names in some contexts a thought. Whether an expression is a name of a thought is not syntactically marked; we often have to guess.

Now not every sentence is an *assertoric* sentence. When Cato the Elder said 'Destroy Carthago!' he did not make an assertion, but gave an order. The sense of an imperative sentence is not a thought. Frege called its sense 'a command', the sense of a request 'a plea' and so forth. For Frege, grammatical mood has significance for the sense expressed. If one utters a sentence in the indicative mood, *and no defeating circumstances obtain* (one utters the sentence on stage), one makes an assertion (SR: 164, 34). If one utters a sentence in the imperative mood, *and no defeating circumstances obtain*, one makes a command etc. Consequently, what someone puts forth with the imperative sentence 'Destroy Carthago!' and the assertoric sentence 'Carthago will be destroyed' differ. The difference in sense explains, among other things, why someone who understands these sentences will challenge their utterances differently when s/he has reason to do so. ('Destroy Carthago! Why should I do that?'; 'Carthago will be destroyed. Why should I believe that?')

Many philosophers of language have not followed Frege in this point. They argue that 'Destroy Carthago' and 'Carthago will be destroyed' express the same thought, but the utterances that express this thought differ in force. The difference in force is responsible for the difference between a command and an assertion. However, the significance of grammatical mood for the content of a sentence can be seen if we compare the following speech-reports:[29]

> Cato the Elder told the Romans to destroy Carthago.
> Cato the Elder told the Romans that they will destroy Carthago.

Both sentences are uttered with assertoric force that extends over the whole utterance. Yet, there is a difference between these sentences in their intuitive meaning that can be traced back to the fact that the subordinate clauses are in different grammatical moods (correspond to different grammatical moods of the utterances that are reported). This is a prima facie reason to hold that sentences in different grammatical mood express senses of different kinds. To the difference in grammatical mood of uttered sentence correspond different ways of referring to the sense expressed in indirect discourse. Now as we cannot exchange co-referential words in the noun-clause 'that Carthage will be destroyed' one cannot exchange them in 'to destroy Carthage'. Hence, neither expression is a name of a truth-value; one expression names a command, another a thought.[30]

Indirect questions are further examples of expressions that don't refer to thoughts. Take:

> John asked who killed Kennedy.

We cannot exchange co-referential terms in 'who killed Kennedy' without risking to turn a true report into a false one. Hence, 'Kennedy' etc. refers to the sense of 'Kennedy', not to Kennedy. But 'Who killed Kennedy?' does not express a thought when uttered in isolation. What is the reference of the indirect question? The sense of the interrogative sentence is at least a first-stab answer.

Frege himself sums up the discussion so far: 'We were able to regard the noun-clause as a noun phrase, indeed one could say as a proper name of that thought, that command etc. as whose name it entered into the compound sentence' (SR: 168, 39. My translation).

6

THE SENSE AND REFERENCE OF AN ASSERTORIC SENTENCE

INTRODUCTION

In Chapter 4 we discussed Frege's argument for splitting conceptual content into sense and reference; in Chapter 5 we examined how his distinction between sense and reference plays out for natural language proper names. The argument was only concerned with the sense and reference of proper names. It assumed that assertoric sentences can differ in cognitive value, but it has not committed Frege to a theory of sense and reference for sentences. A large part of SR is therefore devoted to developing a theory of sense and reference for *assertoric* sentences, that is, sentences in the indicative for which the question can arise whether they say something true or false. All other sentences, optatives, etc., are of no direct interest in SR. In fiction, some assertoric sentences are uttered or inscribed solely with the intention to *make as if* to say something true or false. Frege calls such sentences *pictures* (SR, 163, 33 fn). Pictures have only sense, but no reference. If not stated otherwise, 'sentence' will refer to assertoric sentences that are intended to have sense and reference.

Frege takes for granted that an assertoric sentence expresses a sense, which he calls 'a thought'. He goes on to ask:

(Q1) Does a sentence have a reference (or does it have only sense)?
(Q2) If a sentence has a reference, does it refer to its sense?

(Q1) is answered positively: 'Yes, a sentence that is true or false has a reference'; (Q2) negatively: 'The reference of a sentence is not its sense.' This raises a third question:

(Q3) If a sentence does not refer to its sense, to what does it refer?

Answer: 'A sentence that is true or false is a name of a truth-value.' In his answer, Frege assumes that there are (exactly) two truth-values, the True and the False. The thought expressed by a sentence *s* is a mode of presentation of the truth-value of *s* and *s* itself is a name of its truth-value. Frege's defence of this answer takes up the main part of SR (162–76, 32–50).

Not many philosophers have been convinced that sentences are names of truth-values. Russell, for instance, wrote to Frege:

> I have read your essay on sense and reference, but I am still in doubt about your theory of truth-values, if only because it appears paradoxical to me. I believe that a judgement, or even a thought, is something so entirely peculiar that the theory of proper names has no application to it.
>
> (PMC: 155–6; BW: 233)

Russell's worry is straightforward: sentences are simply not proper names that refer to (pick out) objects. Moreover, the alleged referents are hitherto unheard of objects: the True and the False.

Dummett takes Frege's view about sentence reference not 'merely' to be paradoxical; it also has disastrous effects. In Chapters 2 and 3 we saw that Frege started logic with judgements and judeable contents. Judgeable contents are expressed by assertoric sentences. These have therefore a unique and fundamental role. Logic starts by analysing sentences and thoughts. But, says Dummett,

> [i]f sentences are merely a special case of complex proper names, if the
> True and the False are merely two particular objects amid a universe of
> objects, then, after all, there is nothing unique about sentences: what-
> ever was thought to be special about them should be ascribed, rather,
> to proper names – complete expressions – in general.
>
> (Dummett 1981a: 196)

In this chapter I will do my best to make Frege's paradoxical view
of sentence reference plausible. I will first argue that it has no disastrous consequences. I will then go on to give reasons that sentences can be split up into a name and a sign of force. Finally, I will
try to motivate the assumption that there are truth-values that can
serve as the references of sentences.

DISASTER PREVENTION

Let us for the sake of the argument assume that a sentence is a
name of a truth-value and its sense a mode of presentation of a
truth-value. Does this assumption have disastrous effects?
Following Dummett, Sullivan has presented an argument that can
serve as a representative example for the 'disastrous consequences' allegation.

If thoughts are modes of presentations of truth-values,
thoughts cannot have the distinctive status Frege wants to ascribe
to them. Under this assumption

> it should be possible for me fully to grasp or understand a sense which,
> as the sense of a name of a truth-value, is a thought, while it is no part
> of my understanding that *what* I have grasped *is* a thought. It cannot be
> demanded that this should be part of my understanding, because
> whether a sense is a thought is a matter, not of its internal form or
> nature, but of its particular semantics. It is a matter of what object in
> particular it determines as its referent, and it cannot be a requirement
> of understanding that I must know that. The merger theory contrives to
> turn its being a thought into an extrinsic property of sense.
>
> (Sullivan 2004: 479)

If a thought is mode of presentation of a truth-value, one needs to
know which object is presented in order to know whether one has

grasped a thought or not. This seems indeed bizarre. I don't know yet whether 'Intelligent beings live on Mars' is true, false or neither true nor false, but I know that this is sentence expresses a thought.

Can Frege answer this objection? Some modes of presentation of the True (False) are such that one can grasp them without knowing that they represent a truth-value. Take the mode of presentation expressed by 'the object I am currently thinking of'. As things stand this is a mode of presentation of the True. However, it is not a thought. In order to answer the objection Frege must therefore distinguish those modes of presentation of the truth-values that are thoughts from other modes of presentations of the truth-values by a feature that makes it obvious to someone who grasps them that they present truth-values.

Sullivan assumes that someone who grasps a thought is in a position to know that it is a thought because thoughts are modes of presentations that have an 'internal form or nature'. It is also part of the nature of each thought that it has an opposite:

> To each thought corresponds an opposite, so that rejecting one of them is acknowledging the other. One can say that to make a judgement is to make a choice between opposites. Rejecting the one and acknowledging the other is one and the same act.
>
> (PW: 185; NS: 201. In part my translation.)

A thought never comes alone: every thought p has an opposite, not-p, such that acknowledging the truth of the thought that p is rejecting the truth of the thought that not-p (and vice versa). We grasp the thought p if we know under which conditions it is true. This automatically gives us a hold on the conditions under which the thought is false. These conditions, in turn, are the conditions under which its opposite is true. Hence, one cannot grasp a thought without also being in a position to grasp its opposite. When I grasp the thought that London is a big city I am thereby also able to grasp the thought that London is not a big city. I will grasp the thought and its opposite. One way of entertaining this thought, is asking the question 'Is London a big city *or not*?' This bipolarity is a distinctive feature of thoughts not shared by other modes of presentation of the two truth-values. For example, I can grasp the mode of presentation expressed by 'the True' without grasping its negation, because there is no negation of the True. Since grasping a thought is knowing its truth-conditions, someone who grasps a thought thereby knows whether it has an opposite, that is, whether it is a thought. Thoughts are singled out as those modes of presentations of the True (False) that have opposites and knowing a thought's opposite is part of grasping it.

SENTENCES AND TRUTH-VALUE NAMES

The view that sentences are truth-value names might not have disastrous consequences. But it still strikes us as paradoxical: a sentence is simply no singular term.

To see Frege's point in saying that assertoric sentences are names (singular terms), we need to go back to beginning of *Begriffsschrift*. According to §3 of *Begriffsschrift*, every Begriffsschrift sentence consists of a sentence-nominalisation ('John's being fat') and the predicate 'is a fact'. Importantly, in a sentence such as 'John's being fat is a fact', *'the subject contains the whole content*, and the predicate serves only to represent this as judgement' (CN: 113; BS: 3–4. My emphasis). The subject term 'John's being fat' contains the whole content of 'John's being fat is a fact'; the predicate 'is a fact' carries only assertoric force.

Now expressions such as 'John's being fat' or 'that John is fat' cannot be used like an indicative sentence. They are subordinate clauses. In SR Frege argues that such subordinate clauses are *'Nennworte'* (see SR: 168–9, 39–40). *'Nennwort'* is the school grammar term for 'expression that refers to a particular object' In Frege's own terminology subordinate clauses are complex proper names. Frege seems to be right about this. It is a characteristic feature of proper names that one can existentially generalise in their position ('John smokes. Therefore: there is someone who smokes, namely John.'). The expression 'that John is fat' has this feature:

> It is the case that John is fat.
> Therefore, there is something that is the case, namely that John is fat.

The expression 'that John is fat' refers to something in Frege's general sense of 'reference', that is, one can use 'that John is fat' to speak about something. For example, the teacher may ask 'What is true, that 2 + 2 = 4 or that 2 + 2 = 5?' When the pupil answers 'That 2 + 2 = 4 is true' she uses 'that 2 + 2 = 4' to pick out an object and the rest of the sentence to characterise it. What do we pick out with 'that 2 + 2 = 4'? Early Frege answered: the circumstance of 2 + 2 being 4 ('that p' refers to the content of 'p'). We say of this circumstance that it is a fact. Mature Frege still holds that 'that 2 + 2 = 4' is a name, but the reference is no longer the content of '2 + 2 = 4'. More about this in the next section. The idea that some complex proper names can have the same content as complete sentences will be preserved in Frege's later work. It is the key to understand his view that sentences refer.

Let us first have a look at the changes in Frege's views that are visible in *Basic Laws of Arithmetic* and its companion pieces. He will replace circumstances with truth-values. Frege's modifications of the *Begriffsschrift* theory of sentences depend on the plausibility of the assumption that there are truth-values. I will come back to this assumption in due course and take it for granted at this point. He will also discard the idea that 'is a fact' is a predicate that carries assertoric force. Post-*Begriffsschrift* he used the '⊢' to make assertions. The judgement-stroke is a *sui generis* sign, not a predicate or concept-word: 'The assertion sign cannot be used to construct a functional expression; for it does not serve, in conjunction with other signs, to designate an object. "⊢ 2 + 3 = 5" does not designate anything; it asserts something' (FC: 149, 22 fn). If we simply inscribe '2 + 2 = 4' *without making thereby an assertion* we write down a truth-value, says Frege. '2 + 2 = 4' should be paraphrased as 'The truth-value thereof that 2 + 2 = 4' or, closer to natural language, '2 plus 2 being 4' (PMC: 64; BW: 98. See also GGA I: 24).[1] One asserts that 2 + 2 = 4 by combining the assertion-sign with such expressions: '⊢ 2 + 2 = 4' does not refer, it asserts something.

In the revised Begriffsschrift it is true 'by design' that every expression that expresses the same thought as an assertoric sentence of a natural or scientific language without asserting it is a truth-value name. For example, 'the truth-value thereof that

2 + 2 = 4' and the sentence '2 + 2 = 4' express the same thought. Frege says the same about subordinate clauses such as 'that London is in the UK' and complete sentences such as 'London is in the UK' of natural language. For example, in SR he tests the hypothesis that subordinate or 'that'-clauses are names of truth-values. If the words composing the subordinate clause have their normal reference, '*the sense of the subordinate clause is a complete thought*, in which case it can be replaced by another of the same truth value without harm to the truth of the whole – provided there are no grammatical obstacles' (SR: 173, 46. In part my translation. My emphasis). Frege holds that, if the sense and reference of a sentence-nominalisation such as 'that 2 + 2 = 4' has not shifted, *its sense is a thought* (SR: 166, 37). For example, in 'It is the case that 2 + 2 = 4' the sense of the 'that'-clause is a thought, the same thought that is expressed by '2 + 2 = 4'. Hence, a singular term that purports to refer can express the same sense as an assertoric sentence.

How can one justify the thesis that a sentence-nominalisation and the sentence nominalised have the same sense? Frege's criterion of sense identity works only for assertoric sentences and it cannot be applied across grammatical categories (see Chapter 4, pp. 140ff.). How can he make a positive case for his view?

I am not aware that Frege has provided an argument for this important thesis. He seems to trust that nominalising a sentence – putting a sentence in dependent form – is a grammatical transformation that leaves its sense unchanged. However, one can try to support his view by appealing to connections between propositional and nominal attitudes. Consider Frege's own example from *Begriffsschrift*: the sentence 'Archimedes perished at the conquest of Syracuse' and the singular terms 'that Archimedes perished at the conquest of Syracuse' and 'the violent death of Archimedes at the conquest of Syracuse'. Frege claims that the singular terms have the same content as the sentence. Now everyone who understands (1) 'Archimedes perished at the conquest of Syracuse' and (2) 'that Archimedes perished at the conquest of Syracuse' must judge what (1) says if, and only if, he predicates truth or being a fact of the reference of (2) (and the other way around). The relation between these contents is analogous to thought identity. Frege can argue that it is similar enough to allow him to say that the sense of an assertoric sentence in pure form is a mode of presentation of an object.[2]

We can now give an argument that supports Frege's view that sentences refer:

1   A sentence-nominalisation such as 'that p' is a complex proper name that purports to refer to an object.
2   The assertoric sentence 'p' and the sentence-nominalisation 'that p' expresses the same sense (thought).
3   If two expressions have the same sense, they refer to the same object, if they refer at all.
4   Therefore: An assertoric sentence 'p' refers to the same object as the sentence-nominalisation 'that p'.
5   Therefore: An assertoric sentence is a complex proper name that purports to refer.

Frege subscribes to the premises of this argument and its conclusion. But Russell et al. will take the argument to be a *reductio ad absurdum* of its premises. A sentence is not a name!

Frege's conclusion starts to look less paradoxical if we take the following quotation into account:

> If I attach the word 'salty' to the word 'sea-water' as a predicate, I form a sentence that expresses a thought. To make it clearer that *we have only the expression of a thought, but that nothing is meant to be asserted, I put the sentence in the dependent form 'that sea-water is salty'*. Instead of doing this I could have it spoken by an actor on the stage as part of his role, for we know that in playing a part an actor only seems to speak with assertoric force.
>
> (PW: 251; NS: 271. My emphasis and correction.)

In natural language we cannot separate the mere expression of a thought from its assertion. Take a sentence s in the indicative mood that expresses the thought that p. If one utters s and (1) s is not part of a complex sentence and (2) no defeating factors obtain, one has asserted that p (PW: 198; NS: 214, CP: 247, 377). About (1): If 'Sea-water is salty' is the antecedent a conditional ('If sea-water is salty, sea-water will not quench thirst'), uttering the sentence is not asserting that sea-water is salty. About (2): if I utter 'Sea-water is salty' in a scientific discussion and Laurence Olivier makes as if he asserts the very same sentence on stage, we both express the same thought, but only I have asserted it. One can only express thoughts with unembedded assertoric sentences without at the same time asserting them, *if one does something that defeats the assertoric force carried by the grammatical mood*. This seems to be a limitation of natural language.

Frege suggests in the quote above that nominalising a sentence does the same 'job' as uttering it on stage. If we put a sentence *s* into dependent form – that is, transform *s* into *that s*, the nominalised sentence does not carry assertoric force, yet expresses the same thought as *s*. Using 'that' nominalisations is the only grammatical transformation available in natural language to express a thought without asserting it (PW: 198; NS: 214). This is not quite right. For the propositional question 'Is sea-water salty?' is supposed to express the same thought as the assertoric sentence 'Sea-water is salty' (T: 355, 62). Frege's view should rather be that only a 'that'-clause can express a thought without *any* force at all. The sentence-nominalisation 'that sea-water is salty' and the sentence 'sea-water is salty' express the same thought; in addition to expressing the thought, the sentence puts it forth as true. An assertoric sentence is made up out of a part that only expresses a content or thought and an additional feature that provides the assertoric force. In natural language the additional feature is the indicative mood. In Frege's revised Begriffsschrift, assertoric force is carried by the assertion sign and the content is completely expressed by a sentence-nominalisation. The sentence-nominalisation is a name that has sense and purports to refer; the assertion sign has neither, combined they assert something. Frege's conclusion should then better be expressed as:

5*   In a perspicuous symbolism, assertoric sentences are replaced by a combination of a complex proper name that *only* expresses a thought and refers to an object and a sign that *only* carries assertoric force, but does not refer.

The perspicuous symbolism will assign to *two* component expressions the *two* roles that *one* assertoric sentence performs: expressing a thought and asserting it. Natural language approaches the perspicuous symbolism: the grammatical mood of a sentence carries only assertoric force, but it is not a component of a complex expression.

Now 5* is no longer paradoxical: a sentence nominalisation is indeed a complex proper name. In a further step, the sentence-nominalisations can be replaced by variables that range over the things the nominalisations refer to. In this way one can formulate the laws of logic (see Chapter 1, p. 43f.).

From now on I will assume that Frege investigates in 'On Sense and Reference' whether complex signs that express thoughts *without asserting them* refer to something. Frege's own explanation of 'sentence' justifies us in making this assumption: 'A sentence is for me a composite sign that is intended to express a thought' (PW: 153; NS: 236. My translation). The sentence is intended to express a thought, not to assert it. According to this explanation, 'Sea-water is salty' is not a sentence, 'that sea-water is salty' is one. For an indicative 'sentence' asserts something if its assertoric force is not overridden. For Frege, 'sentence' or, as he says, 'proper sentence' is not a category of grammar, but of logic (see GGA I: 391, 37). A subordinate clause can express a thought unasserted and hence, qualifies as a proper sentence.

Let us use an example to sum up the discussion of this section: The thought expressed *with assertoric force* by 'The morning star is a body illuminated by the sun' is expressed *without assertoric force* by the singular term 'that the morning star is a body illuminated by the sun'. This singular term seems to refer to a content or thought. For instance, when I say 'That the morning star is a body illuminated by the sun was an important fact discovered in astronomers' I seem to speak about a fact or a truth. This is, in essence, Frege's view in *Begriffsschrift*.

A SENTENCE DOES NOT REFER TO A THOUGHT

In SR Frege changes his mind. He presents an argument for the conclusion that the content or thought is not the reference of the sentence:

We now inquire concerning the sense and reference of an entire assertoric sentence. Such a sentence contains a thought. Is this thought, now, to be regarded as its sense or reference? Let us assume for the time being that the sentence has a reference! If we now replace one word of the sentence by another having the same reference, but a different sense, this can have no effect upon the reference of the sentence. Yet we can see that in such cases the thought changes; since, e.g. the thought of the sentence 'The morning star is a body illuminated by the sun' differs from that of the sentence 'The evening star is a body illuminated by the sun.' Anybody who did not know that the evening star is the morning star might hold the one thought to be true, the other to be false. The thought, accordingly, cannot be the reference of the sentence, but must rather be considered as its sense.

(SR: 162, 32. In part my translation.)

He makes four assumptions:

(1) Sentences have sense and reference.
(2) A sentence expresses a thought.
(3) The thought that *p* expressed in sentence *s* is different from the thought that *q* expressed in sentence *s** if one can hold true *s* without holding true *s** (or the other way around).
(4) Reference principle: If α and β have the same reference, they can be substituted for one another in every complex expression that has a reference without changing its reference (see SR: 162, 32).

As already pointed out, we must read for 'assertoric sentence' 'what expresses the content of an assertoric sentence without asserting it' or 'complex expression supposed to express a thought'.

Now assumption (1) will be tested by Frege in further discussion. He takes (2) to be obvious, but expands on it in a footnote: 'By a thought I don't understand the subjective deed of thinking, but its objective content which is capable of being the common property of many' (ibid., fn).

Consider Frege's illustration of the 'capable of being the common content of many' idea.[3] In asking the propositional question 'Was Frege born in Wismar?' I put something, a content, forth and request my audience to determine whether it is true or false. In order to answer my question correctly, you must take a stand on what I have asked. Frege plausibly assumes that you must therefore grasp *the same content* that I expressed with my words. Otherwise how could you answer my propositional question correctly? Now mental acts such as inquiring whether Frege was born in Wismar, judging that Frege was born in Wismar etc. and mental images and feelings that accompany such acts are unshareable: you cannot make the very same judgement that I just made. You can only make a judgement of the same type as I just did. And it is plausible to say that your and my judgements are only of the same type if their content is the same thought. Hence, the practice of answering propositional questions forces us to assume that there are shareable contents and to distinguish them from unshareable mental acts and ideas. This practice gives us also an intuitive grip on when one grasps a shareable content, a thought. In order to answer a propositional question one needs to know under which conditions 'yes' ('no') is the right answer to it. Someone who knows under which conditions 'yes' ('no') is the right answer grasps the thought contained in the propositional question.

Frege takes the notion of a thought for granted in SR; later he will devote the paper 'The Thought' (1919) to it. We will have reason to raise and answer further questions about thoughts in the eighth section of this chapter. Assumption (3) is one part of Frege's criterion of thought identity, which we already have discussed in Chapter 4 (pp. 140ff.).

We can now sum up the argument like this: if the thought contained in a sentence 'Fa' were its reference, substituting 'a' or 'F' with co-referential expressions could not change the thought. However, such substitutions can change the thought contained. Hence, if a sentence has a reference, it is not the thought.

One way to respond to this argument is to retract the view that sentences refer. They express thoughts, but do not name them. A second way is to find new references for them. Frege goes the second way. In the next section I will therefore outline how he aims to introduce these objects, the True and the False.

TRUTH-VALUES IN 'FUNCTION AND CONCEPT'

One can start to understand Frege's view that sentences refer to truth-values by considering why he introduces truth-values. In order to do so we need to revisit 'Function and Concept'.[4] In this paper he aims to extend the realm of functions from numerical functions (mapping numbers onto numbers) to functions such as $x^2 = 1$. He writes about this function:

> Now if we replace x successively by -1, 0, 1, 2 we get:
> $$-1^2 = 1$$
> $$0^2 = 1$$
> $$1^2 = 1$$
> $$2^2 = 1$$
>
> Of these equations the first and third are true, the others false. I now say 'the value of our function is a truth-value', and distinguish the truth-value the True from the False. I call the first, for short, the True; and the second, the False. Consequently, e.g. '$2^2 = 4$' refers to the True just as, '2^2' refers to 4. And '$2^2 = 1$' refers to the False. Accordingly,
>
> '$2^2 = 4$', '$2 > 1$', '$2^4 = 4^2$'
>
> all refer to the same thing, viz. the True, so that in:
>
> '$(2^2 = 4) = (2 > 1)$'
>
> we have a correct equation.
>
> (FC: 144, 13. In part my translation.)

Let us get clear about Frege's basic points. Take the designator of a numerical function. If we complete '$1 + \xi$' with '1' we 'generate' a complex designator for the value of the function for the argument 1, the number 2. 2 is the value of the function $1 + x$ for the argument 1. The analysis of the designator '$1 + 1$' into functional expressions and completing expressions mirrors the determination of the semantic value of this designator.

Frege now wants to extend this analysis to equations such as '$2^2 = 4$'. In order to do so, he assumes that the equation can be decomposed into functional (for example, '$\xi^2 = 4$') and non-functional expressions (for example, '2'). The functional expression refers to a function, the non-functional one to an argument. He calls the function that a well-defined predicate such as '$\xi^2 = 4$' refers to, a *concept*. Like '1 + 1', the equation '$2^2 = 4$' is supposed to refer to the value the concept '$\xi^2 = 4$' assumes for the argument 2.

If the concept '$\xi^2 = 4$' has a value for 2, Frege can extend his theory of functions to equations and sentences in general. What can the value be? This value must be an object. The argument-sign '1' completes the function-sign '$\xi^2 = 1$' to a complete expression, a sentence. Complete expressions can only refer to complete 'entities', that is, objects. (See Chapter 7 for discussion of this point.) Consequently, if sentences refer at all, they can only refer to objects. Frege really needs to discover two new *objects* to extend function theory in the way he wants to.

But are there such objects? It is uncontroversial that the formula '$1^2 = 1$' is true. Now saying, as he does, that if it is true, the True is the value of the function $\xi^2 = 1$ for the argument 1 is either a harmless but unfruitful way of coding that the equation is true or an as yet unwarranted reification. Quine, for example, takes the first option: 'It is convenient to speak of truth and falsity as *truth values*; thus the truth value of a statement is said to be truth or falsity according as the statement is true or false' (Quine 1974: §2). However, a convenient way of speaking about a statement's truth (falsity) does not introduce new objects: truth-values. At best, it introduces new words for the property of being true (false). If Frege wants to make his functional analysis of sentences plausible, he needs to provide an argument that makes the positing of truth-values as objects plausible and not merely introduce a new way of speaking about the property of *being true*. He tackles this task in SR.

WHY SENTENCES REFER TO TRUTH-VALUES

Frege has to answer several interrelated questions: if a sentence does not refer to a thought, what does it refer to? In FC, sentences referred to truth-values. But this seemed only to be another way of saying that a sentence says something true. In SR he tries to make the view that sentences refer to truth-values and that these truth-values are objects plausible by starting from plausible assumption about the references of sentence parts.

He considers the sentence 'Odysseus was set ashore at Ithaca while sound asleep'. Frege argues that if one takes this sentence seriously, one must acknowledge a referent for 'Odysseus'. For it is obvious that 'Odysseus was set ashore at Ithaca while sound asleep' cannot say something true if 'Odysseus' does not refer. The name must refer to something otherwise there is nothing to which the predicate 'ξ was set ashore at Ithaca while sound asleep' can apply or not. If one is not concerned with the truth of what the sentence says, one does not need to acknowledge a reference for the name 'Odysseus', only a sense. He argues further:

> The fact that we concern ourselves at all about the reference of a part of the sentence indicates that we generally recognise and expect a reference for the sentence itself. The thought loses value for us as soon as we recognise that the reference of one of its parts is missing. We are therefore justified in not being satisfied with the sense of a sentence, and in inquiring also as to its reference. But now why do we want every proper name to have not only a sense, but also a referent? Why is the thought not enough for us? Because, and to the extent that, we are concerned with its truth-value. [...]
> We have seen that the referent of a sentence may always be sought, whenever the referents of its components are involved; and that this is the case when and only when we are inquiring after the truth-value.
> We are therefore driven into accepting the *truth-value* of a sentence as its reference.
>
> (SR: 163, 33)

What is a truth-value? 'By the truth-value of a sentence I understand the circumstance that it is true or false. There are no further truth-values. For brevity I will call the one the True, the other the False' (ibid.). Frege concludes: 'Every declarative sentence concerned with the references of its words is therefore to be regarded as proper name, and its reference, if it exists, is either the True or the False' (ibid.). Frege takes this argument not to prove that sentences refer to truth-values. Rather, it makes the 'hypothesis' plausible that a sentence refers to a truth-value.

The hypothesis that a sentence refers to a truth-value is then strengthened by a further consideration that appeals to the reference principle. If a sentence refers to a truth-value, it must be substitutable *salva veritate* by other sentence that have the same truth-value. Now if we replace in 'It is true that 2 + 2 = 4' the contained sentence-nominalisation with the nominalisation of another true sentence, say 'that 3 + 1 = 4' we arrive again at a true sentence: 'It is true that 3 + 1 = 4.' According to Frege, this intersubstitutivity is grounded in sameness of reference. If we accept the hypothesis that sentences refer to truth-values, the explanation is that both that-clauses refer to the True and therefore they can be exchanged for each other *salva veritate* in sentences in which the have their standard reference. How convincing is this argument?

First, the truth-value of the sentence *s*, Frege says, is the circumstance that *s* is true (false). If this were his considered view, he would face the question why saying that *s* refers to the True (False) is more than an artificial way to say that the circumstance that *s* is true (false) obtains (that *s* is true). For he uses the truth-predicate 'is true' in saying what the truth-value of a sentence is. In fact he makes things even worse: if the truth-value of the sentence *s* is the circumstance that *s* is true (false), and circumstances are distinct if they have different constituents, there are as many truth-values as there are sentences. How can Frege then hold that there are exactly two truth-values? He is best not taken here as telling us what truth-values are, but only under which circumstances a sentence *s* has a truth-value: the sentence *s* has a truth-value if, and only if, *s* is either true or false.[5]

Second, the argument pivots on the premise that our concern about the reference of a sentence part is an indication that we recognise and expect a reference for the sentence itself. Fair enough. We concern ourselves about the reference of 'Odysseus' when we want to find out whether 'Odysseus was set ashore at Ithaca while sound asleep' is true. But this only shows that we take the truth of the thought expressed to depend on whether 'Odysseus' has a reference or not. If there is no reference, the sentence cannot say something true. In neutral and non-committal terms we can say that we are concerned with the reference of 'Odysseus' when we are interested in *whether the thought is true or not*. Frege himself uses the neutral locution when he tries to shed light on truth-values in later work: 'The only thing for which this [the fact that a sentence part has a reference] is essential is that which I call truth-value, namely *whether the thought is true or false*' (PW: 194; NS: 211. My translation and emphasis). We have no reason to assume that if we are interested in whether a part of a sentence *s* has a reference, we are so interested because we are primarily interested in whether *s* itself has a reference. The neutral principle covers Frege's example perfectly well:

> The neutral principle: we are interested whether a part of a sentence *s* has a reference, if we are interested in the question whether the sentence says something true or false.

Frege's argument begs the question against someone who takes sentences to have no reference, but plausibly takes them to be true or false and their possession of these properties to depend on the reference of the sentence parts.

Third, Frege builds on the idea that we find it natural to enquire *after the truth-value* of sentences. Now surely we often enquire whether a sentence *is true (false)*. But before reading Frege, you won't have enquired after *the truth-value* of a sentence. (Did you ever ask yourself what the truth-value of a claim is?) His argument assumes that we already know what truth-values are and operate with them.

Frege's argument does not help us to understand what a truth-value is, rather it exploits an understanding of what a truth-value is and argues that such things, truth-values, can be the references of sentences. Truth-values are the 'unmoved movers' in Frege's modified Begriffsschrift. He specifies in *Basic Laws of Arithmetic* I to which functions expressions such as the conditional-stroke and the negation-stroke etc. refer by determining under which conditions Begriffsschrift sentences containing them refer to the True (False). How does he suppose his reader to apprehend the truth-values? Frege wants to answer this question by bringing to bear consideration from the theory of judgement.

JUDGEMENT AND TRUTH-VALUE IN 'ON SENSE AND REFERENCE'

Every thinker who pursues the truth must make judgements and inferences. The objects to which these activities commit us are, in principle, available to anyone able to think and reason. The objects are the True and the False. Frege's Begriffsschrift assumes these objects and defines all logically relevant concepts in terms of them.[6] According to him, a proper understanding of what judging is will give us an independent grip on truth-values:

> *These two objects [the True and the False] are acknowledged, if only implicitly, by everybody who judges, who takes something to be true, and therefore even by the sceptic.* The designation of the truth-values as objects may appear to be an arbitrary fancy or a mere play upon words from which no profound consequences may be drawn. What I mean by an object can be more exactly discussed only in connection with concept and relation. [...] But so much should already be clear that in every judgement [Footnote: A judgement, for me is not the mere grasping of a thought, but the acknowledgement of its truth [*Anerkennung der Wahrheit*]] no matter how trivial, the step from the level of thoughts to the level of reference (the objective) has already been taken.
>
> (SR: 163–4, 34. My translation and emphasis.)

So far taking truth-values to be objects seemed to be just an arbitrary fancy, that is, an artificial way of coding that a sentence is true (false). Frege's general message is clear: it is an insight that truth-values are objects and one can draw profound consequences from it, namely that concepts are functions from objects to truth-values and that sentences are names of truth-values.

Frege suggests an argumentative strategy for justifying the positing of truth-values. Everyone who makes judgements, even the sceptic, implicitly acknowledges the truth-values. The sceptic he has in mind is obviously not the ancient sceptic who withholds judgement totally, but a sceptic who doubts the existence of other minds or the external world. Such a sceptic will make inferences to the effect that he has no reasons that justify judgements about other minds, external objects etc. But the sceptic will make judgements and draw inferences. Thereby, Frege argues, the scep-tic has committed himself to the True and the False. If we make explicit our tacit knowledge of what it is to judge, we will see that we are already committed to the two truth-values. When it comes to truth-values, judgement is the key. This should not come as a surprise. Judging is the 'logically primitive activity' and judging involves the notion of truth. The crucial point for our purposes is that we come to know truth-values by elucidating the activity of judging. Even if only implicitly everyone who has made a judge-ment has acknowledged the True (the False). He draws on this implicit acknowledgement of the True (False) in judgement and tries to render it more explicit.[7] How can we develop this outline into an argument for his view?

The general drift of this part of SR is that our grip on the notion of judgement is better than our grip on the relation between a thought and truth-value. Judging that p is a mental relation between the thought that p and a truth-value. Hence, we can learn something about thoughts, truth-values and their relation by making our understanding of judgement more explicit. Let us therefore now work through Frege's remarks about what judge-ment is or is not.

1 *Judging that* p *is not thinking that the thought that* p *is true.* In Chapter 3 (p. 76) we saw that Frege suggested that judging is sub-suming a circumstance under the concept ξ *is a fact*. In 'On Sense and Reference' he gives one reason to hold that asserting that p is not uttering a sentence that says that the thought that p is true (a fact) and he suggests a more general reason against a predicative understanding of judgement.

Asserting is not linguistically predicating truth of a thought. Uttering a sentence that says that (the thought) p is true is neither necessary nor sufficient for asserting that p. I can assert that 2 is prime simply by uttering the indicative sentence '2 is prime' in the right circumstances, no truth-predicate is necessary.[8] I can also utter '2 is prime *is true*' without asserting that 2 is prime (I may make the utterance as an actor on stage). Frege concludes that it is not the truth-predicate, but '*the form* of the assertoric sentence' by means of which one states the truth. If one utters a sentence in the indicative in the absence of factors that defeat its force, one makes an assertion.

Assertion is a speech act; judgement a mental act. What counts against a view of assertion will not automatically count against a view of judgement (and vice versa). But he goes on to give a more general argument:

> By combining subject and predicate, one reaches only a thought, never passes from sense to reference, never from a thought to its truth-value. One moves at the same level but never advances from one level to the next. A truth-value cannot be a part of the thought, any more than, say, the sun can, for it is not a sense but an object.

(SR: 164, 35)

No activity that consists in combining a subject and a predicate can be a judgement. For in judgement one moves from a thought to its truth-value, while a combining activity can only move from one thought to a more complex thought.

Subject and predicate in the logical sense are parts of thoughts; roughly they are the senses of singular terms and predicates distinguishable in a sentence expressing the thought. Frege argues that judging cannot be combining a mode of presentation of a thought and the sense of 'is true' to a complex thought. There is Frege-independent and a Frege-immanent reason for this negative thesis.

First, the Frege-independent reason for rejecting the predication view. Let us assume that judging that p is predicating truth of the thought that p. What is predicating truth? We have two options: (1) predicating truth is what is common in judging that p is true, assuming that p is true, wondering whether p is true, etc. or (2) predicating truth is a distinctive mental act with 'assertoric force'.

If we accept (1), one can predicate truth of the thought p and yet not judge p. One only entertains now, as Frege says above, the more complex thought (p is true). Predicating truth of the more complex thought will result in an even more complex thought. One can now again predicate truth of this complex thought, and so forth. Hence, if one wants to explain judgement in this way, one faces a regress of ever more complex thoughts. The conclusion is that predicating truth is thinking complex thoughts, but not judging.

If we accept (2), one cannot predicate truth without *eo ipso* judging that *p*. But in (2) the judgement is not explained with recourse to the predication of truth; all the explanatory work has been done by the distinctive force of the mental act and no work by the concept of truth. For example, if one were to think a thought that does not contain the sense of 'is true' with this force one would still make a judgement. The result is that the property (concept) ξ *is true* does no work in a theory of judgement.

Second, the Frege-immanent reason appeals to a conception of what judgement is or should achieve if it is the logically primitive activity. In 'Comments on Sense and Reference' Frege expands on topics introduced in 'On Sense and Reference'. In this paper he criticises intensionalist logicians as follows:

> The intensionalist logicians are only too happy not to go beyond the sense [...]. They forget that logic is not concerned with how thoughts, regardless of truth-value, follow from thoughts, *that the step from thought to truth-value – more generally, the step from sense to reference – has to be taken* [...].
>
> (PW: 122; NS: 133. My emphasis.)

Logic studies inference, argues Frege. An inference is a judgement mediated by other judgements. It takes one from acknowledged truths to acknowledged truths. An inference from *p* to *q* cannot be exhaustively described in terms of the thoughts *p* and *q*. You have only inferred *q* from *p* if you acknowledge the truth of *q* and your acknowledgement is justified because you acknowledge the truth of *p*. This view of inference underlies Frege's prima facie counter-intuitive restriction that one cannot infer anything from a mere assumption. The mere assumption of *p* cannot justify acknowledgement of the truth of *q*: I can only infer from the assumption that *q* is true if *p* is.[9]

Now if judging is predicating truth, an inference takes one only from some thoughts to a more complex thought that contains the sense of the truth-predicate. But when I infer *q* from *p*, I am not aiming to think the thought that q is true; that I could do without inference. Intuitively, I want to apprehend the truth of q via the truth of q. Frege aims to capture this view and systematise it when he writes about judgement. He calls the act, which is supposed to achieve this aim, 'judgement'. His description of this act already assumes that there are truth-values; the alternative description as acknowledgement of truth does not assume this. It can therefore be accepted by someone who has yet to be convinced that there are truth-values.

Judging, then, is not predicating truth. The notion of a property or concept of truth does not do any work in a theory of judgement. However, he takes it to be clear that there is a relation between judgement, truth and thought. Judgements are evaluable as correct or incorrect depending on the truth or falsity of the contents judged. The prescriptions for judgements are given with the laws of truth. We evaluate judgements according to these prescriptions if we criticise someone who judges falsely or infers a falsehood from a truth. For the laws of truth to yield prescriptions for judgement, judging and truth must be related. How can this relation be characterised and what are its relata if truth is not a property of thoughts? Let us look at answers suggested by Frege.

2 *Judging that* p *is acknowledging the thought* p *as true.* Before and after SR Frege frequently characterises judging as acknowledging a thought *as true.*[10] The 'as' construction suggests that judging is a way of acknowledging a thought. For example, if I regard someone *as a friend*, I regard him in a certain way, namely in the way one regards friends. I will not pursue this idea further. For if judging is a way of acknowledging, it brings no rational commitment to truth-values with it. Adverbial theories of thought and intentionality are especially developed to dodge such commitments. In general, one can think in a particular way without being mentally related to something. Since 'acknowledging as true' does not help Frege's cause, I will pursue now alternative construals.

3 *Judging that* p *is acknowledging the truth of (the thought)* p. In SR Frege characterises judgement also as follows:

- Acknowledging the truth of a thought (SR: 164, 34 fn).
- Advancing from a thought to its truth-value (SR: 164, 34; SR: 177, 50).
- Distinguishing parts in a truth-value by going back to the thought (SR: 165, 35).

I will now argue that among these characterisations the first one helps him to argue that there are truth-values. I addition, it will illuminate the second and third characterisation.

Let us then start with 'judging is acknowledging the truth'. Frege takes judgement to be indefinable (SR: 165, 35). He does therefore not intend to define judgement, but to elucidate it, that is, give his readers pointers to arrive at the right notion. The first elucidation requires his readers to draw on their understanding of 'acknowledging' and 'truth'. I will assume that we have a working knowledge of the meaning of 'true' and 'is a truth'. So we need first to get clear how his readers would have understood 'anerkennen'.[11] In his time the German verb 'anerkennen' had (and still has) at least three meanings: a legal one (one can acknowledge or honour a claim), an evaluative one (one can acknowledge the achievements of person; give someone a prize in recognition of his or her good work) and an ontic one. The evaluative view of judgement was prominent in Frege's time. Its background is Herman Lotze's influential book *Logik*, first published in 1841. Lotze (1817–81) argued that the distinction between truth and falsity is a distinction in value with which logic starts (see Lotze 1880: 4f.). Lotze's student Windelband took it to be uncontroversial that 'is true' is a value predicate (Windelband 1920: 196). If 'is true' is a value predicate, it is natural to hold that judging is an evaluation. Frege has studied briefly with Lotze in Göttingen and Frege's '17 Key-sentences in Logic' is in part a critical commentary on Lotze's *Logik*. However, for reasons that will soon emerge it is implausible to assume that Frege held a version of the evaluative view of judgement.[12]

JUDGING AS ACKNOWLEDGING THE TRUTH

Let us now introduce the ontic understanding of acknowledgement. Frege has studied the treaty '*Was Sind und Was Sollen die*

Zahlen' by the mathematician Richard Dedekind (1831–1916).
Dedekind criticises there the view that only natural numbers exist
with the following words: 'But I see absolutely no merit – nor did
Dirichlet – in actually undertaking this tedious transcription and
in declining to use and acknowledge numbers other than the natural numbers' (Dedekind 1888: 338).[13] None of Dedekind's readers will have struggled to understand his message: Someone who
acknowledges numbers other than the natural ones admits them
into his or her ontology. I will call this meaning of 'acknowledge'
the *ontic sense*.

Frege himself frequently uses 'acknowledge' in the ontic sense.
For instance, he says in 'Foundations of Geometry II': 'One has to
acknowledge [*anerkennen*] ur-elements that are indefinable' (CP:
300, 301. My translation. See also PW: 68; NS: 76). The object-
construction '*S* acknowledges *a*' is also used in SR: 'Someone who
does not acknowledge a reference [*Wer eine Bedeutung nicht
anerkennt*] can neither ascribe nor withhold a predicate of it' (SR:
162, 33. My translation).

I will focus on the ontic meaning because an appeal to the legal
and normative meaning of 'to acknowledge' won't help Frege to
argue for the existence of the True and the False. Let us assume
that judging is acknowledging the truth of a thought in the ontic
sense. How would this assumption further Frege's argumentative
purposes?

1 If judging is acknowledging the truth of a thought, Frege
has a good reason to say that judging implicitly commits us to
truth-values as objects and that we can recognise this by reflecting
on our ability to judge. When we correctly say what we do
when we judge and want to shed light on this activity, we will
say things like 'I have committed myself to *the truth of* p' or
'I acknowledge *the truth of* p'. In one way of decomposing
these statements, we decompose them into a singular term
'the truth of *p*', a psychological verb and a designation of the
judger.

Frege holds that expressions that contain the definite article
'the' as a semantically relevant part introduce objects. Here is a
representative quote:

In the sentence

'The direction of *a* is identical with the direction *b*'

the direction of *a* appears as an object [*erscheint als Gegenstand*] [...].
(Footnote: *This is shown by the definite article. Concept is for me a possible predicate of a singular judgeable content, object a possible subject of such a content.*)

(FA: 76. My emphasis and translation. See also FA: §51, §57, §66 fn and §68 fn)

The definite article represents something as an object and it therefore signals reference to an object. Why this is so will be discussed further in Chapter 8. Let us here work with the intuitive idea.

Taken together the previous points imply that 'the truth of the thought *p*' stands for an object, the True. This object is acknowledged in judgement.

2 If judging is acknowledging the truth of a thought, there is no regress of predicating truth, but truth is still connected to judgement in such a way that judgements are assessable in terms of norms of truth.

We can make this conclusion plausible by developing the first point further. In saying 'I believe in the non-existence of dinosaurs', one does not indirectly posit a new object: the non-existence of dinosaurs. Why should this be different for 'the truth of the thought *p*'? Answer: One can paraphrase 'the non-existence of dinosaurs' in 'I believe in the non-existence of dinosaurs' away: 'NN believes in the non-existence of dinosaurs' is true if, and only if, NN believes that there no dinosaurs. But one cannot paraphrase 'the truth of the thought that *p*' away in 'I acknowledge the truth of the thought *p*'. If we expand '*S* acknowledges the truth of *p*' to '*S* acknowledges that *p* is true' or '*S* acknowledges *p* as true', the regress of predicating truth is inescapable. For what could acknowledging that *p* as true be other than predicating truth of it? The same point applies to any attempt to reduce acknowledging the truth to a propositional attitude. Consider the most plausible proposal and assume that acknowledging *A* is the same as judging *that A* exists or *that* there is something with which *A* is identical.

This assumption raises again the question whether judgement is predication of the second-order concept of *existence* or *being identical with A*. A new regress of predication threatens. If acknowledging *the truth of* p is acknowledging an object, this regress does not get going. Hence, reflections on judgement make plausible that there is an object, the True, which we acknowledge when we judge. Although this might not be actually Frege's argument, it is Fregean in spirit in elaborating his criticism of a predicative understanding of judgement.

At this point it is helpful to compare Frege with his contemporary Franz Brentano. Brentano's main interests are in the philosophy of mind. His main work is *Psychology from an Empirical Point of View* (1874). In this book he proposes a theory of self-knowledge: our immediate self-knowledge consists in *acknowledgements* of mental events. An acknowledgement of a mental event should not be construed as a predication of existence, 'but *consists rather in the simple acknowledgement* [*in der einfachen Anerkennung*] of the mental phenomenon which is present in inner consciousness' (Brentano 1874: I, 201. My translation and emphasis). This understanding of acknowledgment is in line with the idea that acknowledging the truth of a thought is not predicating truth of it. Brentano himself makes this point using the 'acknowledgement' terminology:[14]

> If we say that every acknowledging judgement [*anerkennende Urteil*] is an act of holding-true, and every rejecting judgement an act of holding-false, this does not mean that the former consists in predicating truth of what is held-true and the latter in predicating falsity of what is held false. [...] what the expressions denote is a particular kind of intentional reception of an object, a distinctive kind of mental reference to a content of consciousness [...].
>
> (Brentano 1874: II, 89. Translated in Kremer 2002: 565.)

There are important and deep differences between Brentano and Frege, but in one important point, they come surprisingly close.

3 If judging is acknowledging the truth of a thought, Frege has given the metaphor of advancing from a thought to its truth-value

a clear point. When I pose a propositional question, I grasp a thought. I cannot pose such a question, without acknowledging the thought expressed by the interrogative sentence. I *can* acknowledge the thought that 2 + 2 = 4 without *eo ipso* acknowledging the truth of the thought that 2 + 2 = 4. When I have acknowledged the truth of this thought, I have decided the question posed. I have acknowledged the thought *and* its truth. I have advanced from the thought to an object that is related to it.[15]

If judging is acknowledging the truth of a thought in the ontic sense, Frege has a good reason to assume that there are truth-values. He has discovered a new kind of object through philosophical reflection on judgement. The True and the False are the objects to which every thinker is rationally committed just by making judgements. The False enters the picture together with the True because acknowledging the truth of the thought p is the same act as rejecting its falsity. We can go even further: the True and the False are the *only* non-mental objects every thinker is rationally committed to just by making judgements. A Cartesian sceptic might doubt that there is an external world, that s/he has a body etc., but in so far as s/he makes inferences and judgements, s/he has implicitly committed her/himself to the True and the False. Now the laws of truth, says Frege, 'are the most general laws, which prescribe universally the way in which one ought to think if one is to think at all' (GGA I: xv) The truth-values are the objects we are committed to if we think at all, the laws of truth are the laws that prescribe how one ought to think if one is to think at all. Every thinker who makes judgements at all acknowledges thereby the True and the False. Logic is the science of the laws that ground prescriptions how one must judge if one is to judge at all (see Chapter 1, pp. 20–1). Hence, the True and False are the fundamental objects of logic: '[I]n logic we have only two objects to begin with: the two truth-values' (see PMC: 191; BW: 121. In part my translation).

The laws of truth are the laws of the truth-values, they govern thinking in so far it is trying to acknowledge the truth. Hence, the truth-values can be indirectly characterised by the laws of truth. Let me explain. Here are some prescriptions for judgement:

(Pr1) One is never allowed to: acknowledge the truth of the thought *p* and reject its truth at the same time.

(Pr2) One is allowed to: acknowledge the truth of the thought *p* if one has acknowledged the truth of the thought (*p* and *q*).

In the next step we have to ask which laws must hold if the most general prescriptions for judgement are correct. For example, which law of truth would make prescription (Pr2) correct? Answer: 'A thought proper is either true or false. When we make a judgement about a thought, then we either accept it as true or reject it as false' (PW: 149; NS: 161).

If a thought either determines the True or the False, simultaneously acknowledging and rejecting the truth of a thought is incorrect. Hence, it is a law of logic that nothing is both the True and the False. From the laws of logic we can now gather properties of truth-values. For example, that there are two truth-values, that the True and the False exclude each other etc. Uncovering prescriptions for correct judgement is an indirect method to find out about the True (False).

There is, however, a serious drawback. Acknowledgement is a factive notion like seeing. As one cannot see something that is not there one cannot acknowledge what is not (see N: 377, 148). Hence, one can only acknowledge the truth of a thought if the truth of the thought is. If the truth of a thought does not exist or obtain, one cannot acknowledge it. Now when I answer a question, I am trying to acknowledge the truth of a thought. Compare acknowledging the truth with hitting the target, and trying to acknowledge the truth with aiming to hit a target.[16] As every hitting of the target is a successful attempt to hit the target, every acknowledging the truth is a successful attempt to acknowledge the truth. But not every attempt to acknowledge the truth is an acknowledging of the truth. Hence, we can say that a judgement is successful if, and only if, it is an acknowledgement of the truth and unsuccessful if, and only if, it is a mere attempt to acknowledge the truth. There is no regress of explanation because acknowledging the truth is a success notion and cannot be qualified in the dimension successful/unsuccessful. As a toy duck is not a duck, an unsuccessful acknowledgement of the truth is not an acknowledgement of the truth. But since every acknowledgment of the truth is an attempt to acknowledge the truth, all acknowledgements of the truth are subject to the prescriptions that result from the laws of truth.

If one can only acknowledge the truth of a thought if it is a truth, what account should one give of error or mistaken judgement? Consider a case in which you and I honestly disagree about a question. You assert honestly that *p*, while I honestly assert that not-*p*. Since our assertions are honest, one should assume that we both have made a judgement. But if judging is acknowledging the truth, given that *p* and not-*p* cannot both be true, at least one of us hasn't made a judgement. This is a prima facie strange conclusion.

The problem disappears if we bring in again the notion of a try or an attempt. As Frege himself says we are only bound by the laws of truth if we *want* our thinking to reach the truth.[17] In the example just given I have tried to acknowledge the truth of *p*, and failed to do so without realising it. There is a clear and intuitive sense of 'mistake' in which I made a mistake. I have failed to do what I tried to do. The falsity of the thought makes my trying to acknowledge the truth a failure. Hence, one can give a good sense to the idea of a mistaken judgement if acknowledging the truth is a factive attitude.

But it is at best controversial to say that judgement is factive. Here we must bear in mind that judging is, as he puts it, the *logically* primitive activity. Logic studies inferences, conceived as judgements with a distinctive kind of justification:

> To make a judgement because we are cognisant of other truths as providing a justification for it is known as *inferring*. *There are laws governing this kind of justification, and to set up these laws is the goal of logic.*
>
> (PW: 3; NS: 3. My emphasis.)

In setting up these laws we are concerned with an act, inference, in which a truth is acknowledged, that is, in which one takes a step from a thought to an object systematically correlated with it. In logic, we must take the step from thought to this object (NS: 133; PW: 122). Psychology also studies judgement, but if we want to arrive at a notion of judgement which is useful for the science of the laws of truth, we need to distinguish between the logically and merely psychologically important aspects of judgements and set the latter aside. I think that in his work on judgement Frege sets the non-factivity of our ordinary notion of judgement aside to arrive at a conception of judgement suited for logic.

HOW ARE THOUGHTS AND THE TRUE (FALSE) RELATED?

We have now motivated the assumption that there are truth-values and we have an initial grasp of what they are. But we need to improve our understanding of truth-values. What we know so far leaves open that every thought has a truth-value distinct from the truth-value of all other thoughts. For example, a philosopher who believes in circumstances can accept what Frege said so far and argue that a true thought is a mode of presentation of a particular circumstance that obtains.

How can one make plausible that every true (false) thought is a mode of presentation of the same truth-value? Let us start from Frege's third characterisation of judgement in SR:

> Judging can be regarded as the advance from a thought to its truth-value. This is of course no definition. Judging is something entirely peculiar and incomparable. One might also say that judging is distinguishing parts within the truth-value. This distinguishing is done by going back to the thought.
>
> (SR: 164–5, 35. My translation.)

The circumstances of the *Begriffsschrift* contained arguments and functions as constituents. In which sense does the True (the False) have parts? Frege himself hedges his talk of parts of the truth-values:

> However, I have used here the word 'part' in a special sense. I have in fact transferred the relation between the parts and the whole of the sentence to its reference by calling the reference of a word part of the reference of the sentence if the word itself is part of the sentence. This way of speaking can certainly be attacked, because with respect to

reference, the whole and one part do not suffice to determine the remainder, and because the word 'part' is used already in another sense for bodies.

(SR: 165, 35–6. In part my translation.)

If, in general, the reference of the part of an expression is part of the reference of the whole expression, in any plausible sense of 'part', the reference of 'the capital of Sweden', namely Stockholm, contains Sweden as a part. This is a bizarre consequence. Similarly, on this assumption the reference of 'It is not the case that ( )' is different from the reference of 'It is not the case that it is not the case ( )' although the references of both expressions have the same part.

In his *Begriffsschrift* lectures Frege will therefore backtrack from the assumption that parts can be discerned in truth-values:

The references of the parts of a sentence are not parts of the reference of the sentence.
However: the sense of a part of a sentence is a part of the sense of the sentence.
The reference of a sentence is its truth-value.

(FLL: 87; VB: 20. See also PW: 255; NS: 275)

What about Frege's first point that the thought expressed by a sentence contains the senses of the sentence parts as constituents?

We have already discussed in Chapter 2 (pp. 60ff.) that a sentence is a picture of the thought it expresses. Frege often argues that the sentences S and S^* express different thoughts because they contain non-synonymous sentence parts (see FC: 145, 14). For example, the sentences '17 + 28 = 45' and '45 = 45' contain different non-synonymous sentence parts, *therefore* they express different thoughts. This argument requires the truth of the Picture Thesis.[18] According to the Picture Thesis, the thoughts expressed by the two sentences have different constituents and are therefore different. If the thoughts expressed are complex objects that *contain* the senses of the parts of the sentences in an order, the thoughts cannot be identical. In contrast, if the thoughts were values of functions the fact that two sentences were made up from non-synonymous parts would leave open the possibility that the thought expressed is the same. For different functions can determine the same value for different arguments.[19]

Frege's characterisation of judging as decomposing a truth-value is indefensible, but has an important core that is worth preserving and that can be preserved even if truth-values are atomic. His considered view is that one decomposes thoughts into complete and incomplete parts when one sees them as premises and conclusions in an inference from the general to the particular.[20] Take a simple inference:

(P) $\vdash a = a$.
Therefore: (K) $\vdash$ Hesperus = Hesperus.

In inferring (K) from (P) I appreciate that these thoughts have a common part, namely the sense of the predicate '$\zeta = \zeta$'. (K) is an instance of (P), among other things, because both contain this sense in a particular way. But discerning a common thought part in the premise and conclusion is not sufficient to appreciate that one can infer the one truth from the other.

One makes an inference if one acknowledges *the truth of one thought* because and justified by one's acknowledging of *the truth of another thought*. If we take this and the previous point together, we arrive at the thesis that in order to make an inference from (P) to (K) one must see the thoughts expressed as sharing parts *such that sharing those parts guarantees that (K) is true, if (P) is true*. But one can only see this connection between the structure of the thoughts and their truth, if one implicitly assumes that the thought parts are modes of presentations of those objects and functions, which, when the second is applied to the first, determine the truth of the thoughts under consideration. Instead of 'judging is distinguishing parts in a truth-value' Frege would do better to say:

> In judging that *p* and inferring that *p* from premises one distinguishes complete and incomplete parts in the thought and one acknowledges those objects and concepts that determine the truth-value of the thought if it is so decomposed into parts.

The awareness of and commitment to these objects and functions is manifest in our caring about whether the parts of the sentence that expresses the thought are referential when we care about truth. Consider Frege's example: when we acknowledge the truth of the thought expressed by 'Odysseus was set ashore at Ithaca while sound asleep' and we decompose the thought such that the sense of 'Odysseus' is part of it, we thereby acknowledge the reference of 'Odysseus' and subsume it under the concept ξ *was set ashore at Ithaca while sound asleep*:

> [A]nyone who seriously took the sentence to be true or false would ascribe to the name 'Odysseus' a referent, not merely a sense; for it is the referent of the name which is held to be characterised by the predicate.
>
> (SR: 162, 32–3)

To summarise: if one makes judgements, one decomposes thoughts into modes of presentations of concepts and objects. If the concepts presented in a thought under one decomposition are applied to the objects presented in this decomposition, the result is the truth (falsity) of the thought. A definite description such as 'the truth of the thought that $2 + 2 = 4$' does not stand for a property of the thought, it stands for the object that is functionally determined by the objects and functions presented by the thought named in the definite description.

If the truth-value of a thought is functionally determined by the objects and functions presented by the thought parts, *and not by the thought parts themselves*, one can exchange thought parts that present the same objects without changing the truth-value:

> The result of replacing the sense of '*a*' in the thought that *a* is F with a mode of presentation that determines the same object as the sense of '*a*' is a different thought with the same truth-value as the thought that *a* is F.

This substitution principle together with further premises yields the conclusion that every true thought presents the True, every false thought the False.

Frege's investigation of judgement reveals a network of inter-linked concepts from which he will develop logic: judgemental content, concepts and truth-values are all introduced at the same time. His theory of concepts and truth-values makes explicit a part of the ontology of judgement. If we come to see that judging is not predicating truth, but acknowledging the truth and reject-ing the falsity of a thought, we have discovered truth-values and other 'entities' distinctive of the Fregean approach to logic.

If the parts of a thought present objects and concepts at all, there is a systematic pairing of thoughts and truth-values. For every thought, whose parts determine object and functions, there is one truth-value. Since the truth-value of the thought that p is the same value as the truth-value of the thought that q if, and only if, the thought that p can be generated from the thought that q by substituting modes of presentations that determine the same objects (functions) for each other, this is compatible with the view that there are just two truth-values. Compare: talking about 'the sum of $2 + 2$' and 'the sum of $3 + 1$' may suggest that we are deal-ing with different objects, but we don't.

BACK TO SENTENCE REFERENCE

Frege has introduced the True and the False as the objects we are committed to when we make judgements, independently of what the subject-matter of our judgements is. But he has still not estab-lished that a sentence-nominalisation that contains the sense of an assertoric sentence refers to a truth-value. Even worse. Frege's general notion of reference cannot justify that sentences refer to truth-values. When using a subordinate clause we do not want to speak of truth-values. Our common sense view is that there is a property of truth and that singular terms such as 'that p' refer to objects that have this property or lack it. Our common sense view may be false, but it still determines what we want to talk about with 'that p'. Hence, Frege cannot make a good descriptive case for his view of sentence reference. He can only argue that the truth-value of sentence is the object that determines its semantic role (see Chapter 4, p. 130). I take it that this problem is, in part, responsible for the fact that Frege's theory does not appeal to us.

We are more likely to reject an argument for it than to accept the view. He might persuade us to give up our common sense view of sentence reference and accept his proposal in order to bring our view of sentence reference in line with broader logical concerns. Perhaps we *ought* to refer with sentences to truth-values, but we don't do it.

7

THE SENSE AND REFERENCE
OF A CONCEPT-WORD

In Chapters 5 and 6 we discussed the sense and reference of singular terms in general and those of (unasserted) sentences in particular. The third basic category in the logical grammar of Frege's Begriffsschrift is that of a concept-word. What is a concept-word? What is the sense of a concept-word? Do concept-words have reference? If so, what is the referent of a concept-word? In this chapter I will present Frege's answers to these questions and assess the arguments he provides in support of them.

WHAT IS A CONCEPT-WORD?

Frege's writings contain two conceptions of concept-words. We have already encountered the first one in his early work. In a Begriffsschrift sentence such as '⊢ 3 > 2' one can distinguish in different ways variable ('3', '2') and invariable parts ('... > 2', '3 > ...') (see BS: §9). 'Variable' means in this context 'thought of as replaceable by other expressions'. The variable parts of sentences are the argument-expressions. If one varies in '⊢ 3 > 2' only one numeral, the invariable sentence-remainder is what Frege will later call a concept-word. If one varies more than one numeral, the invariable sentence-remainder is a relation-word. The methodology used in the *Begriffsschrift* suggests that concept-words are sentence-fragments that can be completed by singular terms to sentences. Such concepts-words have gaps that can be filled. In Frege's later work the variable/invariable terminology is replaced by the complete (saturated)/incomplete (unsaturated) terminology.

Frege also uses another notion of concept-word. He articulates it in FA: 'As soon as one uses a word with the indefinite article or in the plural without any article, it is a concept-word' (FA: 64. See also FA: 77 fn 2; CO: 188f., 199f.; PW: 122; NS: 133; GGA I: 19). He introduces 'concept-word' here as a successor for 'common name' (*'Gemeinname'*, *'Gattungsname'* or *'Nomen appellativum'*). 'Common name' misleadingly suggests that 'man' designates each man, 'concept-word' doesn't (see FA: 64; PW: 124; NS: 135). Frege's criterion for concept-words helps to identify such words in natural language. If we apply the criterion, 'a man' and 'men' turn out to be concept-words. Frege's criterion is silent on verb phrases. Is 'smokes' a concept-word in 'John smokes' or not? One can say of John that he is *smoking*. Hence, 'smoke' or 'smoking' seem to be concept-words, although not captured by Frege's criterion.

According to the sentence-remainder conception of concept-words, 'Peter is a man' splits up into the singular term 'Peter' and the incomplete remainder 'ξ is a man'. According to the generic name conception, the sentence is split up into a singular term 'Peter', the copula 'is' and the concept-word or generic name 'a man'. The expression 'ξ is a man' is incomplete, that is, there is a gap in which a singular term can be inserted to make a sentence. In contrast, there is no such gap in 'a man'.

The sentence-remainder and the generic name conception co-exist in Frege's work. For example, in a letter to the philosopher Paul Linke Frege moves with silken ease between saying that a concept-word is a complex combining the copula 'is' with a generic name or *nomen appellativum* and that the generic name itself is the concept-word (PW: 96–7; BW: 154–5). The sentence-remainder conception is rooted in Frege's method of decomposing sentences into constituents (see Chapter 3, pp. 84ff.). The generic name conception is rooted in the ordinary notion of predicating or saying something of something. He suggests that these concept-words can be predicated of something: one can say of something that it is *a man* or of some things that they are *men* (CO: 184, 194). Some Frege-exegetes take the coexistence of these conceptions to be a 'great fault-line in Frege's philosophy of language', others have chosen to favour one or other conception in their attempts to repair Frege's theory of concept-word reference.[1] When working through his views on the sense and reference of concept-words we have to keep the question in mind which conception of concept-word will fit with them best. In the next section I will start by discussing Frege's characterisation of concept-words and concepts as unsaturated.

UNSATURATEDNESS IN FREGE'S MATURE PHASE

After Frege has split up conceptual content in sense and reference, concepts are no longer the common constituents in different conceptual contents. Concepts are now functions that return for every object as argument either the True or the False as value, but never both or neither. If the function $x^2 = 1$ returns for an argument the value the True, Frege says that the argument falls under the concept ξ *is a number whose second power is 1*; if the function returns for the argument the value the False, the argument does not fall under this concept. Appealing to these connections between functions from objects into truth-values and the understanding of concepts as subsuming things, he goes on to say: 'We thus see how closely that which is called a concept in logic is connected with what we call a function. Indeed, we may say at once: a concept is a function whose value is always a truth-value' (FC: 145–6, 15). In a further step, Frege identifies the properties of an object with the concepts under which it falls (see CO: 190, 201).

Frege continues to characterise functions in general and concepts in particular as unsaturated or incomplete. But in which sense can a function be said to be incomplete?[2] In none, I think, is the right answer. For instance, the concept ξ *is a number whose second power is 1* is not completed by an argument to a whole.

Frege indeed held that functions, in general, are completed by objects to a 'complete whole' (FC: 140, 6). But the value of the function $\xi + 1$ is the number 2. Now 2 does not contain in any sense 1 or $\xi + 1$. Hence, functions in general and concepts in particular are neither complete nor incomplete.

Frege seems to agree when he says in 'Comments on Sense and Reference':

> [The name of a function always has empty places.] Accordingly I call the function itself unsaturated, or in need of supplementation, *because its name has first to be completed with the sign of an argument if we are to obtain a complete reference.*
>
> (PW: 119; NS: 129. My emphasis.)

And in 'Introduction to Logic' he contrasts unsaturated senses with concepts thus: 'We can, *metaphorically speaking*, call the concept unsaturated too; or we can say that it is predicative in character' (PW: 193; BW: 210. My emphasis). If concepts are incomplete *only* because their names are incomplete, their incompleteness has no explanatory value. Even worse, if 'a man' or 'positive square root of 2' refer to concepts, concepts are not even in a derivative sense unsaturated. For these expressions have no gaps.

We have seen in Chapter 3 (p. 101) that Frege appeals to the unsaturatedness of concepts to distinguish between a list of things and a circumstance. But if a sentence refers to a truth-value and not a circumstance, it is no longer necessary to explain the unity of circumstances by assuming that concepts are unsaturated. Truth-values don't contain objects and functions. Hence, there is no question of the unity of the truth-value. However, there is still a problem of the unity of a thought: a thought is distinct from a list of senses. According to Frege, the distinction consists in thoughts containing unsaturated senses: 'Not all parts of a thought can be complete; at least one must be 'unsaturated', or predicative; otherwise they would not hold together' (FC: 193, 205).

This is only part of the answer, for incomplete senses and words can also appear on lists. In the case of incomplete concept-words the complete names must be 'inserted' in the gaps of the concept-words. In Frege's mature philosophy senses are the *basic* unsaturated things, physical objects expressing senses are only unsaturated in a derivate sense:

> As a mere thing, of course, the group of letters 'and' is no more unsaturated than any other thing. It may be called unsaturated in respect of its employment as a symbol meant to express a sense, for here it can have the intended sense only when situated between two sentences: its purpose as a symbol requires completion by a preceding and succeeding sentence. *It is really in the realm of sense that unsaturatedness is found, and it is transferred from there to the symbol.*
>
> (CT: 393, 39. My emphasis.)

The inscription 'and' is neither the remainder of something complete nor something that completes such a remainder. It is therefore neither saturated nor unsaturated. The English *word* 'and' (in contrast with the group of letters 'and') is in need of completion by two sentences if it is used to express the concept of sentence conjunction.

This suggests that unsaturated expressions are distinguished from saturated ones in that one can use the former only in connection with further words to express their sense, while one can use the latter to express their sense on their own. Let us consider paradigm complete expressions such as 'the smallest prime' or 'Aristotle'. Can they express their sense independently of a sentence? Geach has answered this question positively. Proper names can be used in simple acts of naming independently of sentences to acknowledge the presence of a thing ('Hey, Joe!') (see Geach 1962: §20). However, can all singular terms be so used? ('Hey, the smallest planet in the solar system!'). More importantly, if proper names have an independent use, Fregean concept-words such as 'poison' or 'men' have a similar independent use (see Vendler 1984: 657). Hence, proper names and concept-words seem both saturated. I will come back to this point later in the chapter (p. 262).

Let us briefly summarise the main points. Frege inculcated upon his readers the need to heed the distinction between concept, or, more generally, function, and object. His research is guided by the maxim: 'Never to lose sight of the distinction between concept and object' (FA: xxii). Concepts are supposed to be unsaturated or incomplete, objects saturated or complete. However, the characterisation of concepts as incomplete is no longer warranted by Frege's mature theory that identifies concepts with functions from objects to truth-values, relations with functions from sequences of objects to truth-values. If concepts are not unsaturated or only saturated in a derivative sense, should one not give up the distinction between concept and object and argue that everything is an object? Frege does not go this way. There is, according to him, a fundamental distinction between concepts and objects that is independent of the unsaturated/saturated distinction: '[T]he relation of equality, by which I understand complete coincidence, identity, can only be thought of as holding between objects, not concepts' (PW: 120; NS: 130–1. See also PW: 182; NS: 198).

In the following section it will become clear that the difference between concepts and objects is the distinction between 'things' that stand in the relation of identity and those that do not. In order to develop this point in more detail, we need to have first more of Frege's theory of sense and reference in view. The next section starts us off.

DO CONCEPT-WORDS *REFER*?

In Frege's mature work, the notion of reference connects concepts and concept-words: '(CR) A concept-word refers to a concept if the word is used as it is appropriate for logic' (PW: 118; BW: 128. My translation). From a contemporary perspective (CR) is controversial. Some recent theories of reference and truth give up the idea that concept-words refer at all. For example, one can say under which conditions a concept-word is true of (correctly predicated of) an object without holding that the concept-word itself has a reference:

$(\forall x)$ (The English expression 'x is a horse' is true of x if, and only if, x is a horse).

This semantic axiom for 'x is a horse' tells us only when the predicate is true of an object, no reference is assigned to it. Why do we need to say anything more about 'x is a horse' in a theory of reference and truth?[3]

The following passage from his 'Introduction to Logic' (1906) can be read as Frege's response to the challenge:

> It is inconceivable that it is only for the proper names that there can be a question of reference and not for the other parts of the sentence which connect them. If we say 'Jupiter is larger than Mars', what are we talking about? About the heavenly bodies themselves, the references of the proper names 'Jupiter' and 'Mars'. We are saying that they stand in a certain relation to one another, and this we do by means of the words 'is larger than'. This relation holds between the references of the proper names, and so must belong itself to the realm of reference. It follows that we have to acknowledge that the sentence-part 'is larger than Mars' is referential ['*bedeutungsvoll*'] and not merely significant ['*sinnvoll*']. If we split up a sentence into a proper name and a remainder, then the remainder has for its sense an unsaturated part of a thought. But we call its reference a concept. In doing so we are of course making a mistake, a mistake language forces upon us. By introducing the word 'concept', we countenance the possibility of sentences of the form 'A is a concept', where A is a proper name. We have here stamped as an object what – as being completely different in kind – is the precise opposite of an object. For the same reason the definite article at the beginning of 'the reference of the remaining part of the sentence' is a mistake too.
>
> (PW: 193; NS: 209. In part my translation.)

Frege starts his argument by appealing to the general notion of reference as that what we are talking about. When we say that 'Jupiter is larger than Mars' we are talking about Jupiter, Mars and, Frege wants to continue, a relation holding between them. Before fleshing out this argument, it is worth pausing a moment to look at the mistake he discusses at the end of quote. We make a mistake when we conclude from our argument that *the reference of 'is larger than' is a relation* and *the reference of 'is larger than Mars' is a concept*, since the expressions 'the reference of "is larger than" ("is larger than Mars")' seems to refer to a relation (concept). Concepts (relations) cannot be referred to by singular terms. Frege tries to avoid mentioning the reference of 'is larger than Mars'; he merely says that the concept-word is referential (see also PMC: 136–7; BW: 218–19). The problem arises for every argument for the conclusion that concept-words refer. I will discuss the view on which this problem is based and possible solutions later in the chapter (p. 254).

Can one develop Frege's outline of an argument to a convincing argument for the conclusion that concepts refer? Without further elaboration, his description of the referential import of an assertoric utterance of 'Jupiter is larger than Mars' is hardly convincing. Bell (1979: 49), for example, argues that Frege did not make a good case for concept- and relation-word reference. Concept- and relation-words must of course be ascribed a semantic role. Their semantic role can be specified by taking such words to stand for functions from objects (sequences of objects) to truth-values (see Dummett 1981a: 219, 224) But concept-words don't refer in the intuitive sense that we don't use them to talk about something.

Now Frege uses the natural language phrase 'to call someone something' to motivate that one indeed refers with a concept-word to something:

> If we did designate Hans by 'man' and likewise Kunz, we should indeed be committing this mistake [of assigning the same symbol to different things]. Fortunately this is not what we do. *In calling Hans a man, we are saying that Hans falls under the concept man* [...].
>
> (CP: 205, 326. My emphasis.)

You ask me 'What is Hans?' When I answer 'A man', I don't want to 'pick out' Hans with my utterance, I wanted to speak of or mention something that subsumes of characterises Hans. Hence, 'a man' is used to refer to something. If you ask me 'What is John to Peter?' and I answer 'A brother', I have mentioned something that characterises John and Peter *in that order*. The general notion of reference as *what one wants to speak about with some words in their normal use* seems to apply her without great strain (see Chapter 4, p. 129).

The view that concept-words refer can be supported by considering existential generalisations.[4] If I refer with '*a*' in a sentence '... a ...', then one can infer from what this sentence says that there is something such that '... it ...'. Singular terms are a special case. If I refer with 'Hans' to something in 'Hans is a man', I can infer from what I said with my utterance that there is something that is a man. Consider now the following similar inferences:

> Hans is a man. Therefore, there is something which Hans is, namely a man.
> Hans is a man and Peter is a man. Therefore, there is something that Hans and Peter both are, namely men.

If we can trust these appearances, 'a man' ('men') refers to something over which we can quantify. The considerations proposed so far support the generic name conception of concept-words. We call Hans 'a man' not '... is a man' and we don't quantify into the position of '... is a man'.[5] For example, in the examples above 'something' cannot be replaced by '... is a man' *salva grammaticale*. This is as it should be. If concepts are not unsaturated, why should they not be referred to by concept-words that are themselves not unsaturated? Given that the sentence remainder view of concept-words creates more problems than it solves, I am happy to recommend to Frege to revise it.

In *Begriffsschrift*, Frege has already presented ideas about concept-words that underpin his view that they refer (see Chapter 3, p. 907) Consider again my answering the question 'What is Hans?' by saying:

> Hans is [a man]$_F$.

The question puts the concept-word 'a man' in focus. Basically, every expression occurring in a sentence can be in focus if it is uttered as a response to a particular question. The part of a sentence that is in focus is considered to be variable. If I say 'Hans is [a man]$_F$', there is set of relevant alternatives: 'Hans is a woman', 'Hans is an alien' etc. in which the position of 'a man' is filled by other expressions. The variable part or parts of a sentence introduce a thing; the invariable sentence remainder characterises it. In this way Frege disentangles the notion of *what a sentence is about* from *being the referent of the grammatical subject of the sentence*. In our example 'a man' is the variable sentence-part; it introduces something the speaker wants to speak of and say something about. Consider moving 'a man' into the position of a grammatical subject:

> A man, that is what Hans is.

Here it is even clearer that 'a man' introduces the topic of the utterance.

The same idea can be applied to Frege's example in 'Introduction to Logic'. Consider the question/answer pair:

> What is Jupiter with respect to Mars?
> Jupiter is [larger than]$_F$ Mars.

The relation-expression is in focus, it is the variable part that introduces something that is characterised by the invariable sentence part, in this case 'Jupiter is ... Mars'. When asking the above question, one puts the relation-word in focus. This is sufficient for it to refer to something. For example, one might continue by saying: 'This relation holds also between the Earth and the Moon.' 'This relation' picks up its reference from the grammatical antecedent 'larger than' in my utterance. How can it pick up a reference if 'larger than' has none? As we have already seen Frege would endorse that 'larger than' refers, but he would reject the idea that 'this relation' refers to the same thing as 'larger than'.

Now Frege wants to say that in 'Jupiter is larger than Mars', 'Jupiter', 'Mars' and 'larger than' all refer. So far, we have found reasons to say that 'larger than' refers, but what about 'Jupiter' and 'Mars'? If we see the sentence as predicating something of Jupiter and Mars, we must take it that there is a question in the background concerning these objects. We want to know something about them and hence we mention them in our background question. If we add the referential import of the question to the utterance, all three objects are referred to.

To sum up: something can be talked about in a sentence and referred to by a part of this sentence, although the relevant sentence part is not a singular term in subject position. Since concept-words can be in focus, we can use Frege's general notion of reference to justify the ascription of reference to concept-words. He holds that it is impossible to speak about an *object* without using an expression to refer to it (see FA: 60). But one can *only* refer to a *concept* if one does not use a singular term. I can succeed in predicating a property of something without using a singular term referring to it. Frege himself makes this point with respect to sentences that contain only concept-words:

> In the sentence 'There is at least one square root of 4' it is impossible to replace the words 'square root of 4' by 'the concept *square root of 4*'; i.e. what is suitably predicated of the concept does not suit the object. *Although our sentence does not present the concept as subject, it predicates something of it; it can be regarded as expressing that a concept falls under a higher one.*
>
> (CO: 188–9, 199–200. In part my translation; my emphasis.)[6]

'There is at least one square root of 4' predicates something of a concept and hence there must be a part of the sentence that *refers* to a concept, although a concept is not named by a singular term. Which part refers to a concept? Consider the question:

> What is there at least one of?

Among the true answers to this question is:

> There is at least one [square root of 4]$_F$.

In this statement the concept-word 'square root of 4' is in focus. In *Begriffsschrift* terminology one can say that 'square root of 4' is the variable part in the statement, further variations of this part are:

> There is at least one [square root of 9].
> There is at least one [city by a lake].
> And so on.

Frege can now argue that in 'There is at least one [square root of 4]$_F$' the concept-word 'square root of 4' refers to something. Intuitively speaking, when uttering the sentence in response to a particular question one wants to say something about a 'thing'; one picks it out and says about it that there is at least one of it. In using 'square root of 4' in the normal way but with a special intonation, the speaker intends to make a claim about something.

So far we have an argued (1) that concept- and relation-words refer and (2) that the generic names view of concept- and relation-words is correct. We still need a reason to hold that concept-words refer to *concepts*.

WHY CONCEPT-WORDS REFER TO *CONCEPTS*

In his 'Comments on Sense and Reference' Frege suggests an argument for the conclusion that concept-words refer to concepts. He says:

> A concept word must have a sense too and if it is to have a use in science, a reference; but *this consists neither of one object nor of a plurality of objects: it is a concept.* [...] A concept-word can be logically incontestable although there is no object to which it refers through its sense and reference (the concept).
>
> (PW: 124; NS: 135. My emphasis and translation. See also PMC: 63; BW: 96; and CP: 226, 228)

Frege points us to an important distinction between concept-words and proper names. An empty proper name is logically contestable: a sentence containing an empty proper name that has not shifted its reference is neither true nor false. Given his view of inference, nothing can be inferred from it. In SR he is particularly concerned about proper names that appear to refer to something, but are in effect empty. He wants to eliminate this source of logical mistakes in his Begriffsschrift (see SR: 169, 41).

In contrast, a concept-word can be logically incontestable even if there is no object of which it is true. For example, the sentence 'Every supercharged particle will spin in a vacuum' can express a true law, although there are no supercharged particles and no vacuum. For Frege only vague and incompletely defined concept-words are logically contestable (see Chapter 5, p. 152).

The logical incontestability of concept-words that are not true of anything gives Frege a reason to take these words to refer to concepts. Consider his example. The concept-word '(a) round square' is not true of any object. Yet, the concept-word refers to something: '"Round Square" [...] is not an empty name, but the name of an empty concept, and thus one not devoid of reference in sentences like "There is no round square" or "The Moon is not a round square"' (CP: 227, 454).

Let us expand on this idea. First, '(a) round square' refers to an object. Take Frege's example again and consider the inference:

> The Moon is not a round square.
> Hence, there is something the Moon is not, namely a round square.

This seems like a good existential generalisation into the position of 'round square'. Hence, we should take 'a round square' to refer to something. But it may sound as if we commit ourselves to a Meinongian non-existent object. But we don't. The 'is' is the 'is' of predication. So we say that there is a thing that cannot be truly predicated of the Moon.

Second, what do we know about the reference of 'a round square'? So far we know that the reference of 'a round square' cannot be truly predicated of any object. One way to capture this fact is to use Frege's notion of function from objects to truth-values. If the reference of 'a round square' cannot be truly predicated of any object its reference is a function that maps every object to the value the False. Concept-words, which are not true of any object, can occur in true statements because they refer to concepts that map every object to the False.

Now we face a new question. How can a concept-word be true of many things and at the same time refer to a concept? Take 'The Earth is a planet'. If I answer the question 'What is the Earth?' I apply 'a planet' to the Earth. In order to do so I refer to the concept *a planet*. Since the concept *a planet* maps the Earth to the True, I have said something true of the Earth. The concept-word 'a planet' is true of many things because the concept referred to maps many objects to the True. I take this to be idea behind passages like the following one: 'The word "planet" does not relate *immediately* to the Earth, but to a concept, under which, among others, the Earth falls. Hence, the relation to the Earth is only mediated by the concept [...]' (CP: 227, 454. My translation and emphasis).

To sum up: concepts emerge as plausible referents for concept-words. However, Frege's own view of concept-word reference is unstable. It gives us a good reason to doubt that a concept-word refers to a concept. I will expound the problem in the next section.

WHY CONCEPT-WORDS MAY BE TAKEN TO REFER TO EXTENSIONS

Frege himself brings out the problem I will be concerned with. In explaining why a concept-word refers to a concept, he appeals to their extensions:

> A concept-word refers to a concept if the word is used as is appropriate for logic. In order to explain this I mention a fact that seems to speak in favour of the extensionalist logicians and against the intensionalist logicians, namely that concept-words that have the same extension can replace each other in every sentence without change of truth-value, that concept-words therefore only behave differently with respect to inference and logical laws insofar as their extensions differ. The logically primitive relation is the relation of an object falling under a concept: all relations between concepts can be reduced to it. In falling under a concept, an object falls under all concepts that have the same extension. This implies what has just been said. As proper names of the same object can replace each other without changing the truth, the same holds of concept-words if the extension is the same. Of course such replacements will change the thought, but this is the sense, not the reference. The reference, namely the truth-value, remains unchanged. *One could easily come to think that the extension is the reference of the concept-word, but then one failed to recognise that extensions are objects and not concepts. But nonetheless this contains a grain of truth.*
>
> (PW: 118–19; NS: 128–9. My translation and emphasis.)

A representative extensionalist logician (*Umfangslogiker*) is Frege's contemporary Ernst Schröder (1841–1902). In his *Algebra der Logik* Schröder proposed that a common name refers to a class.[7] For instance, 'a horse' refers to the class whose members are all and only horses and 'Red Rum is a horse' is true if, and only if, Red Rum is an element of this class.

Now Frege suggests that there are good reasons to hold that concept-words refer to extensions, not to concepts, only back-tracking in the final sentences of the last quote. If the extension of a concept is a class, Frege himself seems to advocate a theory of concept-word reference similar to the one proposed by Schröder. Let us first see what the good reasons are to say that a concept-word refers to an extension.

I will start by introducing the notion of an extension. Every concept has an extension. Unlike aggregates or collections, extensions are *not* composed of the objects that fall under the concept:

> [T]he extension of a concept is not a collection in [Husserl's] sense. A concept under which only one object falls has a determinate extension, as does a concept under which no object falls, or a concept under which infinitely many objects fall, but in these cases there is no collection at all according to Mr. Husserl.
>
> (CP: 202, 322)

Frege introduces his readers to the notion of an extension by means of examples drawn from analytical geometry. If we take the arguments of the functions $y = x^2 - 4x$ and $y = x (x - 4)$ to be the numerical value of the abcissa and the value to be the corresponding numerical value of the ordinate, the functions yield the same graph (FC: 142, 9). Functions that have the same graph have the same course-of-values. In a next step one might want to identify the course-of-values with the set of ordered pairs of numbers that determine the graph. The course-of-values of a function that is a concept is an extension. If we identify an extension with a set of ordered pairs, the first element of the ordered pair is an object, the second element a truth-value. For illustration take the concept-word 'an inhabitant of Germany in 1884'. The extension or course-of-values of the function *an inhabitant of Germany in*

1884 has the same identity-conditions as the set of ordered pairs that contains amongst others the following pairs:

    <Husserl, the True>
    <Frege, the True>
    <Cantor, the True>
    <Russell, the False>
    And so on.

The extension of a concept under which nothing false can be modelled as the set of all ordered pairs whose first element is an object and whose second element is the False.

Are extensions sets of ordered pairs? Difficult to say, but my educated guess is, no, they aren't. A set of ordered pairs is a self-subsisting object; it is not abstracted from other objects. We might, so to say, start with the objects and generate the set-theoretic object from them according to a particular method. But extensions are abstracted from concepts, they are, as Frege says, *derived*: 'The class, namely, is something derived [*etwas Abgeleitetes*], whereas in the concept – as I understand the word – we have something primitive' (PMC: 191 fn 69; BW: 121. See also PMC: 192 fn 71; BW: 122). What is meant by 'derived'? If two concepts return for the same objects as arguments the same values, Frege will say that the concepts are mutually subordinated. Mutual subordination is an equivalence relation that shares important properties with the identity relation:

Identity:

$(\forall x)\,(x = x)$
$(\forall x, y)\,(x = y \rightarrow y = x)$

$(\forall x, y)\,(x = y \,\&\, y = z \rightarrow x = z)$

Mutual subordination:

$(\forall x)\,(\forall F)\,(Fx \leftrightarrow Fx)$
$(\forall x)\,(\forall F, G)\,(Fx \leftrightarrow Gx \rightarrow Gx \leftrightarrow Fx)$
$(\forall x)\,(\forall F, G, H)\,(Fx \leftrightarrow Gx \,\&\, Gx \leftrightarrow Hx \rightarrow Fx \leftrightarrow Hx)$

The analogies between identity and mutual subordination 'almost inescapably force us', says Frege, to transform sentences in which we assert that two concepts are mutually subordinated into identity statements between a new kind of object: extensions of concepts in particular, courses-of-values of functions in general (PW: 182; NS: 197):

> (Axiom V) (∀x) (Fx ↔ Gx, if, and only if, the course-of-values of ξ is F = the course- of-values of ξ is G.)

This axiom takes us from a relation between functions to new objects. Thereby, we derive the later from the former. Frege does not reduce extensions to something more fundamental. What we know about courses-of-values in general and extensions in particular is what can be derived from Axiom V about them. Here is one thing we come to know by attending to Axiom V: if an object falls under a concept *F*, it falls under all concepts that have the same extension as this concept. Take, for instance, the concept-words 'a renate' and 'a cordate'. These concept-words have the same extension: every renate is a cordate and every cordate is a renate. If an object that falls under a concept *F*, falls under all concepts co-extensional with *F*, concept-words that refer to co-extensional concepts can be substituted for each other *salva veritate* in sentences in which they have their normal sense and reference. For example, the first and second sentences of the following pairs have the same truth-value:

> John is a renate./John is a cordate.
> All normal human beings are cordates./All normal human beings are renates.

All concept-words under which nothing falls have the same extension, hence, they can be exchanged *salva veritate* when they have their normal reference:

> John is not a unicorn./John is not a green goblin.
> There are no unicorns./There are no green goblins.

The sentence-pairs illustrate that two concept-words can be intersubstitutable *salva veritate*, and yet exchanging them generates sentences that differ in cognitive value. For example, someone who knows that there are no green goblins can extend his or her knowledge when s/he comes to know that there are no unicorns.

On the basis of the previous points one can give now the following argument for the conclusion that concept-words refer to extensions:

> (P1) If two expressions have the same reference, they can be substituted *salva veritate* in all sentences in which their reference has not shifted.
>
> (P2) If two concept-words have the same extension, they can be substituted *salva veritate* in all sentences in which their reference has not shifted.
>
> (C1) Hence, for concept-words sameness of extension is nothing but sameness of reference.
>
> (C2) Hence, the reference of a concept-word is nothing but the extension of a concept.

Whatever extensions are, they seem to have the right properties to be the references of concept-words.

This argument for the conclusion that concept-words refer to concepts is further strengthened if one adds the Fregean thesis that identity is a relation that holds *only* between objects (see p. 232). If identity does not hold between concepts, and concept-words refer to concepts, concept-words cannot be co-referential. For co-reference is having the *same* concept as reference. If concept-words cannot refer to the same concept, exchangeability of co-referential expressions *salva veritate* does not apply to concept-words. But how can one then apply the sense/reference distinction to concept-words? For the distinction seems only to have a point if two expressions can have the same reference, yet differ in sense. According to Frege, sameness of extensions comes to the rescue here:

> [C]oincidence in extension is a necessary and sufficient criterion for the occurrence between concepts of the relation that *corresponds to* identity between objects. [Footnote: For identity in the proper sense of the word does not occur between concepts. Cf. my essay on concept and object in *Vierteljahreszeitschrift für wissenschaftliche Philosophie*.]
>
> (CP: 200, 320. My emphasis.)

Since coincidence of extension is a relation between concepts that is analogous to identity between objects, there is a distinction analogous to the sense/reference distinction for concept-words.

Frege is then frequently understood as holding that concept-words refer to extensions. The following quote from Carnap is a representative example:

> I think that Church [in 'Review of Carnap, Introduction to Semantics', *Philosophical Review*, 301] is in accord with Frege's intentions when he regards a class as the (ordinary) nominatum of a predicator (of degree one) [...] and a property as its ordinary sense.
>
> (Carnap 1956: 125)

A minor quibble: Church talked about '*Begriffsumfangsnamen*' which are not concept-words, but, well, proper names of extensions. Many philosophers have followed Carnap and defended the view that concept-words refer to extensions (classes).[8] The sense of the concept-word is conceived as a condition an object has to fulfil for the concept-word to truly apply to it, i.e. for an object to be a member of the extension referred to.

But although there is a grain of truth in it, Frege takes the view that concept-words refer to extensions to be false! In the next section I will discuss why he rejects this view.

WHY CONCEPT-WORDS CANNOT REFER TO EXTENSIONS IN PARTICULAR AND OBJECTS IN GENERAL

Frege endorses two complementary theses:

> Proper names can *only* refer to objects, not to concepts; concept-words can *only* refer to concepts, not to objects (see, for instance, CO: 184, 195).

Both theses follow from a general principle that Frege states in a letter to Russell:

> This difference between the signs [i.e. between complete and incomplete signs] must correspond to a difference in the realm of reference;

> *although it is not possible to speak of it without turning what is in need of*
> *completion into something complete and thus falsifying the real situation*
> [...] The decomposition of the sentence corresponds to a decomposi-
> tion of the thought, and this in turn corresponds to something in the
> realm of reference, and I should like to call this a primitive logical fact.
>
> (PMC: 142; BW: 224. In part my translation. My emphasis.)

Unsaturated signs have unsaturated senses and references, saturated signs have saturated senses and references.

I will discuss the first thesis in the following sections under the
label 'Frege's concept-paradox'. In the quote above Frege already
states this paradox; I will come back to it in the next section. In
this section I will only be concerned with the second thesis that
concept-words can only refer to concepts and not to objects.

If concept-words can only refer to concepts, Frege has a general
reason to reject all views that make a concept-word refer to an
object such as an extension (set). For example, the concept-word
'an inhabitant of Germany in 1884' cannot refer to the extension
of the concept *an inhabitant of Germany in 1884*. The extension
is an object. It can be referred to by singular terms and it has identity-conditions: the extension of concept F is the same as the
extension of concept G if, and only if, the concepts are mutually
subordinated.

Frege takes it to be a primitive logical fact that the reference of
an unsaturated sign is itself unsaturated. One will need further
reasons to become convinced of this logical fact. In CO he seems
to appeal to the substitutivity of co-referential expressions to
argue that concept-words cannot refer to extensions (see
CO: 189, 201). Assume that 'an inhabitant of Germany in 1884'
refers to the set whose members are all and only the persons
that inhabit Germany in 1884. This set can be referred to, as I
have just done, by the designator 'the set whose members are all
and only the persons that inhabit Germany in 1884'. But 'an
inhabitant of Germany in 1884' and 'the set whose members
are all and only the persons that inhabit Germany in 1884' cannot
be exchanged *salva veritate* in sentences in which these designators have their normal reference. Since this result can be gener-
alised, concept-words can't refer to extensions, only to the

concepts that determine the extension. However, we will see in the next sections that there is reason to doubt that co-referential expressions can be exchanged in all sentences in which they have their normal reference *salva veritate*. Hence, we cannot appeal to this principle about reference to disqualify the extension as the referent of a concept-word.

The reason why a concept-word cannot refer to an object such as an extension is that there is a connection between *singular* term reference, that is, reference to *one object*, and *identity*. We have already discussed in Chapter 4 (p. 112) a necessary condition for an expression to purport to refer to *one determinate* object. In Frege's sense/reference terminology we can express this condition as follows:

> (Singularity) The expression 'a' can only refer to an *object* (that is, be a *singular* term) x if knowledge of the sense of 'a' consists in part in a criterion of re-identifying x.

Given Frege's explanation of what a proper name is nothing more than satisfaction of (Singularity) is required for an object to be a proper name purporting to refer to an object (see Chapter 4, p. 112).

The previous sections have given us reasons to believe that concept-words refer, but don't satisfy (Singularity). For Frege has *not* given us a criterion for deciding whether a concept is the same as 'another'. For example, in FA (§69, 1) he is clear about that *different* concepts can have the *same* extension and he is happy to leave the matter there. Identity-conditions for concepts are never provided. Moreover, it seems plausible that one can understand a concept-word completely *without knowing any identity-conditions for objects that may be its referent*. For example, one does not need to know anything about sets and their general identity-criteria, nor about any other *object* that may be assigned to 'smokes' as its reference in order to use 'smokes' predicatively (see Husserl 1891: 13). Concept-words such as 'a man' or 'smokes' are true of many things, for example, each man. Knowing the sense of the concept-word requires knowing when it is true of something.

In short, it requires knowledge of the *criteria of application* of the concept-word. The sense of a concept-word is specified by a criterion of application. For example, the sense of '(a) renate' is given by saying that something is a renate if, and only if, it has kidneys. The sense of '(a) cordate' is given saying that something is a cordate if, and only if, it has a heart. The sentence 'Something is a renate if, and only if, it is a cordate' differs in cognitive value from the sentence 'Something is a renate if, and only if, it is a renate' because '(a) renate' and '(a) cordate' differ in sense, but have the same extension. The criteria of application include in many cases knowledge of criteria of distinctness for the things of which the concept-word is true. For instance, I only master '(a) renate' if I know how to apply it and to distinguish one application from another. But according to Frege, the *objects* of which the concept-word is true (to which it applies) are not its reference. The concept-word '(a) renate' refers to one thing, but this 'thing' is also not a collection of all objects of which the concept-word is true. The conclusion is that concept-words are neither plural terms that refer to many *objects*, nor singular terms that refer to *one object*. Concept-words refer, but not to one object or some objects; they refer to concepts.

CONCEPT-WORDS, CRITERIA OF APPLICATION AND CONSTITUTIVE MARKS

But how can a concept-word refer to something if its sense provides *only* criteria of application to objects it is true of and *no* criteria of identity for what it is supposed to refer to? Here is how Dummett puts this point:

> [T]he sense of a predicate consisted in the way in which its application to objects is determined, and there is nothing in the way of an identification of a concept as the referent of the predicate to correspond to the identification of an object as the referent of the name. It seems, indeed, virtually impossible to make any sense of the conception of identifying a concept as the referent of a predicate, because we can make no suggestion for what it would be 'given' a concept.
>
> (Dummett 1981a: 241)

Dummett concludes that predicates, i.e. Frege's concept-words, can only be said to refer by 'force majeure'. In short: they don't refer. The conclusion seems warranted. Given that that the sense of a concept-words consists in a criterion of application we seem only be entitled to say that it is true of some things. Moreover, how can one say that a concept-word refers to one concept if its use does not draw on any knowledge of features that distinguish the concept from others?

Frege's distinction between properties and characteristic marks ('*Merkmale*') provides a partial answer to these questions (see FA: §51 and CO: 191, 202). Consider an example he gives in a letter to the mathematician Heinrich Liebman:

> Concepts are usually composed out of component concepts, the characteristic marks. *Black silk cloth* has the characteristic marks *black*, *silk* and *cloth*. An object that falls under this concept has the characteristic marks as its properties. What is a *characteristic mark* with respect to a concept is a *property* of an object falling under a concept.
> (PMC: 92–3; BW: 150. I have changed the translation.)

The concept *black silk cloth* is composed out of other concepts: 'I compare the individual characteristic marks of a concept with the stones that constitute a house [...]' (PMC: 93; BW: 151). Frege identified the properties of an object with the concepts under which it falls. The properties under which an object must fall to be a black silk cloth are the marks of the concept *black silk cloth*. Characteristic marks that compose a concept are not its properties. (The concept *black silk cloth* is not black etc.)

Frege's notion of constitutive marks is inspired by the traditional doctrine of concepts according to which a concept-word has a comprehension and an extension. A definition of the concept-word analyses the comprehension by displaying its constitutive marks. Constitutive marks are, according to the traditional understanding, component senses, not, as Frege, thinks, parts of concepts, that is, references. The view that some concepts are composed of others raises a further question. A Fregean concept is a function from objects into truth-values. How can such a function be composed out of other functions as 'a house is made of stones'? I take it that the function $x^2 + 2 - x$ contains two functions, similarly as the concept *black silk cloth* contains several concepts.

Now back to our initial question. How can one say that a concept-word refers to a concept if knowledge of its sense is exhausted by a criterion of application? Answer: in many cases the criterion of application of a concept-word tells us which properties an object must have to fall under the concept referred to by the concept-word. *These properties, in turn, are the characteristic marks of this concept.* Let us assume for the sake of the argument that the criterion of application of 'a man' is specified by saying that something is a man if, and only if, it is a rational biped. *Rational* and *biped* are the properties one must have to fall under the concept *man* and they are the characteristic marks of the concept *man*. Hence, if one knows the criterion of application for a concept-word one knows the constitutive marks of a concept, that is, one knows the composition of this concept out of other concepts. This puts one in an optimal position to refer to the concept. For what could one know about a concept that was more distinctive than its composition out of other concepts? In order to refer to concepts one does not need to know identity-criteria because we know their constitutive marks. Strawson will later generalise this idea: 'The sense of the general term gives the individual essence of the general thing. So there is no need for *general* criteria of identity for things of the kind to which the general thing belongs' (Strawson 1976: 195).

However, Frege's answer is incomplete: what about simple concepts that do not contain other concepts as marks? He says that most concepts have characteristic marks and he seems to be happy to leave it at that (PMC: 92; BW: 150). If *most* concepts have characteristic marks, some concepts are simple. What can we say about them and the concept-words that refer to them?

Strawson has argued that the criterion of application in these cases will consist in the ability to recognise and re-identify instances of the concept. Possessing these abilities enables one to think about the concept whose instances one can recognise and identify (see Strawson 1976: 194).

The Fregean answer to the questions raised above is therefore that one can refer to a concept because knowing the sense of a concept-word is knowing a criterion of application. This criterion determines which properties a thing must have for the concept-word to be true of it *and* it specifies thereby the characteristic marks of the concept the concept-word refers to.

If Frege's answer can be completed in the way Strawson proposed, it will also address an objection Russell levelled against Frege:

> [Frege's] theory of indication is more sweeping and general than mine, as appears from the fact that *every* proper name is supposed to have the two sides [sense and reference]. It seems to me that only such proper names as are derived from concepts by means of *the* can be said to have meaning, and that such words as *John* merely indicate without meaning. If one allows, as I do, *that concepts can be objects and have proper names*, it seems fairly evident that their proper names, as a rule, will indicate them without having any distinct meaning; but the opposite view, though it leads to an endless regress, does not appear to be logically impossible.
>
> (Russell 1903: 502. My emphasis.)

The regress Russell is concerned with gets going if one assumes that the sense of a proper name such as 'Aristotle' must be complex like the sense of 'the inventor of formal logic'. The expression of the complex sense, in turn, contains concept-words such as 'inventor' and 'logic'. If these concept-words have again a sense, the same game gets going again.

Russell assumes that the sense of a proper name must be complex, i.e. it must be identical to the sense of a definite description. This seems prima facie plausible. A sense is a mode of presentation or determination. How can one determine an object if not in terms of properties that distinguish it from something else? If so, the mode of determination seems to be complex because it appeals to the distinguishing properties.

In Frege's theory the regress stops with concept-words. If I know the criterion of application for a concept-word, and the concept is complex I know in which way the concept is composed from concepts. This enables me to refer to the concept; I don't need to know further distinguishing properties that apply to the concept. A similar story needs to be told along Strawsonian lines for simple concepts.

Let us summarise what we have learned so far. There are conceptual connections between *being a singular term*, *being an object* and *standing in the relation of identity*. An expression can only be a singular term purporting to refer to an object if knowledge of its sense consists, in part, in knowledge of identity-conditions for the reference of the term. Therefore something can only be the reference of a singular term if it stands in the relation of identity. These two points together can now be used to illuminate what an object (in contrast to a concept) is. An object is something that can be referred to by singular terms and which therefore must stand in the relation of identity to something (namely, itself). Concept-words purport to refer to concepts, but one does not need to know conditions of identity for the things they refer to in order to refer with them. Hence, concept-words don't refer to objects.

This argument is not watertight. If we had a conception what objects and concepts are that is independent of the ways of referring to them via singular terms and concept-words, we could argue that a difference in the conditions for reference to something need not constitute a difference in what is referred to. However, Frege argues that numbers are (self-subsisting) objects by attending to the ways we refer to them (see FA: §57 and §62). We develop our understanding of the different kinds of things by systematising how we refer to them. If we apply this strategy to concept-words, concepts will turn out to be so different from objects that they cannot be referred to by singular terms.

Now Frege says that concepts cannot stand in the relation of identity. So far we have only reasons to hold that one can refer with a concept-word to a concept without knowing a criterion of identity. The stronger conclusion that concepts don't stand in the relation of identity is not yet warranted. One explanation for the observation that one can refer to concepts without knowing a criterion of identity and that such a criterion has not been found yet is that the things referred don't stand in relation of identity.

Frege has made so far a good case for the claims that (3) concept-words refer to concepts, (4) that concept-word reference is distinct from singular term reference and (5) that concepts are not objects.

So far, so good, but he is still in an uncomfortable position: Extensions are not the references of concept-words, but sameness of extension still explains the intersubstitutivity *salva veritate* of concept-words in terms of identity of extensions (see p. 244 earlier in the chapter). Hence, one might argue that we have here a case in which reference in the sense of 'what one wants to speak about' and semantic role come apart. Concept-words refer to concepts, but their semantic role is specified by assigning extensions to them. Frege is aware of this tension. In his review of Husserl's *Philosophy of Arithmetic* Frege toys with the idea that a concept-word refers directly to a concept and indirectly to the extension of the concept (CP: 201, 322). However, without further clarification of the direct/indirect distinction this is not an answer.

Frege's late work suggests a more radical solution. He became sceptical of the idea that there are extensions. Singular terms such as 'the extension of the concept *F*' don't refer (PW: 269; NS: 288–9). If there are no extensions, one must define the conditions of interchangeability of concept-words without appealing to extensions: concept-words are exchangeable *salva veritate* in sentences in which these words have their normal sense and reference if, and only if, the concepts predicatively referred to have the same values for the same objects. Extensions need not play an important role in the theory of sense and reference. Hence, Frege need not make new distinctions to accommodate them.

The most pressing concern for Frege after he dispenses with extensions is the question what numbers are. Numbers are objects and extensions are logical objects. Hence, it is attractive for a logicist to identify the former with the later. For example 0 is the number of the concept $\xi \neq \xi$, that is *the extension* of the concept *extension of a concept equinumerous with the concept* $\xi \neq \xi$ (GGA I: 57ff.). If there are no extensions, there are no objects with which the numbers could be identical. In a late manuscript Frege raises therefore the question whether there are simply no numbers in arithmetic (PW: 256–7; NS: 277). Perhaps we only have a series of second-order concepts: *there is exactly 1 F, there are 2 Fs, ...*

The further exploration of this view is a task for philosophers of mathematics.[9]

THE CONCEPT-PARADOX OR WHY PROPER NAMES CANNOT REFER TO CONCEPTS

A concept-word has a referent, but we cannot refer to its referent with a proper name, for example, by saying 'The reference of the concept-word "a horse" is the concept *horse*' without committing a mistake:

> [L]anguage brands a concept as an object, since the only way it can fit the designation for a concept into its grammatical structure is as a proper name. ... Strictly speaking, it requires something contradictory, *since no proper name can designate a concept*; or perhaps better still, something nonsensical.
>
> (PW: 177–8; NS: 192. In part my translation and emphasis. See also PMC: 161; BW: 243)

Why shall we believe (6) no (complex or simple) proper name can designate a concept?

Frege himself expounds the concept-paradox often by saying that a saturated expression cannot refer to an unsaturated thing and an unsaturated expression cannot refer to an object (see, for example, PW: 177; NS: 192). In this formulation the concept-paradox seems unmotivated. Burge, for example, takes the concept-paradox to be the result of a 'serious mistake':

> A difficulty in Frege's position did emerge when he committed himself to asserting the German analogue of the sentence 'The concept (or function) *horse* is not a concept (or function)'. Since the subject term 'The concept *horse*' has the grammatical role of a name, Frege thought that it could not stand for a concept (or function). This is deeply counterintuitive. I believe that this constitutes one of Frege's most serious mistakes. *Church showed, in his calculus of lambda-conversion, that there is no reason why a syntactically saturated expression – one with no open argument places or free variables – cannot denote a function, including a concept. The key point is to distinguish their grammatical roles.*
>
> (Burge 2005: 21. My emphasis. See also Burge 2007: 598)[10]

The standard answer to Burge's challenge appeals to the so-called *reference principle*:[11] 'If α and β have the same reference, they are inter-substitutable *salva veritate* in all extensional sentences and *salva congruitate* in all sentences' (Wright 1998: 240). Frege himself subscribes to the '*salva veritate*' part of this principle in 'On Concept and Object'.[12] Concept-words and singular terms have different grammatical roles and can therefore not be intersubstituted *salva congruitate*. According to the reference principle, they have referents of different kinds.

But the reference principle cannot bear the weight of the argument for the conclusion that 'is a horse' and 'the concept *horse*' differ in reference. The argument is not persuasive, for two expressions α and β might not be intersubstitutable *salva congruitate* in all sentences and yet have the same reference. This point can be made plausible by independent examples.[13] Take the sentence:

The horse Black Beauty was a horse.

Since Black Beauty is an object there is no reason to doubt that the reference of 'Black Beauty' is Black Beauty. If the reference principle is true, these expressions should be inter-substitutable *salva congruitate*. But as the sentence below shows, they aren't:

The horse the reference of 'Black Beauty' was a horse.

Hence, one can't justify the conclusion that 'the concept *horse*' and 'is a horse' don't co-refer and that the first term refers to an object by appealing to the reference principle. For exchanging 'is a horse' in 'Shergar is a horse' with 'the reference of "is a horse"' results in a similarly ungrammatical string.

It seems to me that the standard motivations miss the true source of the concept-paradox. Frege told us that concepts don't stand in the relation of identity (PW: 120; NS: 130–1; PW: 182; NS: 198). Now *identity* and *singular* reference are interconnected. It is a platitude that mutually illuminates the notion of singular reference and identity that, necessarily, if the singular terms α and β are non-empty, the identity statement 'α = β' is either true or false. If α and β are singular terms, they can be used to make an identity statement that is either true or false; if they refer, then the referents are or are not identical. This is part of what it is to be a singular term that stands for something. Assume now that 'the concept *smoking*' referred to what 'smokes' refers to and that 'the concept *running*' refers to what 'runs' refers to. Under this assumption the sentence 'The concept *smoking* = the concept *running*' must be either true or false. But if concepts are not the sort of thing that can stand in the relation of identity or difference, the identity-sentence 'The concept *smoking* = the concept *running*' is neither true nor false. But this contradicts our assumption that the designators 'the concept *running*' and 'the concept *smoking*' are singular terms referring to concepts. Hence, the assumption that concepts can be named by singular terms turns out to be inconsistent, just as Frege said. He concludes that singular terms that purport to refer to concepts either (1) refer to an object or (2) don't refer at all. In his early work Frege went for (1): 'the concept *horse*' refers to an object. Why? If one trusts his report, it was common practice among the mathematicians of his time to say 'The function F = the function G'.[14] He can now argue that they either make a systematic mistake or use 'the function F' to express truths about objects related to concepts. As long as he had faith in mathematical practice, he endorsed the second option that makes mathematical practice come out right.[15]

Concepts cannot be referred to by singular terms. Why does Frege suppose that concept-words *can* refer to concepts? The platitudes that characterise the semantic features of concept-words don't rely on the notion of identity. Among these platitudes are, for example, if '(a) man' and '(a) rational' are non-empty, then 'Either every man is rational or not every man is rational'. Since the semantics of concept-words is disconnected from the notion of identity, they can take concepts as their referents.

The thesis that singular terms cannot refer to concepts can be motivated without appeal to the saturated/unsaturated distinction. Hence, the concept-paradox is not, as Burge has it, the result of a serious mistake. The concept paradox is 'founded in the nature of things' (namely the nature of concepts; they don't stand in the relation of identity) and 'the nature of language' (namely the semantics of singular terms that connects singular reference and identity).

The thesis that singular terms cannot refer to concepts has bizarre consequences. We have seen that an expression is a proper name referring to an object if knowing its sense includes knowledge of identity-criteria. From this follows (PN):

> (PN) A word used with the definite article or a demonstrative pronoun is a proper name. A proper name refers to an object, if it refers at all.

Frege's repeatedly points out that the definite article in the singular always indicates an *object*, and cannot indicate a *function*.[16] Why? An expression of the form 'the *F*' only denotes something if there is a unique *F*. *Unique* satisfaction is characterised in terms of identity: an expression is only uniquely satisfied by something x if every object y that satisfies the expression is identical with x. If the relation of identity does not apply to functions (concepts), functions cannot be denoted by expressions starting with the definite article. Expressions of this sort have satisfaction-conditions that can only be fulfilled by objects, not by functions (concepts). Concepts can only be the referents of expression that are not singular in this sense. Hence, as he puts it in FA, a word that is used with the indefinite article or in the plural without the article is concept-word (FA: 64).

According to (PN), 'The number n belongs to the concept *F*' is not about a concept, but about an object! Either concepts are objects or Frege's theory of concept-word reference is false. His comments in 'Concept and Object' are therefore spot on:

> While Kerry therefore does not succeed to close the divide between concept and object, one could attempt to use my own remarks to this effect. *I have said that a statement of number contains a statement about a concept; I talk of properties ascribed to a concept and I let a concept fall under a higher one. I have called existence a property of a concept.*
>
> (CO: 188, 199. My emphasis and translation.)

By way of some background, Frege takes the fundamental insight of FA to be 'that the content of a statement of number contains an assertion about a concept' (FA: 59; GGA I: ix). In GGA I this result is assumed and forms the basis of Frege's further investigation. Consider one of his examples. When I utter the sentence 'Venus has 0 Moons' I assert that the number 0 belongs to something. To what? Not to a collection of objects:

> If I say 'Venus has o Moons', there is simply no Moon or agglomeration of Moons for anything to be said of; rather, a property is thereby assigned to the concept 'Moon of Venus' – the property, namely, of including nothing under it.
>
> (FA: 59)

There is no object that completes the concept ξ *is a Moon of Venus* to a circumstance that is a fact. Hence, the number 0 belongs to the concept ξ *is a Moon of Venus*. Frege's fundamental insight is a generalisation of this idea. Hence, number statements like the one above are about concepts.

Now Frege's fundamental insight in the philosophy of arithmetic appears to be incompatible with his view of concept-word reference. He responds by biting the bullet: yes, expressions such as 'the concept *horse*' refer to objects! If the concept-word 'a horse' in (S1):

> (S1) Red Rum is *a horse*

refers to a concept, then

> Red Rum falls under *the concept to which 'a horse' refers*

should be true. But if concepts are exclusively referred to by concepts-words this sentence is false. The same goes for the famous example:

> (S2) The concept *horse* is a concept.

However, it is counter-intuitive that (S2) is false. Frege does not take (S2) to be a counter-example to the thesis that incomplete 'things' can only be referred to by incomplete expressions, but he responds by saying that 'the concept *horse*' stands for an object, if it stands for anything, and not a concept.

If 'the concept *horse*' refers to an object, to which object does it refer? He does not say. Before Russell's discovered that some concepts don't have extensions, Frege assumed that every concept had an extension. Some authors have proposed that 'the concept *horse*' is a proper name of the extension of the concept. Although it might be natural to make this identification, it is controversial.[17] Fortunately, we do not need to enter this controversy for our purposes.

The fact that Frege sticks to his thesis that functions (concepts) cannot be the reference of singular terms has counter-intuitive consequences which are labelled 'concept paradox'.

Counter-intuitive consequence 1: sentences such as (S2) are false:

> It must indeed be recognised that here we are confronted by an awkwardness of language, which I admit cannot be avoided, if we say that the concept *horse* is not a concept, whereas, e.g. the city of Berlin is a city, and the volcano Vesuvius is a volcano. Language is here in a predicament that justifies the departure from custom.
>
> (CO: 185–6, 197)

Frege's talk of 'deviation from linguistic custom' is an understatement. 'The concept horse is a concept' is a paradigm of a Kantian analytic proposition, i.e. its predicate concept is 'contained' in the subject-concept. Such a proposition can be false (not true) if its subject part is empty: 'The largest prime is prime' is not true, for there is no largest prime. But if the unproblematic sentence 'Shergar is a horse' is true, 'a horse' must have a reference and this reference is a Fregean concept.[18] Hence, 'The concept *horse* is a concept' seems to be an obvious truth, not a falsehood.

Counter-intuitive consequence 2: every communicative intention to mention a concept is necessarily frustrated:

> By a kind of necessity of language, my expressions, taken literally, sometimes miss my thought; I mention an object, when what I intend

is a concept. I fully realise that in such cases I was relying upon a reader who would be ready to meet me half-way – who does not begrudge a pinch of salt.

(CO: 193; 204. See also PW: 119; NS: 130)

While Frege takes this problem to be a mere communicative hitch, Dummett takes it to be a dilemma that 'would be a *reductio ad absurdum* of Frege's logical doctrines' (Dummett 1981a: 212), if no solution were available.

Counter-intuitive consequence 3: If one wants to say what a word refers to, one has to use the two-place predicate 'ξ refers to ζ'. This relation-word refers predicatively to a relation between *objects*; *a linguistic expression* and *its referent*. One can refer singularly to a concept-word, say 'ξ is a horse' by using the name of a concept-word, but one cannot refer with a singular term to its reference. A concept cannot be the referent of a singular term. Wright's question is therefore spot on: 'How is one to explain what, e.g., "is a horse" refers to without recourse to any singular term purporting to refer to the same thing?' (Wright 1998: 243). If one tries to explain what 'ξ is a horse' refers to by referring to its reference with a singular term one always fails. For example, '"ξ is a horse" refers to *the set that contains all and only horses*' is a grammatical sentence of English, but it is by Frege's lights false. Similar problems arise if we consider generic names. The question 'What does "a horse" refer to?' cannot been answered by referring to something with a singular term and using a generic name again is of no help ('"A horse" refers to a horse' (?)) The referent of a concept-word is a concept and a concept cannot be referred to by a singular term. However, if we are not allowed to use a singular term on the right-hand side of the relation-word, we cannot even form a complete English sentence that explains what 'a horse' refers to. Frege seems to be driven to the conclusion that concept-words have a reference, but that one cannot say what their reference is (PMC: 136; BW: 219).[19]

Frege is well aware of the first two problems. Hence, he looked for ways to soften the blow of the thesis that a concept cannot be referred to by a singular term. Later I will look at his responses to them (pp. 262ff.). Limits of space prevent me from looking at more recent attempts of Fregeans to solve the problem on his behalf.[20] I will, however, start in the next section with the third problem and argue that an answer to it can be found in Frege's work.

HOW CAN ONE EXPLAIN WHAT A CONCEPT-WORD REFERS TO?

Frege himself assumed that a semantic stipulation such as the one below gives the relation-word '$\xi = \zeta$' a reference: '$\Delta = \Gamma$' refers to the True if, and only if Δ coincides with Γ' (GGA I: §7). 'Δ' and 'Γ' here are short for names to which the reader can arbitrarily assign a reference. How is this explanation supposed to give '$\xi = \zeta$' a reference? Prima facie, the explanation only tells us when sentences containing the concept-word are true. No reference is assigned to '$\xi = \zeta$' and, if we accept Frege's view that concepts cannot be referred to by singular terms, no reference can be assigned. What can he do to explain to which thing the concept-word refers?

The theory of multiple decomposability comes to Frege's help. The sentence '$\Delta = \Gamma$' can be used to answer the question 'Which things coincide, if, and only if "$\Delta = \Gamma$" refers to the True?' In this case an object is subsumed under the first-order relation of identity. But the same sentence can also be used to answer a different question 'What are Δ and Γ if, and only if, "$\Delta = \Gamma$" refers to the True?' If you answer this question with '$\Delta [=]_F \Gamma$' ('Δ and Γ are equal'), the sentence uttered is decomposed differently: we take the objects as given and supply new information about the relation between them. The expression '$\xi = \zeta$' is used within the sentence predicatively and it is in focus. The expression in focus refers to the object that is characterised by the sentence remainder. We have already seen earlier (p. 235f.) that a sentence part can be in focus and refer to something, although the sentence part is not a *singular term* (CO: 188–9, 199–200). The same thought applies here. If I answer the question mentioned above by making an assertoric utterance of '$\Delta [=]_F \Gamma$', the sentence uttered is about identity, although I do not refer to the relation with a singular term. My answer gives the relation-word '$\xi = \zeta$' a reference-condition, although the word has not been used on its own.

Frege's introduction of the signs of the modified Begriffsschrift in GGA I sheds light on a further problem. He says that an unsaturated sense needs completion in order to exist, whereas a saturated sense does not (CP: 391, 37). Earlier (pp. 231–2) this asymmetry seemed unfounded. Now we can defend Frege's idea. If concepts and functions are not objects, one cannot state what they refer to by using the relation-word 'ξ refers to ζ'. As we have seen one can say what these expressions refer to without 'objectifying' their references by using them predicatively in sentences and decomposing these sentences in an unorthodox way. Consequently, the reference of concept- and relation-words can only be fixed by fixing the reference of a sentence that contains the concept-words and decomposing the sentence. By contrast, it is no problem to use 'ξ refers to ζ' to state the reference of names in Frege's sense. Hence, we arrive at the conclusion that one cannot introduce a concept- or function-designator and explain its sense without using it predicatively within a sentence. This gets us, I think, pretty close to Frege's view that the senses of these expressions 'demand' completion.

FREGE'S MANOEUVRES

Alternative decompositions of statements 'about concepts'

In the previous section we have seen that the doctrine of multiple decomposition helps Frege's theory of concept-word reference. In 'Concept and Object' he takes the doctrine of multiple decomposition also to hold the key to the solution of the concept-paradox:

> In the sentence 'There is at least one square root of 4' we have a predication, not about (say) the definite number 2, nor about −2, but about a concept, *square root of 4*, viz. that it is not empty. But if I express the same thought thus: 'The concept *square root of 4* is realised', then the first six words form the proper name of an object, and it is about this object that something is asserted. But notice carefully that what is predicated here is not the same thing as was predicated about the concept.
>
> (CO: 188, 199. In part my translation.)

Take again:

> (1) There is at least one square root of 4.
> (2) The concept *square root of 4* is realised.

In the decomposition of the thought conveyed by (2) a concept is referred to by a singular term, in the decomposition conveyed by (1) not. There are then paradoxical and non-paradoxical decompositions of a thought. If we simply stick to the right decompositions, we can dodge the paradox. Geach has applied this strategy directly to the problematic sentence (S2):

> (S2) The concept *horse* is a concept.

If one takes (S2) to answer:

> Which concept is a concept?

one decomposes (S2) into the incomplete function word 'The concept ( ) is a concept' and the function word '*horse*'.[21] The concept no longer appears non-predicatively in the new decomposition.

The problem with this proposal is that it requires that the same thought is true decomposed in one way and false decomposed in another way. But it is impossible that a thought that refers to the True also refers to the False. If a decomposition does not change a thought, how could it change its truth-value? Hence, Frege's conception of multiple decomposition of the same thought does not allow him to solve the concept-paradox. Multiple decomposition would only allow him to solve the problem if sentences such as 'The concept *horse* is a concept' were not false. Frege would need to make a case that we take them to be false because we understand phrases such as 'the concept *horse*' as singular terms, while in fact these phrases only serve to put the concept-word in focus. This strategy of dealing with the problem may fruitfully be pursued, but since Frege does not do so, neither will I.

Moreover, the application of the decomposition strategy to

number statements comes at a high price. In *FA* he took the form of a number statement to be

The number *n* belongs to the concept *F*.

If number statements are not to give rise to the concept paradox they must be about a first-order concept that falls under a second-order one. For example, the sentence

There are 4 horses that draw the emperor's carriage

can be split up into a first-level concept (in Frege's notation: *ξ is a horse that draws the emperor's carriage*) that is said to fall in the second-order concept referred to by the concept-word 'There exist exactly four such a such that ... a ...' (with 'a' marking the argument place for first-order concept-words). The number-word '4' does no longer occur as a self-standing term in their decomposition. The sentence is no longer about a number.

Are there predicative concept-names?

In 'Comments on Sense and Reference' Frege argues that 'what the concept "man" refers to' is the predicate in

Jesus is, what the concept-word 'man' refers to,

and the grammatical subject in:

What the concept-word 'man' refers to can be predicated of Jesus.

Hence, one can refer with a singular term to a concept without misrepresenting it as an object. If Frege wants to endorse this argument, he must reject the view that concept-words are 'gappy' sentence-fragments that can be completed by singular terms to sentences. For 'what the concept word "man" refers to' cannot be completed by a proper name to a sentence: 'Jesus what the concept word "man" refers to' is not a sentence. The sentence-remainder is '*is* what the concept word "man"' refers to'. This expression can be used predicatively, but it cannot be the complete subject of a sentence in which something is said about the concept.[22]

Now even if we endorse the generic name conception of concept-words, Frege's proposal will not work. We know already that concepts cannot stand in the relation of identity. But the statement 'What the English concept-word "man" refers to is the same thing as what the concept-word "*Mensch*" refers to' can be read as a true identity statement. How could this be if the two expressions flanking the identity-sign were concept-words referring to concepts? Hence, they must be proper names of objects.

BITING THE BULLET

We made no use of the reference principles and others like it in arguing for the thesis that only concept-words can refer to concepts. Hence, the concept paradox cannot be easily dismissed as based on a fallacious inference from grammatical differences to semantic differences. Our discussion has not only helped to locate the source of the paradox. It also helped to see why Frege takes it to be unsolvable, but tolerable.

Sub-problem 1 is the problem that 'The concept *horse* is a concept' seems to be an analytic truth. The sentence 'The concept *horse* is a concept' looks like 'The city Berlin is a city'. Everyone who understands sentences of this type must assent to them and come to know what they say. How could such a sentence be false? Frege has given a principle-based answer to this question: if concepts don't stand in the relation of identity, they cannot be the referents of proper names. One can understand what 'The concept *horse* is a concept' says and deny it for a strong reason.[23] What looks like a triviality turns out to be a necessary falsehood if we bring more knowledge to bear.

Sub-problem 2 is the problem of getting the distinction between concepts and objects across to a reader. If we want to communicate about concepts, our natural language habits compel us to use proper names as grammatical subjects. The communicative mechanism Frege uses to make his logical point spoils it. He relies on the reader's logical ability to recognise that the literally expressed thought is manifestly false. We need to learn that only attending to concept-words used predicatively can teach us what they refer to.

So far so good. But even if we manage to solve the so-called 'concept-paradox', problems will remain. Frege takes a concept-word such as 'smokes' to refer to at most one concept. How can one maintain that a concept-word refers to at most one concept, if concepts don't stand in the relation of identity? He appeals to the idea that sameness of extension is for concept-words analogous to sameness of reference for proper names. But one cannot say that a concept-word refers to at most one concept if, and only if, it refers to a concept F and every concept it refers to has the same extension as F. For *different* concepts can have the *same* extension. As far as I know he has not tackled this difficulty for his theory of concept-word reference. He needs to provide a relation between concepts that is not identity, but which enables one to define 'at most one concept'. If he can't provide such a definition, concepts will not belong to the realm of the countable. An unwanted consequence, for this would show that there are objects we can refer to, but which don't belong to the realm of the countable. Frege's argument from similarity would, in turn, lose plausibility. I will have to leave discussion of this problem for another occasion.

NOTES

INTRODUCTION

1 See PW: 253; NS: 272. I will refer to the book of the same title in which the Begriffschrift is developed as *Begriffsschrift*.
2 See Barwise and Perry 1983: 3ff.

1 SEARCHING FOR THE FOUNDATIONS OF ARITHMETIC

1 See also Kitcher 1975: 31.
2 See Galloway 1999: §2 for a discussion of how one can see sequences.
3 See Parsons 2005: 135–6 for symbolic construction as construction of symbols. Shabel 1998: 613 disagrees with this reading of Kant's text.
4 The letter is listed in PMC and BW under 'Marty', but the editors' comments in BW: 162 make it very likely that it was misclassified.
5 In later work Frege will hold that vague predicates don't refer to concepts. More on this in Chapter 7.
6 For such prescriptions see GGA I: §48.
7 See Harman 1986: 5.
8 See MacFarlane 2002: 37–9.
9 See MacFarlane 2002: 37.

10 I have changed the translation and distinguished between proof (*Beweis*) and grounding (*Begründung*), '*Satz*' is translated as 'sentence'.

11 This example is used by Bolzano to explain the distinction Frege has in mind. Both Bolzano and Frege are influenced by Leibniz's idea that there is a natural order of truths independently of what we know. See especially Bolzano 1837: §195–222 for a detailed investigation of grounds of truth.

12 This has to be taken with a pinch of salt. Frege takes it to be possible that there is more than one small set of laws from which all truths of arithmetic can be derived (CN: 136, §13; BS: 25. See also PW: 205; NS: 221). Hence, there may be more than one perfect proof. However, in the case of arithmetic truth all these proofs are supposed to use only logical laws and definitions.

13 See also Burge 2005: 358. Proof is psychological notion for Frege. Ideally, the steps in a proof mirror the order of truths.

14 There is a considerable body of literature discussing Frege's rationale for proving the truths of arithmetic. See Benacerraf 1981: 31–2; Kitcher 1979: 236–8; Weiner 1990: 18–30. For a general assessment of the discussion see Jeshion 2001: 939–45. The disagreement between these authors is over the question for which reason Frege pursued logicism. I don't see a reason to enter this debate for Frege seems to pursue the project for different reasons that are mutually compatible.

15 See Burge's reading of the opening passage of BS in Burge 2005: 319ff.

16 See Burge 2005: 329.

17 See CP: 335f., 425f.

18 On this point see Dummett 1991a: 24 and Burge 2005: 365.

19 See also Dummett 1991a: 15. For further discussion see MacFarlane 2002: 27ff.

20 The following paragraph addresses worries raised in Macbeth 2005: 61.

21 According to Frege, the content of '$p \rightarrow q$' is the same as 'not (p & not q)'.

22 For a discussion of sentence-nominalisations see Vendler 1967: chap. 5.

23 See Burge 2005: 21–2.

24 See Goldfarb 2001: 29

25 CN: 144, 155; BS: 33, 43.
26 See Goldfarb 2001: 38.
27 There are further alternatives to Frege's understanding of the generality of the laws of, see Williamson 1999: 263ff. and Rosefeldt 2008.

2 THE BEGRIFFSSCHRIFT AND ITS PHILOSOPHICAL BACKGROUND

1 See letter to Peano, PW: 115; BW: 183.
2 See Frege's talk of '*noch so leichtem Erraten*' ('very easy guessing') in NS: 13. The English translation PW: 12 obscures this point.
3 For the term 'guesswork' see Trendelenburg (1856).
4 See also CN: 84–5, 50–1 and VB: 37.
5 See CP: 247, 347 and Frege's letter to Jourdain, PMC: 79; BW: 118.
6 Leibniz himself uses 'lingua universalis' or 'characteristica universalis'; 'lingua characterica' is Frege's term. Frege might appeal with 'characterica' to indicate that the language under consideration is a script whose signs are inscriptions. See Künne 2010: 113f.
7 For the history of 'Begriffsschrift' see Thiel 1995: 20 and Barnes 2002: 65–80.
8 On Humboldt see Thiel 1995; Barnes 2002 and Künne 2010: 167.
9 See PW: 12–13; NS: 13–14.
10 See Barnes 2002: 78.
11 PW: 260; NS: 280.
12 See PW: 14; NS: 15. My translation. The translation in PW makes of '*anschaulich darstellen*' 'perspicuous representation'. A perspicuous representation is a clearly arranged representation; a representation can be perspicuous without being intuitive *(anschaulich)*. The translation ruins Frege's point that his and Boole's aim is to develop a script that *pictures* logical relations.
13 See Parsons 2005: 135–6.
14 Frege himself remarks that 'in pre-scientific discourse what are called numbers are often no more than numerals' (PW: 266; NS: 285). The series of numerals and the number series are in their distinctive features so similar that for non-scientific purposes we get away with identifying them.

15 In PW: '*Glücklicherweise haben wir durch **unsere logischen Anlagen ein Winkelmass mitbekommen**, …*' has been translated as 'Fortunately as a result of *our logical work* we have acquired a yardstick'. But '*logische Anlagen*' does not mean 'logical work'! It means our 'natural capacities for logic'.

16 See also Burge 2005: 14.

17 Frege must have been aware of these Kantian views. Frege's *Begriffsschrift* is in part a discussion of the Kantian theory of judgement and these distinctions are introduced immediately after the passage from the *Critique of Pure Reason* quoted above. See Wolff 1995: Appendix.

18 On Boole and Frege see Sluga 1987.

19 CN: 112 mistranslates '*zuerkennen*' ('ascribe') as 'acknowledge' ('*anerkennen*'). The distinction will become important in Chapter 6.

20 A script is only a Begriffsschrift if its sentences express *only* the conceptual content of judgements voiced by means of them.

21 For discussion of Frege's examples of such definitions see Dummett 1991c: 26 and Sullivan 2004: 3.3.4.

22 Austin does not translate '*verlangt*' in '*verlangt immer eine Ergänzung*'.

23 See for example Klement 2004: 3.

3 FROM SUBJECT AND PREDICATE TO ARGUMENT AND FUNCTION

1 The example is from Rumfitt 1994: 600.

2 See Macbeth 2005: 143f.

3 He provides the explanation later in 'On the Scientific Justification of a Conceptual Notation', CN: 88, 54.

4 See PW: 203; NS: 219.

5 See Sundholm 1998.

6 See especially PMC: 17; BW: 30.

7 Dummett 1981a: 309. See also Geach 1976: 63.

8 Sundholm 1998 distinguishes between inference, implication and consequence.

9 One can try to align validity (an argument is valid if it is necessary that the conclusion is true if the premise is) and inference by explaining validity in epistemic terms. See Campbell 1994: 76.

10 See CN: 130; BS: 19.

11 See also NS: 203; PW: 187 and NS: 274; PW: 254.

12 Ramsey and Wittgenstein agree with Frege on this point. They disagree with him about the question whether this view constitutes the basis for establishing an asymmetry between leftover expressions and proper names. See Ramsey 1925: 409.

13 See Dretske 1970.

14 See Rooth 1996 and Hofweber 2007: 16.

15 See Dummett 1991c: 209 and Kenny 1995: 14ff.

16 See Stevenson 1973.

17 See Baker and Hacker 2003; Heck and May 2006. Glock 1996/7 takes both sides into account.

18 See Heck and May 2005: 8 and Baker 2001: 533.

19 Frege's '*inhaltliche Bedeutung*' should not be translated as 'substantive significance'. '*Inhalt*' refers to conceptual content.

20 See Klement 2002: 68.

21 See Dummett 1981b: 271 and Klement 2002: 85.

22 See Klement 2004: 14.

4 SPLITTING CONCEPTUAL CONTENT INTO SENSE AND REFERENCE

1 Early Wittgenstein disagrees with Frege: '5.533 The identity-sign, therefore, is not an essential constituent of the Begriffsschrift' (my translation. Wittgenstein's use of 'Begriffsschrift' in the original text is not picked up by the translator). For further discussion of Wittgenstein's view see Fogelin 1983.

2 For this and the following see Mendelsohn 1982: 282ff.

3 In the literature there are many so-called 'Fregean arguments'. See, for instance, Sainsbury 1983; Salmon 1986: 11f. and Fine 2007: 34f. Such arguments are inspired by Frege and try to establish the conclusion he argues for. In this section I want to get clear about the argument he actually gives, not about an alternative routes to his conclusion.

4 See May 2001: 28 for further motives for the change to identity.

5 The exception is the judgement-stroke. It has no reference, it acknowledges the truth of a content.

6 See NS: 242; PW: 224.

7 See also §5 of FA on arithmetical equations.

8 See Putnam 1954. For further discussion see Taschek 1995.

9 See Caplan and Thau 2001; for a reply see Heck 2003. Perry 2001 tries to revive Frege's *Begriffsschrift* view for systematic reasons.

10 For another argument see Furth's introduction to the English translation of BS: xix. Mendelsohn 1982: 297f. clarifies and expands it.

11 The question whether one can or needs to identify modes of presentations with scientifically respectable objects does not concern Frege, but it is discussed in the literature. Since Frege himself has not contributed to this debate I will not enter it. For discussion see Dummett 1981a: 227ff. and Evans 1982: §4.2. See also Schiffer 1990 and Peacocke 1999: 121. For Schiffer's different recent view see Schiffer 2003: chap. 2.

12 See also Kripke 2008: 182f.

13 See Burge 2005: 44.

14 As Dummett himself notes 1981b: 152.

15 For further discussion of the two ingredients of the notion of reference see Gaskin 2008: chap. 1.7 and 1.8. See also Bell 1979: 42 and Brandom 1986: §1

16 See Evans 1982: 25.

17 See Sainsbury 2005: chap. 3.6 for a detailed account of communication with empty proper names.

18 Dummett 1978: 131 takes transparency to be an undeniable feature of the notion of meaning. For a discussion of transparency claims see Fine 2007: 60–6.

19 The connection between sameness of sense, inference and taking identity for granted is discussed in Strawson 1957: 95ff. It is used to shed light on sense in Campbell 1994: chap. 3.1 and 3.2.

20 T: 358, 65.

21 Although logical validity of an argument is different from the correctness of an inference (S7) is indirectly involved in logical validity. An argument is logically valid if, and only if, every assignment of objects to its non-logical expressions that makes the premises true also makes the conclusion true. When is it legitimate to assign different objects to different expressions? Can the general terms 'unmarried eligible male' and 'bachelor' be true of different things? No, an assignment of objects is only legitimate if it assigns expressions

with the same sense the same objects. Otherwise, 'Every unmarried eligible male is a bachelor' comes out as contingent truth. Similarly, some arguments are only logically valid if we take the uses of a proper name in both premises to have the same sense. Why? Think of sense as a recipe for picking out a thing from everything there is. If two terms come with the same recipe, we need to assign them the same objects.

22 See Klement 2002: 92.
23 For further detailed discussion see Künne 2003: 42ff.
24 See Grice 1989: part 1 'Logic and Conversation'.
25 For further discussion see Horty 1993 and May 2006.
26 On this point see Beaney 2005; Burge 2005: essay 6; Nelson 2008 and Weiner 2007. On Frege's early view about definition and conceptual analysis see Wiggins 2006.

5 THE SENSE AND REFERENCE OF NATURAL LANGUAGE SINGULAR TERMS

1 My translation. The original translation translates '*vollkommen*' (perfect) as 'complete' (*vollständig*).
2 For further discussion see May 2006.
3 I have changed the translation of '*anerkennen*', '*Satz*' and '*Bedeutung*'.
4 For critical discussion of Frege's theory of vagueness see Williamson 1994: chap. 2.2.
5 For a discussion of different notions of context see, for example, Caplan 2003.
6 Neither does Perry himself accept this response. See Perry 1979: 14.
7 See Evans 1985; Lewis 1980: 95 and Percival 1994.
8 See Evans 1985: 349–50.
9 MacFarlane 2003: 334 fn.
10 See Richard 1981. For an overview over the discussion see Künne 2003: chap. 5.2 and 5.3.
11 For further discussion see Künne 1982; Kripke 2008 and Salmon 2002.
12 For further development of this idea see Textor 2007.
13 See Evans 1982: 192.
14 See Jackson 2005.

15 For a development of this objection see Soames 1998.
16 See Dummett 1981a: 127ff.; Kripke 1980: Introduction: 11ff. replies; Dummett 1981b: Appendix 3 replies to the reply.
17 See Forbes 1990: 536 and Lewis 1999: 352.
18 See Searle 1958 and May 2006: 129ff.
19 The same argument can be found in Russell 1910/11: 206–7; Kripke 1979: 108; Evans 1982: 399f.; Sainsbury 2005: 12ff. and Strawson 1974: 52.
20 See Heck 1995: 79.
21 See PMC: 152; BW: 234.
22 See Bigelow and Schroeter 2009: 102, §5.
23 Strawson 1959: 58.
24 Klement 2002: chap. 5 proposes a Fregean theory that allows one to capture inferences involving propositional attitude sentences.
25 For independent examples of terms with multiple roles or referents see Fine 1989: 267f.
26 See Davidson 1984: 208.
27 For extensive discussion see Burge 2005: essay 4 and his postscript to this essay.
28 As Parsons 1996: 408 does. See Peacocke 1999: 245 and Burge 2005: essay 4 Postscript for attempts to give direct arguments against (Peacocke) and for (Burge) the hierarchy, and Parsons 1996: 402ff. for a failure diagnosis of a possible Fregean argument for the hierarchy.
29 See Pendlebury 1986: 363.
30 For further discussion see Green 1997; Pendlebury 1986 and Segal 1991.

6 THE SENSE AND REFERENCE OF AN ASSERTORIC SENTENCE

1 '*Wahrheitswerth davon, dass*' is in PMC wrongly translated as 'truth-value'. See also Burge 2005: 22.
2 Thanks to Jessica Leech for suggesting this idea.
3 PW: 7; NS: 8.
4 FC was published in 1891. Windelband uses '*Wahrheitswert*' before Frege in 1882. A judgement is an evaluation ('*Beurteilung*') of a connection of ideas: 'All cognitive sentences [*'Sätze der Erkenntnis'*]

contain already a combination of a judgement with an evaluation, they are combinations of ideas whose truth-value ['Wahrheitswert'] has been decided by affirmation or negation' (Windelband 1882: 32. My translation). But although Frege takes truth to be something we strive for, the truth-value is value of a function, not a value in the axiological sense. Otherwise the False could hardly be a truth-*value*.

5 See Künne 2010: 317.

6 See Heck 2007: 40.

7 See Ricketts 2003: 418.

8 See PW: 129; NS: 140.

9 See PMC: 23; BW: 37 and PMC: 182; BW: 118.

10 See also PW: 2; NS: 2; PW: 197–8; NS: 213–14; PW: 251; NS: 271; PW: 258–9; NS: 278–9; PW: 267; NS: 286.

11 For a good overview over the meanings of '*anerkennen*' see Inwood 1992: 245.

12 The evaluative understanding of Frege's '*anerkennen*' is suggested by Gabriel 2003: 19.

13 '*Aber ich erblicke keineswegs etwas Verdienstliches darin - und das lag auch Dirichlet ganz fern -, diese mühselige Umschreibung wirklich vornehmen und keine anderen als die natürlichen Zahlen benutzen und anerkennen zu wollen.*'

14 See further Kremer 2000: 565.

15 I develop this interpretation further in Textor Forthcoming.

16 See Kremer 2000: 555.

17 See GGA I: xvi.

18 See Heck and May 2006: 30.

19 The Picture Thesis and the problems of multiple decomposability are discussed further in Textor 2009.

20 See PW: 201; NS: 217; PW: 187; NS: 203; PW: 254; NS: 274.

7 THE SENSE AND REFERENCE OF A CONCEPT-WORD

1 For the first pronouncement see Gaskin 2008: 155; a representative example of the second strategy is Wiggins 1984.

2 See Beaney 2007: 115.

3 See MacBride 2006: 427ff. for discussion of this option.

4 See Dummett 1981a: 218ff. and Wiggins 1984: 314.

5 See Wiggins 1984: 325–6.

6 I have translated Frege's '*Aussage*' as 'predication'. The '*Aussageteil*' is used in nineteenth-century German for the predicative part of a sentence. '*Aussage*' sometimes does not refer to the speech act of assertion, but to the predicate part of a sentence. Thanks to Wolfgang Künne for discussion.

7 See Schröder 1890: 63–75. A good discussion of Schröder's views on concept-words is Husserl 1891: 13f.

8 See, for example, Carnap 1956: §27.

9 See Rayo 2002 and also Klement 2002: 206–13.

10 See Russell 1903: §49. See also Strawson 1959: 146ff.

11 For an overview see MacBride 2006: 456.

12 CP: 189, 201.

13 See Oliver 2005: 182ff.

14 See GGA II: 148.

15 Frege's reasons for the second option are developed in Burge 2005: 288.

16 See FA: §51; CO: 184, 195.

17 Burge 2005 and Parsons 1986 argue that concept names refer to the extensions that represent the concept. See Schirn 1990 for criticism.

18 We would count 'If there is a concept *horse*, the concept *horse* is a concept' as obviously true, while Frege must count it false.

19 See Heck and May 2006: 11f. for an alternative proposal to solve the problem.

20 See, for example, Dummett 1981a: 214; Wiggins 1984 and Wright 1998. Dummett's proposal is discussed by Wiggins and Wright as well as in Russinoff 1992.

21 See Geach 1955: 534.

22 See also Dummett 1981a: 214f.

23 For further examples of seemingly obvious, yet rationally deniable, propositions see Williamson 2006.

BIBLIOGRAPHY

WORKS BY FREGE

Frege, G. *Conceptual Notation and Related Articles* (CN), Oxford: Clarendon Press, 1972.
—— *Begriffschrift und andere Aufsätze* (1879), Neudruck Darmstadt: Wissenschaftliche Buchgesellschaft, 1977.
—— *The Foundations of Arithmetic* (FA, 1884), Oxford: Basil Blackwell, 1974. (*Die Grundlagen der Arithmetik*, ed. C. Thiel, Hamburg: Meiner, 1988.)
—— *Grundgesetze der Arithmetik*, I (1893), Reprint Darmstadt: Wissenschaftliche Buchgesellschaft, 1962.
—— *Grundgesetze der Arithmetik*, II (1903), Reprint Darmstadt: Wissenschaftliche Buchgesellschaft, 1962.
—— *Collected Papers on Mathematics, Logic and Philosophy* (CP), Oxford: Blackwell, 1984.
—— *Posthumous Writings* (PW), Oxford: Blackwell, 1979. (*Nachgelassene Schriften*, eds H. Hermes, F. Kambartel and F. Kaulbach, Hamburg: Meiner,1983.)
—— *Philosophical and Mathematical Correspondence* (PMC), Oxford: Blackwell, 1980. (*Gottlob Freges Briefwechsel*, eds G. Gabriel, H. Hermes, F. Kambartel, C. Thiel and A. Veraart, Hamburg, Meiner, 1976.)
—— *Vorlesungen über Begriffschrift* (VB). *History and Philosophy of Logic* 17 (1996), iii–xvi, 1–48. (*Frege's Lectures on Logic: Carnap's Jena Notes, 1910–1914*, eds S. Awodey, E. Reck and G. Gabriel. Open Court: LaSalle, 2004.)

OTHER WORKS

Baker, G. (2001) '"Function" in Frege's *Begriffsschrift*: Dissolving the Problem', *British Journal for the History of Philosophy*, 9: 525–44.

—— and Hacker, P.M.S. (2003) 'Functions in *Begriffsschrift*', *Synthese*, 135: 273–97.

Barnes, J. (2002) 'What is a Begriffsschrift?', *Dialectica*, 56: 65–80.

Barwise, J. and Perry, J. (1983) *Situations and Attitudes*, Cambridge, MA: MIT Press.

Beaney, M. (2005) 'Sinn, Bedeutung and the Paradox of Analysis'. In M. Beaney and E.H. Reck (eds) *Gottlob Frege: Critical Assessments Vol. IV*, London: Routledge, 2005, 288–310.

—— (2007) 'Frege's use of Function-Argument Analysis and his Introduction of Truth-Values as Objects', *Grazer Philosophische Studien*, 75: 93–123.

Bell, D. (1979) *Frege's Theory of Judgement*, Oxford: Oxford University Press.

Benacerraf, P. (1981) 'Frege: The Last Logicist', *Midwest Studies in Philosophy*, 6: 17–35.

Bigelow, J. and Schroeter, L. (2009) 'Jackson's Classical Model of Meaning'. In I. Ravenscroft (ed.) *Mind, Worlds, and Conditionals: Themes from the Philosophy of Frank Jackson*, Oxford: Oxford University Press, 2009, 85–111.

Boole, G. (1854) *An Investigation of the Laws of Thought*, Gutenberg: Ebook Project.

Bolzano, B. (1837) *Wissenschaftlehre I-IV*, Sulzbach: Seidel; reprint of the 2nd edition 1929–31, Aalen: Scientia Verlag, 1970.

Brandom, R. (1986) 'Frege's Technical Concepts: Some Recent Developments'. In L. Haaparanta and J. Hintikka (eds) *Frege Synthesized*, Dordrecht: Reidel, 253–95.

Brentano, F. (1874) *Psychologie vom Empirischen Standpunkt*, two volumes, edited by O. Kraus (1924/5); reprint Hamburg: Meiner, 1956.

Burge, T. (2005) *Truth, Thought, Reason: Essays on Frege*, Oxford: Clarendon Press, 2005.

—— (2007) 'Predication and Truth, Review of Donald Davidson', *Truth and Predication*, *The Journal of Philosophy*, 104: 580–608.

Campbell, J. (1994) *Past, Space and Self*, Cambridge, MA: MIT Press.

Caplan, B. (2003) 'Putting Things into Context', *The Philosophical Review*, 112: 191–214.

—— and Thau, M. (2001) 'What's Puzzling Gottlob Frege?', *The Canadian Journal of Philosophy*, 31: 159–200.

Carnap, R. (1956) *Meaning and Necessity*, second edition, Chicago: The University of Chicago Press.

Code, A. and Blackburn, S. (1978) 'On the Power of Russell's Criticism of Frege: "On Denoting", pp. 48–50', *Analysis*, 38: 65–77.

Davidson, D. (1984) *Inquiries into Truth and Interpretation*, Oxford: Oxford University Press.

Dedekind, Richard (1888) 'Was Sind und Was Sollen die Zahlen'. In his *Gesammelte Mathematische Werke III*, ed. R. Fricke, E. Noehter and Ö. Ore; reprint New York: Chelsea Publishing Company, 1969.

Dretske, F. (1970) 'Epistemic Operators', *The Journal of Philosophy*, 67: 1007–23.

Dummett, M. (1978) *Truth and Other Enigmas*, London: Duckworth.

—— (1981a) *Frege: Philosophy of Language* [1973], second edition, London: Duckworth.

—— (1981b) *The Interpretation of Frege's Philosophy*, London: Duckworth.

—— (1991a) *Frege: Philosophy of Mathematics*, Cambridge, MA: Harvard University Press.

—— (1991b) *The Logical Basis of Metaphysics*, Cambridge, MA: Harvard University Press.

—— (1991c) *Frege and Other Philosophers,* Oxford: Oxford University Press.

Evans, G. (1982) *Varieties of Reference*, Oxford: Oxford University Press.

—— (1985) 'Has Tense Logic Rested on a Mistake?' In his *Collected Papers*, Oxford: Oxford University Press, 343–64.

Fine, K. (1989) 'The Problem of De Re Modality'. In J. Almog, J. Perry and H.K. Wettstein (eds) *Themes from Kaplan*, Oxford: Oxford University Press, 197–272.

—— (2007) *Semantic Relationism*, Oxford: Blackwell.

Fogelin, R. (1983) 'Wittgenstein on Identity', *Synthese* 56: 141–54.

Forbes, G. (1990) 'The Indispensability of Sinn', *The Philosophical Review*, 99: 535–63.

Gabriel, G. (2003) 'Freges Anerkennungstheorie der Wahrheit'. In D. Greimann (ed.) *Das Wahre und das Falsche. Studien zu Freges Auffassung des Wahren*, Hildesheim/Zürich/New York: Georg Olms Verlag, 2003, 15–28.

Galloway, D. (1999) 'Seeing Sequences', *Philosophy and Phenomenological Research*, 59: 93–112.

Gaskin, R. (2008) *The Unity of the Proposition*, Oxford: Oxford University Press.

Geach, P.T. (1955) 'Class and Concept', *The Philosophical Review*, 64: 561–70.

—— (1962) *Reference and Generality. An Examination of some Medieval Theories*, Ithaca, NY: Cornell University Press.

—— (1976) 'Saying and Showing in Frege and Wittgenstein', *Acta Philosophica Fennica*, 28: 54–70.

Glock, H.J. (1996/7) 'Critical Notice of Frege by Anthony Kenny', *Grazer Philosophische Studien*, 52: 205–23.

Goldfarb, W. (2001) 'Frege's Conception of Logic'. In J. Floyd and S. Shieh (eds) *Futures Past*, Oxford: Oxford University Press, 25–43.

Green, M. (1997) 'On the Autonomy of Linguistic Meaning', *Mind*, 106: 217–43.

Grice, H.P. (1989) *Studies in the Way of Words*, Cambridge, MA: Harvard University Press.

Harman, G. (1986) *Change of View: Principles of Reasoning*, Cambridge, MA: MIT Press.

Heck, R. (1995) 'The Sense of Communication', *Mind*, 104: 79–106.

—— (2003) 'Frege on Identity and Identity-Statements: A Reply to Caplan and Thau', *The Canadian Journal of Philosophy*, 33: 83–102.

—— (2007) 'Frege and Semantics', *Grazer Philosophische Studien*, 75: 27–63.

—— and May, R. (2006) 'Frege's Contribution to Philosophy of Language'. In E. Lepore and B. Smith (eds) *The Oxford Handbook of Philosophy of Language*, Oxford: Oxford University Press, 3–39.

Hofweber, T. (2007) 'Innocent Statements and their Metaphysically Loaded Counterparts', *Philosophers' Imprint*, 7: 1–33.

Homer (1946) *The Odyssey*, London: Penguin Classics. Reprint of the 1946 edition.

Horty, J. (1993) 'Frege on the Psychological Significance of Definitions', *Philosophical Studies*, 72: 223–63.

Humboldt, W. von (1824) 'Über den Zusammenhang der Schrift mit der Sprache' (printed 1838). In his *Werke*, Bd. 5, Berlin: Preußische Akademie der Wissenschaften, 1906, 31–106.

Husserl, E. (1891) 'Besprechung von E. Schröder, Vorlesungen über die Algebra der Logik'; Bd. I. reprinted in his *Aufsätze und Rezensionen* (1890–1910). *Husserliana* 22, Kluwer: Dordrecht, 1979, 3–43.

Inwood, B. (1992) *A Hegel Dictionary*, Oxford: Blackwell.

Jackson, F. (2005) 'What are Proper Names For?' In J.C. Marek and M.E. Reicher (eds) *Experience and Analysis, Proc. 27th International Wittgenstein Symposium*, Vienna: hpt-öbv, 2005, 257–69.

Jäsche, Gottlob (ed.) (1800) *Immanuel Kant's Logik, ein Handbuch zu Vorlesungen*, Königsberg. Translated in I. Kant, *Lectures on Logic* (*The Cambridge Edition of the Works of Immanuel Kant in Translation*), edited and translated by J. Michael Young, Cambridge: Cambridge University Press, 1992.

Jeshion, R. (2001) 'Frege's Notion of Self-Evidence', *Mind*, 110: 937–76.

Jourdain, P.E. (1912) 'Gottlob Frege' (chapter from 'The Development of the Theories of Mathematical Logic and the Principles of Mathematics', *The Quarterly Journal of Pure and Applied Mathematics* 43: 237–69); reprinted in PMC: 179–206.

Kant, I. (1764) 'Untersuchungen über die Deutlichkeit der Grundsätze der natürlichen Theologie und Moral'. In his *Gesammelte Schriften*, Akademie-Ausgabe II, 273–301.

—— (1781/7) *Kritik der reinen Vernunft*. In his *Gesammelte Schriften*, Akademie-Ausgabe III. English translation by N. Kemp Smith, Basingstoke and New York: Palgrave Macmillan, 2007.

—— (1788) Letter to Johann Schultz (25.11). In his *Correspondence*, trans. and ed. by Arnulf Zweig. *The Cambridge Edition of the Works of Kant*, Cambridge: Cambridge University Press, 1999, 283–7.

Kaplan, D. (1989) 'Demonstratives'. In J. Almog, J. Perry and H.K. Wettstein (eds) *Themes from Kaplan*, Oxford: Oxford University Press, 481–565.

Kemp, G. (1995) 'Truth in Frege's "Law of Truth"', *Synthese*, 105: 31–51.

Kenny, A. (1995) *Frege*, London: Penguin.

Kitcher, P. (1975) 'Kant and the Foundations of Mathematics', *The Philosophical Review*, 84: 23–50.

—— (1979) 'Frege's epistemology', *The Philosophical Review*, 88: 235–63.

Klement, K.C. (2002) *Frege and the Logic of Sense and Reference*, London and New York: Routledge.

—— (2004) 'Putting Form Before Function: Logical Grammar in Frege, Russell, and Wittgenstein', *Philosophers Imprint*, 4: 1–46.

Kripke, S. (1980) *Naming and* Necessity, Cambridge, MA: Harvard University Press.

—— (1979) 'A Puzzle about Belief'; reprinted in N. Salmon and S. Soames (eds) *Propositional Attitudes*, Oxford: Oxford University Press, 1986, 102–48.

—— (2008) 'Frege's Theory of Sense and Reference: Some Exegetical Notes', *Theoria*, 74: 181–218.

Kremer, M. (2000) 'Frege on Judgement and Truth', *The Journal of the History of Philosophy*, 38: 549–81

Künne, W. (1982) 'Indexikalität, Sinn und propositionaler Gehalt', *Grazer Philosophische Studien*, 18: 41–74.

—— (1992) 'Hybrid Proper Names', *Mind*, 101: 721–31.

—— (2003) *Conceptions of Truth*, Oxford: Oxford University Press.

—— (2010) *Die Philosophische Logik Gottlob Freges*, Frankfurt: Klostermann.

Leibniz, G.W. (1764) *Nouveaux Essais sur l'entendement humain*. English translation by J. Bennett: http://www.earlymoderntexts.com, 2008.

Levine, J. (2004) 'On the "Gray's Elegy" Argument and its Bearing on Frege's Theory of Sense', *Philosophy and Phenomenological Research*, 64: 251–95.

Lewis, D. (1979) 'Attitudes de dicto and de se', *The Philosophical Review*, 88: 513–43.

—— (1980) 'Index, Context, and Content'. In S. Kanger and S. Oehman (eds) *Philosophy and Grammar*, Dordrecht: Reidel, 79–100.

—— (1999) [1997] 'Naming the Colours'; reprinted in his *Papers in Metaphysics and Epistemology II*, Cambridge: Cambridge University Press, 332–59.

Lotze, Rudolf Hermann (1880) *Logik. Erstes Buch. Vom Denken*, third edition, Hamburg: Meiner, 1989; reprint of the third edition from 1928.

Macbeth, D. (2005) *Frege's Logic*, Cambridge, MA: Harvard University Press.

MacBride, F. (2006) 'Predicate Reference'. In E. Lepore and B. Smith (eds) *The Oxford Handbook of Philosophy of Language*, Oxford: Oxford University Press, 422–76.

McDowell, J. (1977) 'On the Sense and Reference of a Proper Name', *Mind*, 86: 159–85.

MacFarlane, J. (2002) 'Frege, Kant, and the Logic of Logicism', *The Philosophical Review*, 111: 25–65.

—— (2003) 'Future Contingents and Relative Truth', *The Philosophical Quarterly*, 53: 321–36.

May, R. (2001) 'Frege on Identity Statements'. In C. Cecchetto, G. Chiechia and M.T. Guasti (eds) *Semantic Interfaces: Reference, Anaphora and Aspect*, Stanford, CA: CSLI Press, 1–50.

—— (2006) 'The Invariance of Sense', *The Journal of Philosophy*, 103: 111–44.

Mendelsohn, R.L. (1982) 'Frege's *Begriffsschrift* Theory of Identity', *The Journal for the History of Philosophy*, 20: 279–99.

Nelson, M. (2008) 'Frege and the Paradox of Analysis', *Philosophical Studies*, 137: 159–81.

Oliver, A. (2005) 'The Reference Principle', *Analysis*, 65: 177–87.

Parsons, Ch. (2005) 'Kant's Philosophy of Arithmetic'; reprinted with a Postscript in his *Mathematics in Philosophy: Selected Essays*, Ithaca, NY: Cornell University Press, 2005, 110–50.

Parsons, T. (1986) 'Why Frege should not have said "The concept 'Horse' is not a concept"', *History of Philosophy Quarterly*, 3: 449–66.

—— (1996) 'Fregean Theories of Truth and Meaning'. In M. Schirn (ed.) *Frege: Importance and Legacy*, Berlin and New York: De Gruyter, 371–409.

Peacocke, C. (1999) *Being Known*, Oxford: Oxford University Press.

Pendlebury, M. (1986) 'Against the Power of Force: Reflections on the Meaning of Mood', *Mind*, 95: 361–72.

Percival, P. (1994) 'Absolute Truth', *Proceedings of the Aristotelian Society*, 94: 189–213.

Perry, J. (1977) 'Frege on Demonstratives', *The Philosophical Review*, 86: 474–97.

—— (1979) 'The Problem of the Essential Indexical', *Noûs*, 13: 3–21.

—— (2001) 'Frege on Identity, Cognitive Value, and Subject Matter'. In A. Newen, U. Nortmann and R. Stuhlman-Laeisz (eds) *Building on Frege*, Stanford, CA: CSLI Press, 141–59.

Poincaré, H. (1908) *The Foundations of Science*, trans. G. Bruce Halsted, Lancaster, PA: The Science Press, 1946.

Putnam, H. (1954) 'Synonymy and the Analysis of Belief Sentences', *Analysis*, 14: 114–22.

Quine, W.V.O. (1960) *Word and Object*, Cambridge, MA: MIT Press.

—— (1970) *Philosophy of Logic*, Cambridge, MA: Harvard University Press.

—— (1974) *Methods of Logic*, fourth edition, Cambridge, MA: Harvard University Press.

Ramsey, F.P. (1925) 'Universals', *Mind*, 34: 401–17.

Rayo, A. (2002) 'Frege's Unofficial Arithmetic', *The Journal of Symbolic Logic*, 67: 1623–38.

Richard, M. (1981) 'Temporalism and Eternalism', *Philosophical Studies*, 39: 1–13.

Ricketts, T. (1986) 'Objectivity and Objecthood: Frege's Metaphysics of Judgement'. In L. Haaparanta and J. Hintikka (eds) *Frege Synthesized*, Dordrecht: Reidel, 65–97.

—— (2003) 'Quantification, Sentences, and Truth-values', *Manuscrito: Revista Internacional de Filosofica*, 26: 389–424.

Rosefeldt, T. (2008) 'That-clauses and Non-Nominal Quantification', *Philosophical Studies*, 137: 301–33

Rooth, M. (1996) 'Focus'. In S. Lappin (ed.) *The Handbook of Contemporary Semantic Theory*, London: Blackwell, 271–97.

Rumfitt, I. (1994) 'Frege's Theory of Predication: An Elaboration and Defence, with Some New Applications', *The Philosophical Review*, 103: 599–637.

Russinoff, S. (1992) 'Frege and Dummett on the Problem with the Concept "Horse"', *Noûs*, 26: 63–78.

Russell, B. (1903) *The Principles of Mathematics*, ed. by J.G. Slater, London: Routledge, 1992.

—— (1905) 'On Denoting', *Mind*, 14: 479–93.

—— (1910/11) 'Knowledge by Acquantaince and Knowledge by Description'. Proceedings of the Aristotelian Society 11, 108–28; reprinted in his *Mysticism and Logic*, London: G. Allen and Unwin, 1918: 209–32.

—— (1918) 'The Philosophy of Logical Atomism'; reprinted in his *Logic and Knowledge: Essays 1901–1950*, ed. by R.C. Marsh, London: Macmillan, 1956.

Salmon, N. (1986) *Frege's Puzzle*, Cambridge, MA: MIT Press, 1986.

—— (2002) 'Demonstrating and Necessity', *The Philosophical Review*, 111: 497–538.

Sainsbury, M.R. (1983) 'On a Fregean Argument', *Analysis*, 43: 12–14.

—— (2005) *Reference without Referents*, Oxford: Oxford University Press.

Schiffer, S. (1978) 'The Basis of Reference', *Erkenntnis*, 13: 171–206.

—— (1990) 'The Mode of Presentation Problem'. In A.C. Anderson and J. Owens (eds) *Propositional Attitudes*, Stanford, CA: CSLI Press, 249–69.

—— (2003) *The Things We Mean*, Oxford: Oxford University Press.

Schirn, M. (1990) 'Frege's Objects of a Quite Special Kind', *Erkenntnis*, 32: 27–61.

Schröder, E. (1890) *Vorlesungen über die Algebra der Logik*, Bd. I, Leipzig: B.G. Teubner.

Segal, G. (1991) 'In the Mood for a Semantic Theory', *Proceedings of The Aristotelian Society*, 91: 103–18.

Searle, J. (1958) 'Proper Names', *Mind*, 67: 166–73.

Shabel, L. (1998) 'Kant on the "Symbolic Construction" of Mathematical Concepts', *Studies in the History of the Philosophy of Science*, 29: 589–621.

Sluga, H. (1987) 'Frege against the Booleans', *Notre Dame Journal of Formal Logic*, 28: 80–98.

Soames, S. (1989) 'Semantics and Semantic Competence', *Philosophical Perspectives*, 3: 575–96.

—— (1998) 'The Modal Argument: Wide Scope and Rigidified Descriptions', *Noûs*, 32: 1–22.

Stalnaker, R. (1981) 'Indexical Belief', *Synthese*, 49: 129–51.

Stevenson, L. (1973) 'Frege's Two Definitions of Quantification', *The Philosophical Quarterly*, 92: 207–23.

Strawson, P.F. (1957) 'Propositions, Concepts, and Logical Truths'; reprinted in his *Logico-Linguistic Papers*, London: Methuen, 1971, 89–101.

—— (1959) *Individuals*, London: Methuen.

—— (1974) *Subject and Predicate in Logic and Grammar*, London: Methuen.

—— (1976) 'Entity and Identity'. In H.D Lewis (ed.) *Contemporary British Philosophy*, London: Allen and Unwin, 193–219.

Sundholm, G. (1998) 'Inference, Consequence and Implication: A Constructivists Perspective', *Philosophia Mathematica*, 6: 178–94.

Sullivan, P.M. (1995) 'The Sense of a Name of a Truth-value', *The Philosophical Quarterly*, 44: 476–81.

—— (2004) 'Frege's Logic'. In D. Gabbay and J. Woods (eds) *Handbook of the History and Philosophy of Logic*, Amsterdam: Elsevier, 671–761.

—— (2007) 'How Did Frege Fall into Contradiction?', *Ratio*, 20: 91–107.

Taschek, W. (1992) 'Frege's Puzzle, Sense, and Information Content', *Mind*, 101: 767–91.

—— (1995) 'Belief, Substitution and Logical Structure', *Noûs*, 29: 71–95.

Textor, M. (2007) 'Frege's Theory of Hybrid Proper Names Developed and Defended', *Mind*, 116: 947–82.

—— (2009) 'A Repair of Frege's Theory of Thoughts', *Synthese*, 167: 105–23.

—— (Forthcoming) 'Frege on Acknowledging the Truth', *Mind*.

Thiel, Ch. (1995) '"Nicht aufs Gerathewohl und aus Neuerungssucht": Die Begriffsschrift 1879 und 1893'. In I. Max and W. Stelzner (eds) *Logik und Mathematik: Frege-Kolloquium 1993*, Berlin: DeGruyter, 20–37.

Trendelenburg, A. (1856) 'Über Leibnizens Entwurf einer allgemeinen Charakteristik'. In his *Historische Beiträge zur Philosophie*, Berlin: Bethage, 1867.

Vendler, Z. (1967) *Linguistics in Philosophy*, Ithaca, NY: Cornell University Press.

—— (1984) 'Review of Peter T. Geach *Reference and Generality*', *Journal of Symbolic Logic*, 49, 655–7.

Weiner, J. (1990) *Frege in Perspective*, Ithaca, NY: Cornell University Press.

—— (2007) 'What's in a Numeral? Frege's Answer', *Mind*, 116: 677–716.

Whitehead, A. (1898) *A Treatise on Universal Algebra, with Applications*, Cambridge: Cambridge University Press.

Wiggins, D. (1984) 'The Sense and Reference of Predicates: A Running Repair of Frege's Doctrine and a Plea for the Copula', *The Philosophcal Quarterly*, 34: 311–28.

—— (2006) 'Three Moments in the Theory of Definition or Analysis: Its Possibility, Its Aim or Aims, and its Limits or Terminus', *Proceedings of the Aristotelian Society*, 107: 73–109.

Williamson, T. (1994) *Vagueness*, London: Routledge.

—— (1999) 'Truth-makers and the Converse Barcan Formula', *Dialectica*, 53: 253–70.

—— (2006) 'Conceptual Truth', *Proceedings of the Aristotelian Society*, 106, 1–41.

Windelband, W. (1882) 'Was ist Philosophie'. In his *Präludien. Aufsätze und Reden zur Philosophie und ihrer Geschichte*, Bd. 1, Tübingen: Verlag von J.C.B. Mohr (Paul Siebeck), 1911.

—— (1920) *Einleitung in die Philosophie*, second edition, Tübingen: Verlag von J.C.B. Mohr (Paul Siebeck).

Wittgenstein, L. (1921) *Tractatus Logico-Philosophicus*. In Wilhelm Ostwald (ed.) *Annalen der Naturphilosophie*, 14; reprinted in Volume 1 of *Ludwig Wittgenstein Werkausgabe*, Suhrkamp: Frankfurt a.M. 1984. English translation by David Pears and Brian McGuinness (1961), London: Routledge, 1961.

Wright, C. (1998) 'Why Frege Did not Deserve his *Granum Salis*. A Note on the Paradox of "The Concept of Horse" and the Ascription of Bedeutung to Predicates', *Grazer Philosophische Studien*, 55: 239–63.

Wolff, M. (1995) *Die Vollständigkeit der kantischen Urteilstafel*, Heidelberg: Klostermann.

INDEX